D0182519

MARGARET R · SCHERER

THE LEGENDS OF TROY

THE LEGENDS OF TROY

IN ART AND LITERATURE

BY

MARGARET R · SCHERER

NEW YORK AND LONDON · MCMLXIII

PUBLISHED BY THE PHAIDON PRESS

FOR THE METROPOLITAN MUSEUM OF ART

5 CROMWELL PLACE, LONDON SW7

SECOND EDITION 1964

MADE IN GREAT BRITAIN
PRINTED BY GEO. GIBBONS LTD . LEICESTER

CONTENTS

ACKNOWLEDGEMENTS

THIS book grew out of an interest awakened by one person in one well-remembered place and time. Laura Hibbard Loomis, in a Wellesley class on Chaucer in 1916, showed her students illustrations from a manuscript of Christine de Pisan's *Epistle of Othéa, Goddess of Prudence, to Hector, Chief of the Trojans*, in which Greek gods and heroes went garbed as knights and courtiers of the fifteenth century. Classical and modern illustrations of the tale of Troy were already familiar: now the medieval gap in time and interpretation was at once revealed and bridged. Thereafter any reference to the Trojan story caught my eye and was filed for remembrance.

For help in the long process of shaping this volume my deepest thanks are due to many among my colleagues in the Metropolitan Museum. I am indebted to Marjorie J. Milne and Dietrich von Bothmer for invaluable suggestions of classical works and references and for translations from the Latin *Dictys*; to William H. Forsyth, Margaret B. Freeman, and Carmen Gómez-Moreno for material on medieval tapestries; to Edith A. Standen for suggestions regarding structure and the Trojan story in tapestries and other textiles of later periods; and to Marshall B. Davidson, former Editor of Publications, and Lillian Green for advice and assistance in the preparation of the manuscript.

Outside the circle of my colleagues at the Metropolitan Museum I owe debts of gratitude to William T. Jackson of Columbia University for his careful scrutiny of the sections dealing with the legend in classical literature and for his suggestions concerning bibliographies; to Harry Bober of the Institute of Fine Arts, New York University, and to Gertrud Bing, then Director of the Warburg Institute, London, for their kindness in reading the manuscript and making suggestions; to Erwin Panofsky of the Institute for Advanced Study, Princeton University, for help in an endless succession of problems; to the late Cornelia C. Coulter of Mount Holyoke College for translations from Boccaccio's *Genealogy of the Gods*; to Mary M. Kenway of the Pierpont Morgan Library and to the staff of the Frick Art Reference Library for aid in tracing manuscript illustrations; to Hugo Buchthal of the Warburg Institute for assistance in locating elusive examples; to E. H. Gombrich, present Director of the Warburg Institute, and to his staff for enabling me to use that Institute's reference material; to John L. Caskey of the University of Cincinnati for advice regarding the note on excavations at Troy, Mycenae, and Pylos; to Duveen Brothers and French and Company for information concerning Trojan tapestries; and to colleagues in many museums in Europe and the United States for supplying information concerning works of art in their own collections and elsewhere dealing with the legend of Troy.

I am especially grateful to The Metropolitan Museum of Art for its encouragement and its generous support of this volume.

M.R.S.

INTRODUCTION

MORE THAN THREE THOUSAND YEARS AGO, in a small corner of Asia Minor, a city was besieged and fell: despite painstaking excavations in her ruins, archaeologists today can tell us little more of Troy's fate. Yet through the centuries since, her story has lived on in both literature and art, reflecting in its varying forms the changing patterns of the years. The pictures that follow show better than words the legend's history, for, as narrative art must do, they echo the changes in the story.

Since its first great poet told parts of the action and its aftermath in the *Iliad* and the *Odyssey*, the Trojan war has been an outstanding theme in two widely separated periods and two diverse literatures. Greek epic, song, and drama shaped its outlines in the ancient world; its Latin expressions were largely adaptations of these legends in another tongue. The paintings of Trojan scenes which ancient writers described profusely have long since perished: there remain today a few Roman copies, together with gems, coins, some sculpture, and a wealth of Greek vase paintings, exquisite, direct, and forceful presentations of a story known to everyone in a time when everyone delighted in stories.

The second great period of Trojan narrative came with the Middle Ages, when the legend was retold by romancers to fit the pattern of feudalism and chivalry and by historians as the Greek chapters of universal histories. Medieval sources tell of walls painted with scenes from Troy romance. A twelfth-century Latin treatise, *De Claustro Anime*, 'The Cloister of the Soul', speaking in general terms, reproaches the clergy for adorning their palaces while neglecting the needy: 'The painted walls bear the Trojans in clothing of purple and gold, and the cast-off garments are denied to the Christians. Arms are given to the Greeks, to Hector a shield resplendent with gold; but no bread is granted to the poor clamouring at the gates.' Other documents mention specific examples, though fewer than those noted by the ancient chroniclers of Greek art. Most medieval paintings have long since disappeared, but the legend is still abundantly represented in two characteristic forms of medieval art—manuscript illustrations and the storied tapestries with which kings and princes hung their walls.

With the renaissance rediscovery of ancient literature came a revival of the story's classical form, though its treatment was often eclectic. The patterns set by Greece and Rome have remained, with but few exceptions, the accepted literary standard, no matter how far authors may deviate. Behind such widely different expressions as the plays of Racine and of Giraudoux lie the traditions of Greece. The artist's debt to classical form is equally clear: Rubens' or Tiepolo's boldly modelled forms are infinitely closer to Roman painting than to medieval tapestries. Even in the allusive works of Carrà and De Chirico, almost wholly lacking in narrative content, the echo of a classical pose or the solidity of classical modelling is evident.

That the story should have been told first in epic poetry was inevitable in the heroic age of Greece. The Greeks called their first great poet Homer and differed among themselves as to just when he lived; knowing little more of him today than they did then, we place him in the ninth or eighth century B.C., several hundred years after Troy fell. Some have believed the *Iliad* and the *Odyssey* to be the work of different men, but for convenience' sake they are usually credited to one. As to when the war was fought, the Greeks also disagreed, assigning it to dates that ranged from 1334 to 1150 B.C. The traditional date which finally emerged was 1184.

Besides the *Iliad* and the *Odyssey* there grew up in Greece between the eighth and the sixth century B.C. another group of poems known as the epic cycle, ascribed to more or less supposititious authors and probably composed to fill the gaps left by Homer. These epics have long since been lost, but summaries made in the second century A.D. have been preserved in the ninth-century *Biblioteca* of the Greek grammarian Photius, and a few quotations have survived in the works of ancient authors. In chronological sequence of events, though not in date of composition, these cyclic epics are: the *Cypria*, the *Aethiopis*, the *Little Iliad*, the *Sack of Ilium*, the *Nostoi* or 'Returns', and the *Telegonia*. Their scope is treated both in the text accompanying the plates and in the appendix of literary works.

The great Greek dramatists of the fifth century B.C., Aeschylus, Sophocles, and Euripides, drew from these epics as well as from Homer, from the works of other poets, and perhaps from unrecorded legends. So, also, to note only a few authors invaluable for their preservation of Trojan stories, did Diodorus of Sicily and Dionysius of Halicarnassus in the first century B.C. and such writers of the first to second centuries A.D. as Dio Chrysostom, Apollodorus, compiler of mythological histories, the satirist Lucian of Samosata, and the indefatigable traveller Pausanias, to whom we owe so many descriptions of Greek art lost long ago.

From Greece the story of the war and its aftermath passed to Rome and to the Latin tongue. By the third century B.C. Greek plays were being adapted for Roman use, and Livius Andronicus had paraphrased the

Fig. 1. FRAGMENT OF A TABULA ILIACA WITH SCENES FROM THE TROJAN WAR. Roman relief, perhaps first century A.D. Rome, Capitoline Museum.

This is the largest and best preserved of several such fragments carved, and originally painted, with incidents from the Trojan war. It has been suggested that these may have been visual aids for teaching young Romans the legends of their Founding Fathers.

A Greek inscription with an epitome of the story forms a band across the pilaster at the right. The central scene shows the fall of Troy. Top right, the wooden horse; left, Ajax seizing Cassandra. Centre left, Priam killed at his altar; right, Hecuba seized by a Greek; Helen threatened by Menelaus. Below, Aeneas carries his father and leads his son out of the gate. The blurred figure may be his wife. Outside the city walls the Greek ships lie at anchor at the left; at the right, Aeneas and his companions make ready to sail.

Odyssey in Latin, while the legend of the Romans' descent from Aeneas the Trojan and his followers had become widespread. Naevius' epic *History of the Punic War*, composed in that century, told of Rome's founding by the Trojans as well known, and so too, a little later, did Ennius' *Annals*. Julius Caesar's family was proud to trace its descent from Aeneas, and in Caesar's time Varro, 'most learned of the Romans', wrote a genealogy which derived the ancestry of outstanding Roman families from Troy. The time was ripe for the *Aeneid* to become the national epic of the burgeoning Roman Empire. Second only to Vergil in preserving the Trojan story's classic form during the dark centuries after Rome's decline was his younger contemporary, Ovid, whose *Heroides* and *Metamorphoses* were a mine of Trojan lore for the Middle Ages. The first century A.D. saw also the Elder Pliny, an insatiably curious naturalist, who recorded in his *Natural History* an even wider range of now vanished works of art than the Greek Pausanius was to chronicle a century later in his *Description of Greece*.

As pagan Rome became gradually christianized the Trojan legend remained a living force. Saint Augustine's *City of God* argued from Troy's fall that its pagan gods had given but poor protection, and that, therefore, Rome's sack by the Visigoths in A.D. 410 could scarcely have been caused by her neglect of these divinities. Paulus Orosius, writing his defence of Christianity after the same catastrophe, pays tribute to the story's place in Roman education of his day: '. . . the abduction of Helen, the covenant of the Greeks, the assembly of a thousand ships, then the ten years' siege, and lastly the celebrated destruction of Troy is known to all . . . . The most renowned poet Homer in his glorious song has clearly shown what nations and how many peoples were caught in the path of that hurricane and destroyed. It is not our concern to unfold the story in sequence, since that would take a long time and besides it is well known to everybody.' As for the 'events that followed the arrival of Aeneas in Italy', these, he says, 'have been imprinted upon our memories by the instruction received in our elementary schools.'

The classical legend of Troy was fading even as Orosius wrote, and that from which the medieval Troy romances arose was taking shape. Behind these romances lay two Latin works of the fourth to the sixth century A.D. based on slightly earlier Greek originals which claimed to be accounts by men who had fought in the war and were therefore more trustworthy than Homer. These were the *Diary of the Trojan War* by Dictys the Cretan, who had helped the Greeks, and the *History of the Destruction of Troy* by Dares the Phrygian, who had aided the Trojans. Written in simple, straightforward

Latin, easy to read in a time when the ancient speech was breaking down into vernacular tongues, these literary forgeries rather than the great classical accounts were the main sources of that pioneer of Troy romancers, Benoit de Sainte-More.

Benoit's long French verse romance, the *Roman de Troie*, written about 1160, set the tone for the next three centuries, transforming the epic heroes into knights of Christendom and presenting the defeated Trojans rather than the victorious Greeks as the heroes of the war. Western Europe of the Middle Ages still retained a strong sense of its continuity with the Roman Empire, which had ruled so long and on the whole so well, and remembered the tradition of its origin in Troy. Hence, although Benoit used Dictys to fill in much material untouched by Dares, he followed the latter's pro-Trojan point of view. His attitude towards Homer, as a Greek sympathizer, is characteristic of the romances:

> 'Homer, who was a marvellous clerk,
> Very wise and learned,
> Wrote of the great siege and fall of Troy
> After which it was never again rebuilt.
> But his books do not tell the truth,
> As we know without question
> That he was not born within a hundred years of the time
> When the great host was assembled.
> No wonder then that he should make mistakes,
> When he was not there to see any of it.'

The 'Homer' known to Western Europe at that time was the *Ilias Latina*, a Latin condensation of the *Iliad* made in the first century A.D., with which most readers had to be content until the late fourteenth century.

Three works are outstanding among later versions of the Troy romance. Guido delle Colonne's prose *History*, composed between 1272 and 1287 and based, without credit, upon Benoit, exerted a wider influence upon later writers than did the French romance, owing both to its more compact form and to its use of the international language of medieval Latin. John Lydgate's *Troy Book*, written between 1412 and 1420, and based upon Guido, is an exquisite treatment in English verse reminiscent of his 'master Chaucer'. Its influence was not, however, widely felt outside England. Raoul Lefèvre's French prose *Recueil*, or *Collection of Trojan Histories*, completed in 1464, represents an expanded Guido with a wealth of incident which made it widely popular in the courtly circles of northern Europe.

Fig. 2. JASON, HERCULES, AND THEIR COMPANIONS SET OUT TO DESTROY TROY FOR THE FIRST TIME. From a manuscript of Lydgate's *Troy Book*, English, 1450–1475. Manchester, John Rylands Library, Ryl.Eng.MS. No. 1, fol.25v.

The opening of Chaucer's Prologue to the *Canterbury Tales* was the model for the opening description on this page:

> 'When the sweet storms of April
> Unto the lowest roots distill
> Refreshing rain in many a wholesome shower,
> To bring life up from them into the flower.'

Fig. 3. THE RAPE OF HELEN. Italian maiolica dish (Urbino), 1530–1535, after an engraving of the School of Marcantonio, perhaps from a design by Raphael. New York, Metropolitan Museum of Art, Samuel D. Lee Fund, 1941.

Engravings after the works of well-known painters were a common source of designs for Italian maiolica ware. Tradition ascribes this composition to Raphael, chiefly on the strength of Vasari's remark that, besides *The Judgment of Paris* (Plate 13), Marcantonio engraved 'the very beautiful Rape of Helen, also after a drawing by Raphael.' The same composition was used in Gobelins tapestries of the late seventeenth and early eighteenth centuries.

The presentation here is typically renaissance, with its semi-nude figures engaged in vigorous action, its inspiration that of ancient Rome rather than Greece. There is, however, a lingering trace of the Middle Ages. As in medieval romances, the abduction takes place, not from Sparta, Helen's home, but from the island of Cythera, to which Helen has gone, ostensibly to worship Venus but actually to see Paris, of whose presence she had heard. The temple of Venus shown in the background is a colonnaded structure typical of the renaissance revival of classical antiquity.

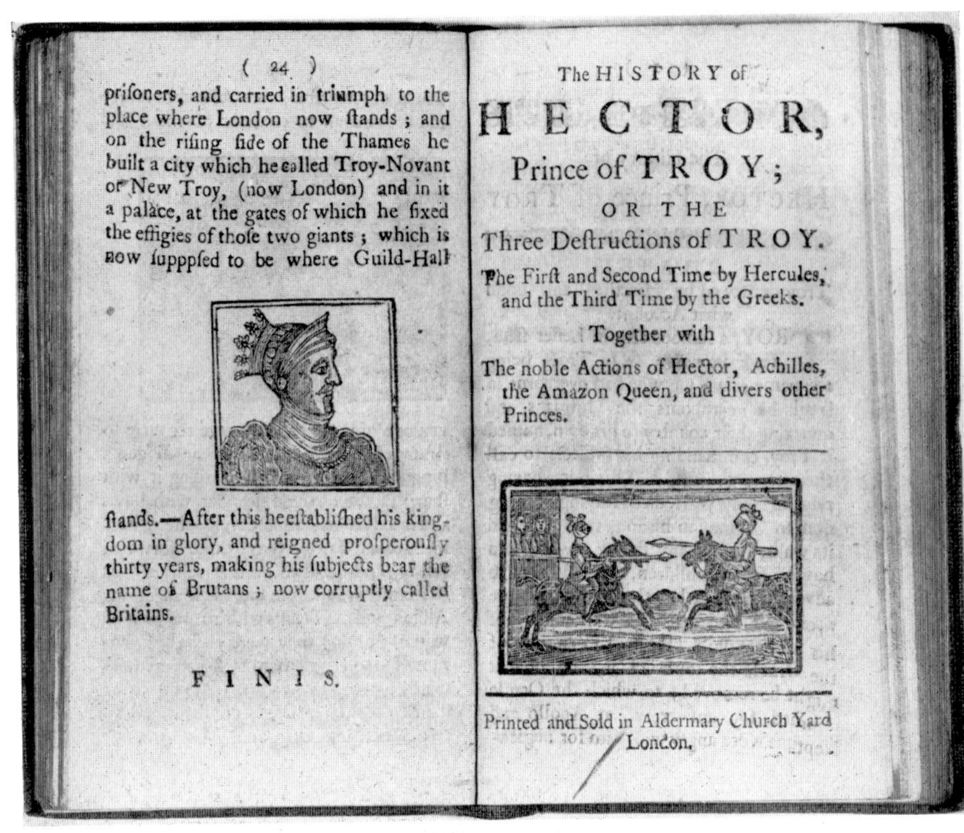

(24)

priſoners, and carried in triumph to the place where London now ſtands; and on the riſing ſide of the Thames he built a city which he called Troy-Novant or New Troy, (now London) and in it a palace, at the gates of which he fixed the effigies of thoſe two giants; which is now ſupppſed to be where Guild-Hall ſtands.—After this he eſtabliſhed his kingdom in glory, and reigned proſperouſly thirty years, making his ſubjects bear the name of Brutans; now corruptly called Britains.

F I N I S.

The HISTORY of

HECTOR,

Prince of TROY;

OR THE

Three Deſtructions of TROY.

The Firſt and Second Time by Hercules, and the Third Time by the Greeks.

Together with

The noble Actions of Hector, Achilles, the Amazon Queen, and divers other Princes.

Printed and Sold in Aldermary Church Yard London.

Fig. 4. TITLE AND END PAGE OF TWO CHAPBOOKS OF THE HISTORY OF HECTOR, PRINCE OF TROY, London, 1728–1769. New York, Pierpont Morgan Library.

The Troy romances were echoed throughout the seventeenth and eighteenth centuries in such simplified, popular forms as ballads and chapbooks, the precursors of today's 'comic' books. Behind this *History of Hector* must have lain some form of Caxton's fifteenth-century translation of Lefèvre's French romance, which emphasized three destructions of Troy. The chapbook account is slanted to emphasize Britain's settlement by Brutus the Trojan, who built his 'New Troy' where London stands.

To the works of these men should be added, especially for English readers, Caxton's translation of Lefèvre between 1468 and 1471. Its publication about 1474 as the first book printed in English made Lefèvre's version the most widely known English form of the Troy romance.

Among the infinite number of the legend's medieval literary expressions it has been possible to mention only a few. Notable omissions are the Scandinavian romances and the large, important group of Byzantine Greek works, which have been passed over as too far outside the main stream of the story's development in Western Europe.

Although the romance form and point of view went out of fashion with the revival of classical learning in the Renaissance, several purely medieval

Trojan themes persisted: Boccaccio, Chaucer, and Shakespeare all told of the loves of Troilus, Priam's son, and the fickle Cressida, a story seemingly unknown before Benoit's time. In the eclectic literature of the Renaissance motives from classical and medieval tradition often mingle, as in Ronsard's *Franciade*, which was devoted to glorifying the legendary descent of the French from the Trojan prince Francus, as Vergil had immortalized that of the Romans from Aeneas in the *Aeneid*. Ariosto's romantic epic, *Orlando Furioso*, continues the work, begun by Boiardo's unfinished *Orlando Innamorato*, of combining Graeco-Roman mythology with elements from the romance cycles of Troy, Arthur, and Charlemagne. And in Spenser's *Faerie Queene* the legend of Britain's settlement by the Trojan Brutus shares honours with allegories from Arthurian romance.

In the main, however, the treatments of the Trojan story in the Renaissance and later, no matter how individual their variations, have had their roots in classical sources. From such sources most writers of the nineteenth century, among them Lang, Landor, and Tennyson, drew the motives for their retellings of Trojan incidents. Yet this century saw a unique return to medieval forms of the Trojan legend, both in literature and in art, in the work of the English Pre-Raphaelite poets and painters. Among the shorter poems of Dante Gabriel Rossetti are several sonnets and ballads on Trojan themes; William Morris began a group of Trojan poems, but left it unfinished. Disenchanted with the industrial age he turned to the romances and planned a long, connected series based on a central theme, in which Troy became once more a medieval city and its heroes knights of chivalry. Only six poems and the rough drafts of a few more were completed, but these contain some of the legend's most poignant and personal nineteenth-century interpretations. The poems had their artistic counterpart in the paintings of Edward Burne-Jones and a few of Rossetti's paintings and drawings.

Since this short-lived Gothic Revival of the tale of Troy, classical authors have been the main source for most treatments of Trojan themes. The *Odyssey*, most fruitful of all, has furnished the inspiration for such widely diverse works as Samuel Butler's *Authoress of the Odyssey*; Robert Graves' *Homer's Daughter*; James Joyce's *Ulysses*; Nikos Kazantzakis' Greek epic, *The Odyssey: a Modern Sequel*; and Ernst Schnabel's *Voyage Home*. The *Iliad's* famous description inspired W. H. Auden's *Shield of Achilles*. Aeschylus' trilogy on the fate of Agamemnon's family underlies Eugene O'Neill's *Mourning Becomes Electra* and T. S. Eliot's *Family Reunion*. Classical in inspiration, too, if not always in spirit, are Masefield's Trojan poetry and prose, the Trojan poems of Stephen Vincent Benét, Archibald MacLeish's radio drama, *The Trojan Horse*, and Jean Giraudoux's *Tiger at the Gates*. Even Christopher Morley's *Trojan Horse*, though based upon the medieval theme of Troilus and Cressida and given a twentieth-century setting, would have been impossible without the Greek tradition, for its Troy, 'earth's most famous town . . . belongs to everybody, and to all times at once', a city embracing classical temples and medieval walls, skyscrapers, radio tower, and a filling station—a city which must be built afresh in each man's mind.

The legend's history in music has been long. Greek drama began in songs sung at the great festivals; music played an important part in the danced mimes of Rome and accompanied the mimes and plays of the Middle Ages. In such renaissance spectacles as George Peele's *Arraignment of Paris* Pallas comes upon the stage appropriately accompanied by 'nine knights in armour, treading warlike almain [a kind of dance], by drum and fife'. Sixteenth-century Italy saw the approach to opera in poems set to music: as early as 1566 Lodovico Dolce's tragedy, *The Trojans*, was sung to music composed by Claudio Merulo. In 1654 Lully, Louis XIV's favourite musician, wrote the ballet music for Caproli's opera, *The Wedding of Peleus and Thetis*, and at his death left the unfinished score for an *Achilles and Polyxena*. One of the earliest English operas had a Trojan theme: Purcell's *Dido and Aeneas* was produced between 1688 and 1690. Early in the next century Elkanah Settle's musical melodrama, *The Virgin Prophetess, or The Siege of Troy*, was set to music by various composers. Its appeal to a mixed and popular audience is indicated by its appearance in one of Hogarth's engravings of Bartholomew Fair.

Trojan opera blossomed in the eighteenth century with Gluck's *Paris and Helen* and his two treatments of the Iphigenia story, a favourite operatic subject for two hundred years. The Trojan theme was continued in the nineteenth century in both light and serious vein, with Berlioz' near-epic opera, *The Trojans*; Offenbach's witty operetta, *Fair Helen*; Saint-Saëns' *Helen*; and *The Egyptian Helen* of Richard Strauss, which stems from the ancient legend that only a phantom Helen went to Troy. In the Moross-Latouche musical comedy of 1954, *The Golden Apple*, the fruit of discord and the fatal judgment reappeared, not at a wedding feast on Thessaly's Mount Pelion, but at a fair in a small town in the shadow of Washington's Mount Olympus. And in 1962 the Trojan legend, from the birth of Paris to the fall of the city, was presented in Michael Tippet's tragic opera *King Priam*.

BEFORE THE ILIAD

1. ATTIC BLACK-FIGURED VOLUTE KRATER: THE FRANÇOIS VASE.
Sixth century B.C. Florence, Museo Archeologico, No. 4209.

The story of the Trojan war begins long before the action of the *Iliad,* with an incident at the wedding feast of Peleus, king of Thessaly, and Thetis, a sea nymph, who were to become the parents of Homer's hero, Achilles. Zeus, king of the gods, merely used this incident to carry out a purpose already conceived. His intent is clearly stated in a passage from the *Cypria*:

'There was a time when the countless tribes of men, though wide-dispersed, oppressed the surface of the deep-bosomed earth, and Zeus saw it and had pity and in his wise heart resolved to relieve the all-nurturing earth of men by causing the great struggle of the Ilian war, that the load of death might empty the world.'

To this end he made use of a quarrel which broke out at the marriage feast. All the deities of Olympus had been invited except Eris, goddess of Discord, who, in revenge for the slight, broke in among the guests and started trouble between Hera, wife of Zeus, Athena, goddess of wisdom, and Aphrodite, goddess of love and beauty. The synopsis of the *Cypria* outlines the story:

'Zeus plans with Themis [the personification of law and order] to bring about the Trojan war. Strife arrives while the gods are feasting at the marriage of Peleus and starts a dispute between Hera, Athena, and Aphrodite as to which of them is fairest. The three

2. THE MARRIAGE OF PELEUS AND THETIS: THE GODS VISIT THE NEWLY-WEDDED PAIR. Shoulder band on the François vase (plate 1).

are led by Hermes at the command of Zeus to Alexandrus [Paris] on Mount Ida for his decision.'

The quarrel with its fateful consequences was now shifted to earth, where it furnished a fruitful cause for war. Alexander, better known as Paris, was a son of Priam, king of Troy, and this city was soon involved.

The *Iliad* does not mention this wedding feast. Homer chose from the mass of existing legend only what fitted his theme: the anger of Achilles and its results, which occupy about seven weeks of the war's tenth year. The summary of the *Cypria* does not describe the banquet in detail. The story that Eris threw among the guests an apple inscribed 'for the fairest' is not found among the extant works of early authors. Several Greek and Latin writers of the second century A.D. tell of it, but it appears earlier in art, being clearly visible in a Greek vase painting of the fourth century B.C. and perhaps present on a much worn ivory carving of the seventh century or earlier. *The Rape of Helen*, an epic composed in the fourth or fifth century A.D. by Colluthus, a Greek of southern Italy, says that Eris picked the fateful apple in the garden of the Hesperides.

The arrival of the gods at the palace of Peleus fills the shoulder band of the François vase, one of the most famous examples of the Trojan story in early Greek art. At the extreme right Peleus welcomes the guests outside his door: immediately above is a scene described near the end of the *Iliad*—the chariot race at the funeral games of Achilles' friend, Patroclus. Immediately below the procession of gods appears an incident from the *Cypria*—Achilles pursuing and finally killing Troilus, son of Priam. The topmost band does not bear upon the Trojan story.

3. THE GODS BRING GIFTS TO PELEUS AND THETIS. Relief on a Roman sarcophagus. Rome, Villa Albani.

Here gods and personified Seasons troop toward Peleus, who sits at the right with the veiled Thetis beside him. First to come is Hephaestus, the celestial smith, who presents a sword and shield. Behind him is Athena bearing a helmet. Then come four Seasons with appropriate gifts, followed by the boy Hesperus, the evening star, who holds an inverted torch to signify the approach of night. He ushers in Hymen, god of marriage, whose torch for the bridal chamber is still unlit. At the extreme left the little winged Eros, god of love, pushes out a goddess. She may be Hera, who has led the procession to the groom's palace but is obliged by custom to leave before Hymen enters the marriage chamber. Or she may be the goddess of Discord, though she lacks the apple, which was, by this time, a familiar part of the story.

Outstanding among late classic authors who told of the feast was the Greek satirist Lucian, of the second century A.D., one of whose *Dialogues of the Sea Gods* makes it the subject of delightfully witty gossip between two sea nymphs, Panope and Galene.

'*Panope.* Galene, did you see what Eris did yesterday at the Thessalian banquet, because she had not an invitation?

Galene. No, I was not with you; Poseidon had told me to keep the sea quiet for the occasion. What did Eris do, then, if she was not there?

Panope. Thetis and Peleus had just gone off to the bridal chamber, conducted by Amphitrite and Poseidon, when Eris came in unnoticed . . . well, she threw down a lovely apple, solid gold, my dear; and there was written on it, FOR THE FAIR. It rolled along as if it knew what it was about, till it came in front of Hera, Aphrodite, and Athena. Hermes picked it up and read out the inscription; of course, we Nereids kept quiet; what should *we* do in such company? But they all made for it, each insisting that it was hers; and if Zeus had not parted them, there would have been a battle. He would not decide the matter himself, though they asked him to. "Go, all of you, to Ida," he said, "to the son of Priam: he is a man of taste, quite capable of picking the beauty; he will be no bad judge."

Galene. Yes, and the goddesses, Panope?

Panope. They are going to Ida today, I believe; we shall soon have news of the result.

Galene. Oh, I can tell you that now; if the umpire is not a blind man, no one else can win, with Aphrodite in for it.'

4. THE GODDESS OF DISCORD THROWS THE APPLE ON THE TABLE AT THE WEDDING FEAST OF PELEUS. Detail of a painted ceiling, 1377–1380. Palermo, Palazzo Chiaramonte.

Between the Roman sarcophagus and the Palermo ceiling painting lay well over a thousand years, during which Homer had become but a name to most of Europe and much ancient literature had perished or had lain forgotten for centuries. Yet from the turmoil of the early medieval world had arisen the new and significant interpretation of the Trojan legend in terms of romances rooted in the works of Dictys and Dares.

Neither Dictys nor Dares had mentioned the wedding feast at Peleus, nor did Benoit de Sainte-More's *Roman de Troie*. Guido delle Colonne notes the feast, but not its occasion, nor does he mention Discord. He has Mercury tell Paris, when he brings the three goddesses for judgment: 'There was thrown among them at a solemn feast an apple, wondrous in shape, of precious material with an inscription in Greek letters that it should be given to the fairest.'

Lydgate's *Troy Book* describes the feast at greater length, though still without calling it a wedding feast. Mercury tells Paris that the three goddesses:

> 'Were at a feast, as I to thee shall tell,
> With all the gods above, celestial,
> That Jupiter held at his own board.
> Not one was absent there except Discord
> And out of spite that she was not present
> To be avenged she made her chief intent,
> And in her mind for many ways she sought,
> Till at the last in such a way she wrought,
> As in the words of poets it is told:
> She took an apple round, of purest gold,

Engraved with Grecian letters up and down
... ...
"To the fairest one among them all",
... ...
And cast it down among them at the board
With haughty mien, speaking no single word.'

Although Lydgate followed Guido's version in the main he too, like the Palermo painter, emphasized Discord's rôle.

Artists as well as writers clothed the heroes and divinities of antiquity in the costumes of their own day, as in this picture of Discord at the feast where only their angels' wings indicate that the goddesses are not mortal guests. This ceiling, decorated with scenes from Trojan and other romances, painted by some provincial artist a little less than half a century before Giotto's time, is one of the few remaining examples of the Trojan story in medieval decorative painting and is by far the best preserved. Somewhat earlier frescoes in the Loggia dei Cavalieri at Treviso are so severely damaged that their subject might be unrecognizable were it not for the names of characters inscribed.

5. DISCORD AT THE WEDDING FEAST OF PELEUS AND THETIS. Illustration by Jean Mielot from a manuscript of Christine de Pisan's *Épître d'Othéa, Déesse de la Prudence, à Hector, Chef des Troyens*, 1461. Brussels, Bibliothèque Royale, MS. fr.9392, fol.63v.

Drawing a moral from an ancient tale was as popular in the Middle Ages as re-telling it in romance. The episode of Discord lent itself admirably to the didactic scheme of Christine de Pisan's *Epistle of Othéa, Goddess of Prudence, to Hector, Chief of the Trojans* (Plate 5). Christine drew much of her material from sources other than romance, such as the fourteenth-century moralized versions of Ovid and collected proverbs or 'Sayings of the Philosophers'. Her book of sugar-coated advice to young squires, composed about 1400, was widely read and translated into several languages; at least two English versions appeared before the end of the fifteenth century. Its general plan is that of a short rhymed text telling some mythological story, a longer prose commentary, usually allegorical, and a short moral, often rather far-fetched. Its various manuscripts are especially rich in representations of classical scenes depicted in terms of life at the French or Burgundian courts in the fifteenth century. As Christine presents the story of the feast:

'Discord is a goddess of evil deeds, and a fable sayeth that when Peleus wedded the goddess Thetis, who became the mother of Achilles, Jupiter and all the other gods and goddesses were at the marriage, but the goddess of Discord was not invited, and therefore out of envy she came unsought. But she did not come for nothing, for she did her part. When the three great goddesses, Pallas, Juno, and Venus, had sat down at a table, Discord came and cast upon the board an apple of gold, whereon was written, "Let this be given to the fairest"; and then the feast was troubled, for each of them said she ought to have it. They went before Jupiter to be judged concerning their strife, but he would not please one to displease another. Wherefore they put the question to Paris of Troy, the which was then an herdsman, as his mother dreamed, when she was great with him, that he would be the cause of the destruction of Troy; he was sent, therefore, to the herdsman in the forest and believed that he was his son. And there Mercury, the which conducted the ladies, told him whose son he was; then he left off keeping sheep and went to Troy to his great kin. The fable shows that a true story is under the poetic form, because great mischief has often befallen through discord and argument. Othéa sayeth to the good knight that he should beware of discord, as it is an evil thing to engage in strife and stir up riot.' Pythagoras sayeth 'Go not where hatreds grow.'

As it is said that discord should be avoided, in the same manner the good spirit should flee all blemishes of conscience and eschew strife and riots. [Cassiodorus] sayeth with authority, 'He shall flee strife and riots, for to strive against peace is madness, to strive against his sovereign is madness, to strive against his subjects is great villany.' Therefore Saint Paul sayeth, 'Not in strife and envying.'

Between the Middle Ages and the nineteenth century successive generations had rediscovered Homer, many Greek and Latin literary classics, and much of the lost art of Greece and Rome. The eighteenth-century classical revival had brought an archaeological reconstruction of antiquity far more meticulous, though less spontaneous, than that of the Renaissance. But with the nineteenth-century romanticists the wheel finally came full circle: a group of artists and authors interested themselves in medieval literary sources and to some extent adopted pseudo-medieval forms. Like artists of the Middle Ages, though self-consciously, Burne-Jones and other English 'Pre-Raphaelite' painters emphasized narrative content and elaborate detail; they even aimed at the angularity and decorative effect of medieval paintings. The classic roundness and solidity of modelling, recovered and perfected in the Renaissance remained, however, a guiding influence in their work. Burne-Jones planned a series of paintings on Trojan scenes,

6. THE FEAST OF PELEUS. Painting, 1872–1881, by Sir Edward Burne-Jones (English). Birmingham, City Museum and Art Gallery.

of which his *Feast of Peleus* was meant to be a part. This *Feast* is neither Greek nor medieval, but the conception of a romantic nineteenth-century artist viewing the ancient world as in a medieval mirror.

The painting is filled with delicate detail. The table, loaded with exotic fruits, is spread upon a shore in Thessaly—or, in the painter's own words, 'in a land no one can define or remember, only desire.' Beyond it unfolds a panorama of woodland and meadow and blue sea, suggestive at once of medieval Flemish painting and of the Oriental landscapes with which Europe had recently become familiar. Discord, bat-winged, departs at the right, casting a malicious glance at the three goddesses. Hermes, wearing the winged cap and shoes which were his classical attributes, kneels near her in the right foreground, holding in one hand the apple with a scroll inscribed DETUR PULCHERRIMAE. Beside him Apollo still fingers his lyre, but casts a troubled glance toward the intruder. Love, slender and winged, stops in his spreading of the marriage bed. In the centre the Fates weave their web of human destiny, over which Atropos the inflexible holds her shears.

Zeus sits enthroned in the centre, raising his hand in an angry gesture toward Discord. At his side Peleus and Thetis cower in dismay. Between them and Discord are Demeter, crowned with ears of wheat, and her daughter, Persephone. At the end of the table nearest Discord sits Dionysus, god of wine, crushing grapes into his cup. To the left of Zeus stand the three contending goddesses, their hands outstretched toward the apple. Hera is next to her lord, the helmeted Athena in the centre, Aphrodite, youthful and appealing, at the left. Nearest her, in the left foreground, Ares, god of war, in the guise of a medieval knight, half rises from his seat as though sensing the beginning of combat.

7. THE JUDGMENT OF PARIS. Attic white-ground pyxis, 465–460 B.C. New York, Metropolitan Museum of Art, 07.286.36. Rogers Fund, 1907.

At the left is Athena with her helmet, facing Hera. Aphrodite is out of sight, behind Athena.

Following the counsel of Zeus the three goddesses went with Hermes to Mount Ida in Asia Minor, where Paris kept his flocks. Hera promised the Trojan prince power and wealth if he would decide in her favour; Athena, victory and renown in war; Aphrodite, the love of the fairest woman in Greece, whom many authors named as Helen, wife of Menelaus king of Sparta. Paris was young and eager; Aphrodite was, after all, love and beauty personified. It was but natural for him to favour her.

Of all incidents in the Trojan war this has been the most continuously stressed in art and literature. It appears in the seventh century B.C., or perhaps a little earlier, on an ivory comb found in Sparta. Homer knew the story, though the *Iliad* mentions it only in passing as '. . . the delusion of Paris, who insulted the goddesses when they came to him.' The summary of the *Cypria* says briefly: 'Alexandrus, lured by his promised marriage with Helen, decides in favour of Aphrodite.' In

8. Reverse of the pyxis shown opposite.
Hermes wears a traveller's hat, carries one of his most common attributes, the caduceus, or wand, and wears the winged boots which carry him swiftly on his errands for the gods. Behind Paris stands a man who may be his father, Priam of Troy.

Euripides' *Trojan Women* Helen herself describes the scene, as she defends her actions to Menelaus after Troy's fall:

> '. . . this Paris judged beneath the trees
> Three crowns of Life, three diverse Goddesses.
> The gift of Pallas was of War, to lead
> His East in conquering battles, and make bleed
> The hearts of Hellas. Hera held a Throne—
> If majesties he craved—to reign alone
> From Phrygia to the last realm of the West.
> And Cypris, if he deemed her loveliest,
> Beyond all heaven, made dreams about my face
> And for her grace gave me. And lo! her grace
> Was judged the fairest, and she stood above
> Those twain . . .'

9. THE JUDGMENT OF PARIS. Roman wall painting from Pompeii, first century A.D. Naples, National Museum.

The three goddesses appear fully clothed in Greek vase paintings of the judgment of Paris. Roman artists, however, usually showed Aphrodite partially nude, as in this wall painting and the relief in Plate 10, and thus Apuleius described the scene as presented in a danced mime in the second century A.D. First came Mercury [Hermes], bearing the caduceus and the golden apple, which he gave to Paris. Next appeared dancers dressed as Juno and Minerva.

'Then came another, which passed the others in beauty, and represented the goddess Venus with the colour of ambrosia; but Venus when she was a maiden, and to the end that she would shew her perfect beauty, she appeared all naked, saving that her fine and comely middle was lightly covered with a thin silken smock, and this the wanton wind blew hither and thither, sometime lifting it to testify the youth and flower of her age, and sometime making it to cling close to her to shew clearly the form and figure of her members; her colour was of two sorts, for her body was white, as descended from heaven, and her smock was bluish, as returning to the sea' [an allusion to the legend that she was born of the sea foam].

The three then danced to appropriate music. Juno's dance, for which she herself played the flute, suggested her promise of power and authority; Minerva's, for which a flute player imitated trumpet tones, recalled the excitement of battle and victory.

'Then came Venus and presented herself, smiling very sweetly,' accompanied by flutes and pipes. She 'moved smoothly forwards more and more with slow and lingering steps, gently bending her body and moving her head, answering by her motion and delicate gestures to the sound . . . and sometimes she seemed to dance only with her eyes. . . . Then the young Phrygian shepherd Paris with a willing mind delivered to Venus the golden apple.'

10. THE JUDGMENT OF PARIS: AT THE LEFT THE THREE GRACES. Relief on a niche of the stage of the theatre at Sabratha, Leptis Magna, North Africa. Roman, second or third century A.D.

Ovid and Lucian of Samosata followed still another version of the scene according to which all the goddesses disrobed at the request of Paris. In one of Lucian's delightfully satiric *Dialogues of the Gods* Hermes and the goddesses, arriving at Mount Ida, are greeted by the young Trojan:

'*Paris*. Good morrow, youngster. And who may you be, who come thus far afield? And these dames? They are over-comely to be wandering on the mountain-side.

Hermes. "These dames," good Paris, are Hera, Athene, and Aphrodite; and I am Hermes, with a message from Zeus. Why so pale and tremulous? Compose yourself; there is nothing the matter. Zeus appoints you the judge of their beauty, "Because you are handsome, and wise in the things of love" (so runs the message), "I leave the decision to you"; and for the prize, read the inscription on the apple.

Paris. Let me see what it is about. FOR THE FAIR, it says. But, my lord Hermes, how shall a mortal and a rustic like myself be judge of such unparalleled beauty? This is no sight for a herdsman's eyes; let the fine city folk decide on such matters. As for me,

I can tell you which of two goats is the fairer beast; or I can judge betwixt heifer and heifer;—'tis my trade. But here, where all are beautiful alike, I know not how a man may leave looking at one, to look upon another . . . . Take it where you will, 'tis a hard matter to judge. . .

Hera. I approve your decision, Paris. I will be the first to submit myself to your inspection. You shall see that I have more to boast of than white arms and large eyes; nought of me but is beautiful.

Paris. Aphrodite, will you also prepare?

Athene. Oh, Paris,—make her take off that girdle first; there is magic in it; she will bewitch you. For that matter, she has no right to come thus tricked out and painted, —just like a courtesan! She ought to show herself unadorned.

Paris. They are right about the girdle, madam; it must go.

Aphrodite. Oh, very well, Athene: then take off that helmet, and show your head bare, instead of trying to intimidate the judge with that waving plume. I suppose you are afraid the colour of your eyes may be noticed, without their formidable surroundings.

Paris. God of wonders! What loveliness is here! . . . . But perhaps it would be well for me to view each in detail; for as yet I doubt, and know not where to look; my eyes are drawn all ways at once.

Aphrodite. Yes, that will be best.

Paris. Withdraw then, you and Athene; and let Hera remain.

Hera. So be it; and when you have finished your scrutiny, you have next to consider, how you would like the present which I offer you. Paris, give me the prize of beauty, and you shall be lord of all Asia.

Paris. I will take no presents. Withdraw. I shall judge as I think right. Approach, Athene.

Athene. Behold. And, Paris, if you will say that I am the fairest, I will make you a great warrior and conqueror, and you shall always win, in every one of your battles.

Paris. But I have nothing to do with fighting, Athene. As you see, there is peace throughout all Lydia and Phrygia . . . . But never mind: I am not going to take your present, but you shall have fair play. You can robe again and put on your helmet; I have seen. And now for Aphrodite.

Aphrodite. Here I am; take your time, and examine carefully; let nothing escape your vigilance. And I have something else to say to you, handsome Paris. Yes, you handsome boy, I have long had an eye on you; I think you must be the handsomest young fellow in all Phrygia . . . . You ought to have been married long ago; not to any of these dowdy women hereabouts, but to some Greek girl; an Argive, perhaps, or a Corinthian, or a Spartan; Helen, now, is a Spartan, and such a pretty girl—quite as pretty as I am—and so susceptible! Why, if she once caught sight of *you*, she would give up everything, I am sure, to go with you, and a most devoted wife she would be. But you have heard of Helen, of course?

Paris. No, ma'am; but I should like to hear all about her now.

Aphrodite. Well, she is the daughter of Leda, the beautiful woman, you know, whom Zeus visited in the disguise of a swan.

Paris. And what is she like?

Aphrodite. She is fair, as might be expected from the swan, soft as down: . . . and only think, she is so much admired, that there was a war because Theseus ran away with her; and she was a mere child then. And when she grew up, the very first men in Greece were suitors for her hand, and she was given to Menelaus . . . Now, if you like, she shall be your wife. . .

Paris. Take the apple: it is yours.'

II. THE JUDGMENT OF PARIS AS A DREAM. From a late-fifteenth-century manuscript of Raoul Lefèvre's *Recueil des Histoires de Troie* (Collection of Trojan Histories). Paris, Bibliothèque Nationale, MS.fr.22552, fol.214v.

Medieval romances customarily interpreted the judgment of Paris as a dream. This was not a new approach: as early as the second century A.D. the Greek Dio Chrysostom had suggested that Paris might have deluded himself 'like a soul which in its sleep follows out its phantasies and imaginings and spins out some long and coherent dream.' A little later Dares' *Historia*, removing as much as possible the pagan supernatural element, said forthrightly that Paris dreamed, and most of the romancers followed this story.

In Lefèvre's romance Paris describes to his father the scene shown in the manuscript illustration (Plate 11):

'It happened to me lately . . . that by your commandment I was in the Lesser Indies [Asia Minor] at the beginning of summer, and that upon a Friday I went me to hunt in a forest right early, and that morning I found nothing that gave me any pleasure. And then after midday I found a great hart that I began to chase so swiftly that I left all my fellowship behind and followed the hart into the most deserted place in all the forest, which forest was called Ida. I followed him so long that I came to a place that was passing obscure and dark. And then I saw no more the hart that I chased. I felt me sore weary and my horse also could go no farther and was all in a sweat. I alighted and tied my horse to a tree and laid me down upon the grass, and laid my bow under my head crosswise instead of a pillow, and soon I fell asleep. Then came to me in a vision the god Mercury, and in his company three goddesses, that is to wit Venus, Pallas, and Juno. He left the goddesses at a little distance and appeared and said to me in this wise:

"Paris, I have brought these three goddesses unto thee, for a great strife and tension has fallen between them . . . . As they ate the other day in a place, suddenly there was cast among them an apple of so marvellous form and fairness and beauty that no such had been seen among them. And there was written about this aforesaid apple in Greek language that it be given to the fairest. And so each of them would have it beyond everything in the world, each saying that she was the most fair and fairer than the others . . . . And each of them promiseth thee certainly a gift for thy reward that thou shalt have without fail for the award of the apple. If thou judge that Juno be the fairest thou shalt be made the most noble man of the world in magnificence; if thou judge for Pallas she shall make thee the wisest man in the world in all sciences; if thou judge that Venus be the fairest, she shall give unto thee the most noble lady of Greece."

When I heard Mercury speak thus to me I said to him that I could not give true judgment unless I saw them naked before me for to see better the fashion of their bodies. And then Mercury had them unclothe all naked, and then I beheld them long. And methought all three passing fair, but yet me seemed that Venus exceeded the beauty of the others, and therefore I judged that the apple appertained to her.'

The judgment is not shown as an obvious dream in the fifteenth-century Italian painting (Plate 12), but it has the dreamlike quality of romance and fairy tale. This picture has much the same atmosphere of dream and mystery as the fourteenth-century English minstrel's romance, *The Siege and Battle of Troy*. The author of this poem had grown so confused that he spoke of four goddesses instead of three and gave all but one masculine instead of feminine names. But his short singing lines evoke an authentic magic. Enveloped in a sudden mist while hunting, Paris lay down to sleep beneath a tree. Then in his sleep he saw:

'Four ladies of Elfin land,
Of them I then knew not at all,
But soon thereafter I knew them well.
And then the ladies began to play;
They had found a ball of gold by the way
It was a full rich ball
Of burnished gold was it all.
And thereon was lettering
Of silver, in fair writing,
So that anyone could read it
Who had ever been at any school.
The letters said "The fairest woman of all
Shall have and hold this costly ball".'

12. THE JUDGMENT OF PARIS. Early fifteenth-century Italian painting. Florence, Museo Nazionale.

Here several incidents are shown at once. At the upper left the goddesses, whose courtly costumes are exaggerated just enough to suggest beings from another world, argue among themselves and toy with the apple, their ample robes spreading about them like a magic carpet. Above them hovers a figure who may be Discord; the deep-shaded grove behind her suggests Italy's thick-leaved orange trees or the gardens of the Hesperides where the fruit was plucked. Opposite the goddesses Paris sits among his flocks listening to the tale unfolded by Mercury; below, in a flower-studded meadow, he gives Venus the apple.

This painting, in the International Gothic style so popular at the turn of the century, is medieval in spirit, but renaissance in form. The figures, though firm and well modelled, are clothed in the fashions of their own time; there is no attempt to recreate a bygone period, or to suggest a feeling for antiquity.

13. THE JUDGMENT OF PARIS. Engraving, about 1510, by Marcantonio Raimondi (Italian), after a design by Raphael. New York, Metropolitan Museum of Art, Rogers Fund, 1919.

Here both subject and composition have been drawn from antiquity, their treatment revitalized by the creative imagination of the High Renaissance. There seems little doubt that Raphael took his inspiration from the Roman sarcophagus illustrated opposite, although its history has not been traced earlier than the late sixteenth century, when it came to the Villa Medici from the Della Valle collection in Rome. In adapting it the artist strengthened the design by reducing the number of scenes and simplifying the figures.

On the sarcophagus Paris sits at the left before his flocks, while nymphs stand behind him. He hands the apple to an Aphrodite clad in transparent drapery. Behind her appear Hera and the helmeted Athena, their arms outstretched. The nude male figure in the centre has been variously interpreted, sometimes as Paris himself in warrior guise ready to steal Helen. To the right the goddesses return to Olympus, where they are met by Zeus upheld by a wind god upon a cloud, while the other deities assemble. Below the Olympians appear the sea god Oceanus and attendant figures. By eliminating most of the return to Olympus, Raphael has simplified the composition and concentrated attention on the judgment scene, of which the gods of heaven and the sea are witnesses. The figures of the three goddesses have been treated with great freedom, showing the influence of another ancient sculpture, the marble group of the Three Graces, then in the cathedral library at Siena. The Three Graces, grouped with two facing toward the spectator and one seen from the back, was a popular theme in Greek and Roman art: it

14. THE JUDGMENT OF PARIS AND THE RETURN OF THE GODDESSES TO OLYMPUS. Front of a Roman sarcophagus, probably second century A.D. Rome, Villa Medici.

appears, for instance, treated in relief, in the theatre at Sabratha (Plate 10). The Siena Graces have exercised an early and enduring influence on renaissance and later art. By the last quarter of the fifteenth century Francesco Cossa had painted them in an otherwise non-classical fresco of the Triumph of Venus in the Palazzo Schifanoia in Ferrara; they were the subject of one of Raphael's early paintings, now in the Chantilly Museum. In these examples they are still the classic Graces, deities presiding over the arts of life. But from the early sixteenth century onward the goddesses among whom Paris judged were represented more and more as variants of these Graces. No doubt the immediate and widespread use of this composition owed much to the popularity of engravings, such as Marcantonio's, in great demand not only for themselves but for use as patterns by designers of ceramics and other decorative arts.

Raphael's design was by no means the first to incorporate figures from antiquity, but it is one of the earliest to use such ancient representations in their original context, and to reunite so harmoniously the classical content with classical form. Patient scholarship had, by this time, opened the door to the rich beauty of the classic past, seen no longer as a backward projection of the present but as an ideal golden age when gods and men alike embodied the perfection of physical beauty. From this vision there gradually emerged the picture of antiquity upon which the modern concept rests. It was left to later centuries to strive for archaeological correctness; for the Renaissance it was enough that its heroes walked like gods and its gods like men.

Raphael had been dead eight years when Cranach painted his *Judgment of Paris*, but the Renaissance moved slowly into Germany and the German artist's picture has a strong medieval flavour. This lingering medievalism may have been strengthened by the amalgamation of the pagan scene with a late and different legend. According to this story Alfred, an imaginary king of Mercia, on a visit to Guillaume d'Albanac, showed such an interest in his host's three beautiful daughters that their father suspected him of dishonourable intentions towards them. He brought them nude into the presence of the sleeping king and demanded that he marry one or see all three slain before his face. Alfred immediately wedded the second daughter.

This scene was often represented in much the same fashion as the judgment of Paris and showed the king being waked from sleep like Paris in the Trojan story. The father was depicted as an old man, frequently bearing a sword. In Cranach's painting this legend has left its trace in the aged appearance of the fantastically garbed Mercury. His hat is decorated with full-fledged birds rather than the traditional wings of classic art, and instead of an apple he holds a crystal globe such as might have been made by a German craftsman of the time. Paris wears heavy plate armour of German design. The goddesses are winsome young German girls posing with naïve awkwardness in the traditional attitudes, but without the customary attributes. The heavy necklaces, the plumed hat, and the scanty drapery serve merely to emphasize their piquant nudity. In the background lies Troy, a many-spired medieval seaport above which towers a castled crag.

Cranach made several versions of his *Judgment of Paris*—paintings in several collections and a woodcut of 1508. All have the same general composition but differ in details, such as the grouping of the goddesses and the attitudes of Paris and Mercury. All the goddesses, however, in their various arrangements, follow the pattern of side, back, and front views. In the woodcut, both they and Paris are older. Mercury remains an old man.

Like Raphael, Cranach was an extremely busy man. The Italian painter was lavishly commissioned by the Pope and the nobility of Rome; Cranach was artist for the Duke of Saxony, and, as such, responsible for a round of official portraits, the decoration of castles, the preparation of banners and costumes for festive occasions, the production of special furnishings, and the general oversight of ducal architecture. Perhaps his stories from classical mythology, with their suggestion of parody, afforded a welcome relaxation. Such subjects were extremely popular in Germany, as throughout the Continent, but the works of Cranach are unique in their humour and seeming naïveté combined with sophisticated technique.

One example, at least, of the furniture which the artist was called upon to decorate must have given him plentiful opportunity for such fancy. A few years after his woodcut of the *Judgment of Paris* he painted a marriage bed for a member of the ducal family. A German poet of the time, Philipp Engelbrecht von Engen, described this bed as covered with pictures from classical mythology and legend. Among these scenes, 'in the midst of the heavenly deities, stood the son of Priam, about to deliver his judgment in a loud voice.' These, wrote the poet, 'were painted, not by Parrhasius, not by Apelles...but by a greater than all these, Lucas.' So magnificently were these paintings executed that 'one believes he sees the figures breathe.'

15. THE JUDGMENT OF PARIS. Painting, about 1528, by Lucas Cranach the Elder (German). New York, Metropolitan Museum of Art, Rogers Fund, 1928.

16. THE JUDGMENT OF PARIS. Painting, 1635–1636, by Peter Paul Rubens (Flemish). London, National Gallery.

The lusty exuberance of baroque painting and its sense of dynamic movement permeate Rubens' *Judgment of Paris* despite the static nature of its theme. The goddesses, posed in a variant of the contrasting attitudes of the Graces, seem caught in briefly-arrested motion. Mercury leans forward eagerly. Only Paris remains in quiet contemplation.

The familiar classical attributes are here. Mercury has his winged hat and caduceus; Juno's peacock spreads his hundred-eyed feathers in the foreground; Minerva's owl sits in a tree above her Gorgon-headed shield; Venus is attended by the winged Cupid, god of love. Yet the painting is not fundamentally an incident from classic myth: its theme is rather the sensuous pleasure inherent in contrasting textures and magnificent human forms seen in a landscape filled with light and life. Transparent white scarves emphasize the flesh tones of Venus and Minerva; a rich crimson robe slips from Juno's splendid shoulders to strike a dominant note of colour. Enveloping the whole is a hazy atmosphere where golden light brightens the horizon beneath a sky alive with driven clouds. A cloud herself, Discord rides above, brandishing the torch that is to set Troy afire.

17. THE JUDGMENT OF PARIS. Painting, about 1915, by Pierre-Auguste Renoir (French). Germantown, Collection of Henry P. McIlhenny.

Atmosphere and texture were Renoir's chief concern in the rendering of this scene. There are the usual contrasted poses, classical attributes, even a tiny columned temple to suggest antiquity. But to the French Impressionist the true theme, the reason for the picture's being, was the play of light and shade upon nude figures in the open air, affording an opportunity to display the radiant flesh-tones and soft atmospheric effects that he loved. This is one of the later examples of a subject which Renoir had already painted several times and which he treated in sculpture as well.

Medieval romances usually began their account of the war with an earlier capture of Troy in the reign of Priam's father, Laomedon. The abduction of Helen, they said, was a result of this capture. In ancient literature this story belonged to the cycle of Hercules myths although it crossed with the legend of Troy. Homer knew the tale: the *Iliad* mentions briefly that Hercules came to Troy

> 'on a time for the sake of Laomedon's horses
> with six vessels only and the few men needed to man them,
> and widowed the streets of Ilion and sacked the city.'

According to a widely accepted ancient account this disaster was caused by the failure of Laomedon to pay the promised wages to Apollo and Poseidon, or to Poseidon alone, for building the walls of Troy. In the *Iliad* Poseidon complains loudly of this breach of faith. The offended gods sent pestilence and a sea monster to ravage the city and its coast, and Laomedon was told that he must expose his daughter Hesione to the beast. Hercules, passing that way, slew it and saved the maiden, but was refused the reward he had been promised—the horses that Zeus had given to Laomedon. Hercules went on his way vowing vengeance, returned with a band of warriors, and killed all the royal family except Priam and Hesione, giving the latter to his comrade Telamon. This legend appeared in art at least as early as the fourth century B.C. when, according to Pliny's *Natural History*, the Greek artist Aristophon painted 'the story of Laomedon and his bargain with Hercules and Neptune'.

Hercules' capture of the city was later linked with the voyage of Jason and the Argonauts in search of the Golden Fleece. As Diodorus of Sicily tells it in his *Historical Library*, Hercules was on his way to seek the Fleece when he stopped to rescue Hesione. He was promised both the maiden and the horses but was unable to take them with him, and when he sent for them later they were refused. He returned when the quest was over, killed most of the royal family, and gave Hesione to Telamon. Ovid's *Metamorphoses* tells much the same story, more briefly.

Dares gave a different reason for the city's first capture. In keeping with his policy of human rather than supernatural explanations, he omitted the story of the divine building of the walls, the vengeance of the gods, and the rescue of Hesione from the monster, and said that the trouble arose from Laomedon's refusal to let the Argonauts land at Troy for provisions. Guido and most of his followers told this version of the incident shown in the tapestry.

In the tapestry Laomedon and his courtiers stand within the city walls at the left; Jason and Hercules, in brocaded robes, are in the foreground; the ship in which they have arrived is moored at the right, labelled *De Gresse* (from Greece). Laomedon's messenger comes through the gateway marked *Troiae* to tell the Argonauts that they must leave. The complicated pattern, angularity of line, and richness of detail are characteristic of Franco-Flemish weaving in the last quarter of the fifteenth century.

Raoul Lefèvre complicated the plot by having Hercules take the city twice. In the first book of his *Recueil* he tells the story of Hesione's rescue, taking it probably from Boccaccio's *Genealogy of the Gods*. The maiden had been exposed, Lefèvre says, not because her father had refused the wages promised for building the walls but because he had appropriated money belonging to the temple: the monster was

18. PRELUDE TO THE FIRST CAPTURE OF TROY:
LAOMEDON FORBIDS JASON AND HERCULES TO LAND FOR PROVISIONS.
Franco-Flemish tapestry, late fifteenth century. Omaha, Joslyn Art Museum, given in memory of Willard Deere Hosford by W. D. Hosford, Jr.

sent in punishment for sacrilege. There is no mention of the Argonauts here, nor does Hercules kill Laomedon. In his second book, however, Lefèvre takes up the familiar tale of Laomedon's refusal to let the Argonauts land, after which Hercules comes back, sacks the city, kills Laomedon, and gives Hesione to Telamon. The third book tells of the war fought for Helen's sake: here, as in most of the romances, the ostensible reason for her abduction is to provide a hostage for Hesione.

Laomedon's son Priam rebuilt the ruined city with the utmost splendour. In ancient Greek tradition Troy, gateway to Eastern trade, was a symbol of wealth and luxury. In Euripides' *Trojan Women* Hecuba emphasizes this when she accuses Helen of wanting to exchange austere Sparta for the more pleasurable city of Asiatic Greece. In the Middle Ages, when Troy's actual site had been forgotten, the legend of its vanished glory was reinforced by the reports of merchants and crusaders concerning its medieval counterpart, Constantinople, seat of the Byzantine emperor, and other Eastern cities they had seen.

The manuscript illustration, opposite, shows Priam's new Troy, not as an Asiatic Greek city but as a Gothic town like those of medieval France and Flanders. Only the suggestion of a dome on the tall tower of the temple recalls such churches of the East as Constantinople's Hagia Sophia. The town is clearly labelled 'The Great City of Troy'. 'The Palace of Ilion' is Troy's citadel in the romances, not another name for the city. 'The Temple' is labelled also, as is the river which the romancer called 'Paucus' but the ancient Greeks knew as Scamander. Lefèvre describes Troy's fabled glory at length, in terms of the French or Burgundian ideal:

'The city was so great that the circuit was three journeys, and at that time in all the world was none so great and none so fair or so finely compassed . . . And there were in the city rich palaces without number, the fairest that ever were, and the fairest houses, rich and well encircled. Also there were in many parts of the city divers fair places and grounds for the citizens to sport and play in. In this city were men of all crafts and merchants who went and came from all parts of the world. In the middle of the city ran a great river named Paucus which bore ships and brought great comfort to the inhabitants . . . There were to be found many games and plays, such as the play of chess, the tables, and the dice, and divers other games. In the most outstanding place, upon a rock, King Priam had his rich palace that was named Ilion, which was one of the richest palaces and strongest that ever was in the world. It was in height five hundred paces without the height of the towers, whereof there were great plenty, so high that it seemed to them that saw them from afar that they reached unto heaven. And in this rich palace King Priam had made the richest hall that was at that time in all the world, wherein was his rich throne, and the table from which he ate and held state among his lords and barons. And all that belonged thereto was of gold and silver, of precious stones and of ivory.'

When he had rebuilt Troy Priam, according to Dares and the romancers, sent Antenor, one of his most trusted counsellors, to Greece to ask Hesione's return. This was refused contemptuously and when Antenor reported the refusal to the Trojan court Priam considered sending a fleet to punish the Greeks and recapture Hesione. It was at the council called to debate this action that Paris told of his dream of the goddesses and the apple and of his conviction that Venus would aid the Trojans.

19. PRIAM REBUILDING TROY. From a late-fifteenth-century manuscript of Raoul Lefèvre's *Recueil*. Paris, Bibliothèque Nationale, MS.fr.22552, fol.206v.

20. HELEN. Fragment of an Attic white-ground krater, 460–440 B.C.
Cincinnati, Art Museum.

Paris sailed for Sparta, home of that Helen whom Aphrodite had named as his prize. The daughter of Zeus and Leda and sister of the demi-gods Castor and Pollux, Helen was so fair that, when little more than a child, she had been carried off by Theseus, king of Athens, from whom her brothers rescued her. She then wedded Menelaus, who had succeeded Tyndareus, her reputed human father, as king of Sparta. Her other suitors, including almost all the chieftains of Greece, had sworn to uphold her choice and to avenge any wrong done to her or her husband.

Comparatively few unmistakable representations remain to show the Greek artists' conception of Helen: among them is this fragment inscribed with her name. It is to poets rather than to artists that Helen owes her immortality. To Homer she was the 'white-armed', the 'rich-haired', the 'shining among women'—stock phrases all. 'Helen, a marvel to men,' the *Cypria* calls her. Long after Homer's day the thought of her softened even Lucian's satire. His cynic Menippus, when Hermes showed him the bones of the illustrious dead in the Underworld, asked only to see Helen:

'*Hermes:* This skull is Helen.
Menippus: And for this a thousand ships carried warriors from every part of Greece?
Hermes: Ah, Menippus, you never saw the living Helen . . . . '

After fourteen centuries these lines echoed in Marlowe's *Faustus*:

'Was this the face that launch'd a thousand ships,
And burnt the topless towers of Ilium?'

Again, in Shakespeare's *Troilus and Cressida*, Helen is a pearl

'Whose price hath launch'd above a thousand ships.'

To Goethe's Faust she was the ideal beauty, impossible to hold even when attained,

21. APHRODITE PERSUADING HELEN. Relief, first century B.C. or first century A.D. Naples, National Museum.

toward which he yet must struggle, content with no lesser beauty. And to Poe her very name brought refreshment:

'Helen, thy beauty is to me
Like those Nicaean barks of yore,
That gently, o'er a perfumed sea,
The weary, wayworn wanderer bore
To his own native shore.

On desperate seas long wont to roam
Thy hyacinth hair, thy classic face,
Thy Naiad airs have brought me home
To the glory that was Greece
And the grandeur that was Rome.'

When Paris reached Sparta, accompanied by the Trojan Aeneas, son of Aphrodite and the Trojan noble Anchises, Menelaus entertained them royally. 'After this,' according to the *Cypria*, 'Menelaus sets sail for Crete, ordering Helen to furnish the guests with all they require until they depart. Meanwhile Aphrodite brings Helen and Alexandrus together.' In this relief Aphrodite has thrown a protective arm about the shoulders of the pensive Helen with the gesture of an affectionate elder sister. Above sits Peitho, goddess of Persuasion. Eros, a slender boy whose wings slash the sky, plants instantaneous love in the heart of Paris. It is a scene in the tradition of the *Iliad*, echoing Priam's words to Helen after nine years of war, 'I hold thee not to blame; nay, I hold the gods to blame.'

22. PARIS AND HELEN. Painting, 1788, by Jacques-Louis David (French). Paris, Louvre.

There is no need for god of Love or goddess of Persuasion here: the figures themselves reveal the artist's interpretation of the situation. Helen's relaxed attitude and dreaming, downcast countenance indicate the yielding of a serious but passionate nature to the pleading of a fiery and volatile suitor. It has been suggested that this conception of the Spartan queen was inspired by Gluck's opera, *Paris and Helen*, produced a few years earlier. Throughout the opera the composer had stressed the contrast between Helen's Spartan seriousness and accustomed discipline and the more impetuous and sophisticated Phrygian from Asiatic Greece. In accordance with this conception of his heroine Gluck represented her as betrothed but not married to Menelaus. The scene recalls the opera's third act in which Helen asks Paris to sing. He sings of love, then falls unconscious, worn out by his ardour. Recovering, he pleads his cause again, and the curtain falls as the lovers take ship for Troy.

The painting is typical of the eighteenth-century classical revival, stimulated by the excavations at Herculaneum and Pompeii in the late 'thirties and 'forties. Helen's pose is derived from that of a classic muse. The couch upon which Paris sits is adapted from Roman examples. In the background is the gallery supported by caryatids made by Jean Goujon 'in the antique style' for the palace of the Louvre in the mid-sixteenth century.

23. THE ABDUCTION OF HELEN. Attic red-figured skyphos, about 480 B.C.
Boston, Museum of Fine Arts, 13.186.

After she had yielded to Paris Helen, according to the *Cypria*, 'put very great treasure on board and sailed away by night.' The loss of treasure as well as wife rankled in Menelaus' breast: in the *Iliad*, when facing Paris for single combat, he reproaches the Trojan with thefts.

In the vase painting Paris leads Helen by the hand while Aphrodite holds out protecting arms. Eros flies before her, Peitho closes the procession, and Aeneas leads the way. Helen's bowed head and halting step suggest the modest attitude of a bride leaving for her husband's home. The delicately painted figures still retain something of the heaviness of feature and almost stylized treatment of drapery that marked the close of the transitional period of Greek art early in the great fifth century.

Here, as in the relief in Plate 21, the gods seem to be acting in unison to shape the actions of the Spartan queen. In Euripides' *Trojan Women*, however, Hecuba taunts Helen for being swayed by human motives:

> 'My son was passing beautiful, beyond
> His peers; and thine own heart, that saw and conned
> His face, became a spirit enchanting thee.
> ... ...

Thou sawest him in gold and orient vest
Shining, and lo, a fire about thy breast
Leapt. Thou hadst fed upon such little things,
Pacing thy way in Argos. But now wings
Were come. Once free from Sparta, and there rolled
The Ilian glory, like broad streams of gold,
To steep thine arms and splash the towers! How small,
How cold that day was Menelaus' hall.'

Helen, defending herself to Menelaus, blames his absence for her flight as well as Aphrodite's power:

'The first plain deed, 'tis that I answer not,
How in the dark out of thy house I fled . . .
There came a Seed of Fire, this woman's seed;
Came—O, a Goddess great walked with him then—
This Alexander, Breaker-down-of-Men,
This Paris, Strength-is-with-him; whom thou, whom—
O false and light of heart—thou in thy room
Didst leave, and spreadest sail for Cretan seas,
Far, far from me! . . . And yet, how strange it is!
I ask not thee; I ask my own sad thought,
What was there in my heart, that I forgot
My home and land and all I loved to fly
With a strange man? Surely it was not I,
But Cypris, there! Lay thou thy rod on her,
And be more high than Zeus and bitterer,
Who o'er all other spirits hath his throne,
But knows her chain must bind him . . . . '

24A. THE JUDGMENT OF PARIS AND THE ABDUCTION OF HELEN.
Left half of a painted cassone panel, Italian, third quarter of the fifteenth century. New York, Metropolitan Museum of Art, Collection of Giovanni P. Morosini, presented by his daughter Giulia, 1932.

Between ancient accounts of Helen's abduction and those in the medieval romances there is a radical change of scene and emphasis. To the Middle Ages the Trojans were so emphatically the heroes of the tale that it was unthinkable for a Trojan prince to offend the chivalric laws of hospitality by stealing his host's wife from the home where he had been welcomed. Dictys began his story of the war with Helen's abduction from Sparta, but most romancers followed the account of Dares, who had Paris steal Helen from the island of Cythera, where she was attending a feast of Venus. Indeed, most of them said that she had gone there, not to worship but to see the handsome Trojan of whom she had heard.

The panel of a painted chest (Plates 24A–B) traces the story of Paris and Helen, from the judgment among the three goddesses at the left to the lovers' exchange of ardent glances in the temple of Venus at the right. The ship in the foreground bears Helen to the temple at Cythera. Just behind it the vessel of Paris arrives at the island. Further away toward the left, on still another ship, Menelaus sails from home.

This painting, the work of a good craftsman rather than a master, belongs to the Renaissance in date, in costume, and in technical competence; spirit and content, however, remain medieval. In this blending of divergent strains it is typical of the cassone paintings of fifteenth-century Italy which form one of the most rewarding sources for scenes from the war of Troy.

As Raoul Lefèvre tells of the lovers' meeting:

'When Paris knew of this feast at Cythera he took his best clothes and did them on and also took the best appearing and most cleanly men he had. And he went to the temple and entered it in a fair, sweet manner, and made his offering of gold and silver with great generosity. Then Paris was looked at hard by all who were there because of his beauty.... So far went the tidings of the comings of these Trojans and of their beauty and fine apparel that Queen Helen heard them speak thereof. And then, after the custom of women, she

24B. PARIS AND HELEN WITH THEIR RETINUE IN THE TEMPLE OF VENUS. Right half of a painted cassone panel, Italian, third quarter of the fifteenth century. New York, Metropolitan Museum of Art, Collection of Giovanni P Morosini, presented by his daughter Giulia, 1932.

had great desire to know by experience if it were the truth that she heard. And she determined to go to the temple under cover of devotion to accomplish her desire . . . . When Paris knew that the Queen Helen . . . was come to the temple, he arrayed himself and his company in the most lordly style he could, and went to the temple . . . . And when he came and saw her he was greatly smitten with love, and began to look at her intently, and to desire to see the fashion of her body, which was so fair and altogether well shaped that it seemed to all who saw her that nature had made her to be beheld and seen. . . . And they looked at each other so long that it seemed as though Helen made a token or sign to Paris to approach her.'

That night the Trojans '. . . took all of those that they found in the temple and all the riches that were therein. And Paris with his own hand took Helen and them of her company and brought them to the ships.'

25. THE ABDUCTION OF HELEN AND HER COMPANIONS. Late-fifteenth-century Italian painting, School of Antonio Vivarini. Baltimore, Walters Art Gallery.

Paris brought Helen and her companions in his ship from Cythera to Tenedos, not far off the coast of Troy. There, after her fears had been allayed, she admitted that she was obliged to obey the will of the gods, who had evidently determined her fate. Paris then took her, her companions, and his men, and set out for Troy.

'And there came toward them, outside the town,' wrote Raoul Lefèvre, 'King Priam with a great company of noble men, and received his children and his friends with great joy. And then he came to Helen and bowed right sweetly to her and gave her great joy and honour. And when they came near the city they found a great multitude of people, who made a great feast of their coming, with many kinds of instruments of music. And in such joy they came to the palace of King Priam and he himself lighted down and helped Helen down from her palfrey.'

Here is the echo of Homeric tradition: in the *Iliad* Helen says of Priam that he 'was gentle always, a father indeed'.

26. THE ARRIVAL OF PARIS AND HELEN AT TROY. From the *Chronique Universelle, dite de la Bouquechardière* (*Universal Chronicle*) of Jehan de Courcy. Flemish, about 1470. New York, Pierpont Morgan Library, M214, fol.84.

In this manuscript illustration Helen, wearing the tall hennin and floating veil fashionable at the French and Flemish courts, is mounted on a white palfrey. Paris rides at her right side. Priam, white-bearded and dignified, is accompanied by his 'great company of noble men', including some high clergy who avert their faces from Helen. In the background the people make music within the city and at the gate. The Flemish artist has shown Troy as a city of his own country, with medieval turrets and crocketed late-Gothic arches; across the river is a Flemish landscape such as fifteenth-century painters loved to show.

While his ship lay at Tenedos Paris had reassured Helen:

' "Think you that I will maintain you dishonestly? Certes, nay, but I shall take you to be my wife. And so shall you be more honoured than you have been with your husband and more praised, for your husband has not come from so noble a stock as I, nor so valiant. Nor has he ever loved you so well as I shall do. Therefore cease from henceforth to make such sorrow".'

Now, home in his father's halls, he made good his promise. As Lefèvre tells

'And when it came unto the morn, Paris, with the agreement and consent of his father, took Helen as his wife, and wedded her in the temple of Pallas. And therefore the feast was extended throughout the whole city, and was continued for eight whole days.'

Nothing marred the merriment save the wailing of Cassandra, Priam's daughter, whose fate it was always to foretell the truth and never to be believed. When she heard of this marriage, as when she had learned of Paris' plan to steal a Grecian woman, she prophesied Troy's doom:

' "O unhappy Trojans, wherefore rejoice you at the wedding of Paris, whereof so many evils shall come and follow? And wherefore see you not the death of yourselves, and of your sons that shall be slain before your eyes, and the husbands before their wives, with great sorrow? O, noble city of Troy, how shalt thou be destroyed and put to naught! O, unhappy mothers, what sorrow shall you see, when you shall see your little children taken and dismembered before you!...O, people blind and foolish, why do you not send the incontinent Helen home again and yield her to her rightful husband, before the swords of your enemies come and slay you with great sorrow?".'

But Cassandra's only reward was imprisonment.

Dictys added an entertaining variant to the account of Helen's reception in Troy, which was not followed by the western romancers. Helen declared that she and the family of Hecuba were distant kin, whereupon the Trojan queen embraced her and won over the king. Helen also influenced all in her favour by saying that she had come to Troy of her own accord and that she had not consented to her previous marriage with Menelaus.

In the tapestry (Plate 27) Paris places a ring on Helen's finger; Priam looks on approvingly from behind the dais. His name is woven into the table top; that of Helen is immediately beneath her robe; that of Paris, above his head. Cassandra stands at the upper left; at the upper right the wedded couple retire to the bridal chamber. The dawning influence of the northern Renaissance is apparent in the ample forms with their rounded modelling and generalized types. Weaving is beginning that approach to painting which was to become the goal of tapestry in the seventeenth and eighteenth centuries.

27. THE MARRIAGE OF PARIS AND HELEN. Franco-Flemish tapestry (Tournai), late fifteenth century. New York, Duveen Brothers.

When Menelaus returned to Sparta and discovered Helen's flight he called upon all the chieftains of Greece to help him recover her. They chose as their leader Agamemnon, king of Mycenae, Menelaus' brother, who had wedded Helen's sister, Clytemnestra. Agamemnon's first task was to gather his warriors. Most came willingly but a few were hard to enlist. Odysseus, king of Ithaca, who had married Helen's cousin, Penelope, was happy with his wife and his little son Telemachus, and he tried vainly to escape by pretending madness. After he had been won over he set himself to persuade others by the ingenuity for which he was famous.

When ready to sail, the Greek allies gathered at Aulis, a small harbour on a bay in north-eastern Greece. According to some authors they then set out for Troy but

28. HOW THE KINGS, DUKES, EARLS, AND BARONS OF GREECE ASSEMBLED WITH ALL THEIR NAVY BEFORE THE CITY OF ATHENS AND CAME TO TROY.
From a late-fifteenth-century manuscript of Raoul Lefèvre's *Recueil.*
Paris, Bibliothèque Nationale, MS.fr.22552, fol.223v.

were driven back by storms; others had it that they were held at Aulis by a dead calm.

The romances, following Dares, changed the place of the Greek gathering from Aulis to Athens, probably because this was then the best-known city of Greece.

The manuscript page shows Athens, with the Greek fleet lying in its harbour, as a purely medieval European city. There is no trace of a lofty Acropolis crowned by the Parthenon, nor of any of the other buildings of ancient Greece that the rare traveller might have seen. There is, however, one distinguishing feature which suggests some acquaintance with Athenian topography. The long strip of land running into the foreground recalls the Piraeus, the peninsula several miles from Athens which formed the city's chief port in ancient times as now. It has three harbours, two of which appear here. In their shelter lie the ships, 'twelve hundred and four and twenty', according to Lefèvre.

An awesome portent took place while the Greek ships lay at Aulis. In the *Iliad* Odysseus recalls it when the warriors are ready to sail for home after the quarrel between Achilles and Agamemnon. It is now the war's ninth year, Odysseus reminds his comrades, and long ago at Aulis Calchas had prophesied that by this time the end should be near. He then describes the portent:

> 'There appeared a great sign: a snake, his back blood-mottled,
> a thing of horror, cast into the light by the very Olympian,
> wound its way from under the altar and made toward the plane tree.
> Thereupon were innocent children, the young of the sparrow,
> cowering underneath the leaves at the uttermost branch tip,
> eight of them, and the mother the ninth, who bore these children.
> The snake ate them all after their pitiful screaming,
> and the mother, crying aloud for her young ones, fluttered about him,
> and as she shrilled he caught her by the wing and coiled around her.
> ... ...
> Kalchas straightway spoke before us interpreting the gods' will
> "Why are you turned voiceless, you flowing-haired Achaians?
> Zeus of the counsels has shown us this great portent; a thing late,
> late to be accomplished, whose glory shall perish never.
> As this snake has eaten the sparrow herself with her children,
> eight of them, and the mother was the ninth who bore them,
> so for years as many as this shall we fight in this place
> and in the tenth year we shall take the city of the wide ways.
> Come then, you strong-greaved Achaians, let every man stay
> here, until we have taken the great citadel of Priam".'

Centuries after Homer's day, Ovid added a characteristic touch: '... the serpent, just as he was, coiled round the green branches of the tree, was changed to stone, and the stone kept the form of the climbing serpent.' The Roman author of the *Metamorphoses* was making use of every opportunity to stress his connecting theme of transformation.

In Dares and the romances Calchas, represented as a renegade Trojan, prophesies a Greek victory; he had indeed forsaken Troy because his prophetic gift had told him the outcome. But the portent of the serpents is omitted.

29. CHEIRON AND ACHILLES.
Roman wall painting from Herculaneum, first century A.D.
Naples, National Museum, 9019.

Above all others the Greeks desired to have with them the young Achilles, son of Peleus and Thetis, of whom great deeds had been prophesied. By all the arts she knew as an immortal nymph, Thetis had tried to make him invulnerable. Some said that she dipped him in the River Styx but forgot the heel by which she held him; others, that fire was her agent but that she was interrupted before the mortal dross had burned away. These, however, were tales later than Homer and the epic cycle: in them Achilles, though half-divine, has all a mortal's vulnerability. And even according to the later legends there remained at least one spot in which he could be wounded fatally—the 'Achilles' heel'.

For his education Thetis entrusted the boy to Cheiron the centaur, half-man, half-horse, wiser than men in all the peaceful arts, so skilled in healing that he was believed to be the teacher of Aesculapius, god of medicine, and such a master of music that he had taught Apollo to play the lyre. At the outbreak of the Trojan war Calchas had prophesied that the city could not be taken without Achilles, and as Thetis knew that if he joined this struggle he would die, she hastened to Cheiron's cave to take her son to a more secure hiding. Statius' *Achilleid* describes the boy and his mother's visit to the centaur in words that might have been inspired by a painting such as this:

'. . . a radiant glow shimmers on his snow-white countenance, and his locks shine more comely than tawny gold. The bloom of youth is not yet changed by new-springing down, a tranquil flame burns in his glance, and there is much of his mother in his looks.' Cheiron sets a banquet before his guest and 'contriving various amusements for her beguiling, at last brings forth the lyre and moves the care-consoling strings, and trying the chords lightly with his finger gives them to the boy.'

30. CHEIRON AND ACHILLES.
Oil sketch for a tapestry, 1630–1632, by Peter Paul Rubens (Flemish).
Rotterdam, Boymans-Van Beuningen Museum.

Rubens was the seventeenth century's painter *par excellence* of Trojan subjects, both in number and quality of works dealing with these themes. This Cheiron and Achilles, in keeping with the artist's temperament, emphasizes the active side of the boy's education. Medicine and music are not neglected, but are symbolically represented by the caryatids at the sides of the design—Aesculapius and Terpsichore, muse of choral song and dance. Music is further stressed by the lyre hanging from a branch at the right. The hunt is suggested by the horn and bow lying on the ground, but the business in hand is a riding lesson. The picture might almost illustrate a passage from Philostratus' *Imagines* describing a painting of The Education of Achilles:

The boy '. . . is sporting on the back of the centaur as if it were a horse . . . for Cheiron is teaching Achilles to ride horse-back and to use him exactly as a horse, and he measures his gait to what the boy can endure, and turning around he smiles at the boy when he laughs aloud with enjoyment, and all but says to him "Lo, my hoofs paw the ground for you without use of spur; lo, I even urge you on; the horse is indeed a spirited animal and gives no ground for laughter".'

The painting combines the gusto of a seventeenth-century Fleming with the bold sweep of the Italian baroque. Yet as between Italy's standards of ideal classic beauty and the vigorous life of the world about him, Rubens unhesitatingly chose the latter. Cheiron's face has the kindly yet determined expression of a jolly but competent Flemish merchant; the boy who rides his back is no graceful stripling but such a youth as the painter might have seen in the streets and fields of Flanders.

31. ACHILLES ON SCYROS. Roman wall painting from the House of the Dioscuri, Pompeii, first century A.D. Naples, National Museum, 9110.

32. ACHILLES ON SCYROS. Painting, 1656, by Nicolas Poussin (French). Richmond, Virginia Museum of Fine Arts, Arthur and Margaret Glasgow Fund, 1957.

Thetis took Achilles from Cheiron, dressed him as a girl, and hid him among the maidens at the court of Lycomedes, king of Scyros, where he fell in love with the princess Deïdamia. The Greeks, meanwhile, sought him far and wide, and eventually Odysseus, wiliest of them all, came to Scyros disguised as a merchant. He offered trinkets to the maidens but put with them a few weapons. These immediately drew the attention of Achilles, and Odysseus recognized him as the prince whom he sought. Achilles, though he knew that death awaited him if he went to war, joined Agamemnon of his own will, bringing with him fifty ships and his own troops, the famous Myrmidons.

The summary of the *Cypria* says nothing of Achilles among the maidens of Scyros, implying that he came straight to war from his father's court, stopping off on the way to marry Deïdamia. The story of his stay at the court of Lycomedes was, however, the more widely accepted. It formed the subject of one of Euripides' lost plays, *The Scyrians*; it appears in one of Bion's idylls; and it was told by Ovid, Statius, Apollodorus, and Philostratus among others.

In the Roman painting, (Plate 31), Odysseus and a companion seize Achilles by the arm as he lays hold upon a sword; in Poussin's version, the hero, decked out in a helmet, looks at himself in a mirror in feminine fashion. Owing to its philosophical significance as a representation of choice, this subject continued to be treated even when Trojan themes as such were out of fashion.

Medieval writers differed from those of antiquity as to the place where the Greeks assembled, but all agreed that something untoward occurred at Aulis. Concerning this happening the old Greek accounts themselves had varied. According to the *Cypria* Agamemnon killed a stag sacred to Artemis and boasted that he was a better hunter than the goddess of the chase. Other sources declared that before the birth of his daughter, Iphigenia, Agamemnon had vowed to Artemis the fairest thing the year should bring forth but that, when Iphigenia proved to be the promised sacrifice, he failed to keep his oath. Whatever the reason, the Greek ships were held at Aulis, unable to set out for Troy.

Calchas the soothsayer now told Agamemnon that before the ships could sail Iphigenia must be sacrificed to Artemis. Despite his anguish Agamemnon agreed, believing the dilemma to be his fault and his responsibility. On the pretext of marrying her to Achilles he sent for Iphigenia; with her, according to some versions, came her mother Clytemnestra, Helen's sister. The mother's horror at her husband's purpose was later to hasten Agamemnon's doom. The *Iliad* makes no mention of the intended sacrifice of Iphigenia, but the story as told in the *Cypria* was a favourite with Greek dramatists.

In Euripides' *Iphigenia in Aulis* Agamemnon tries in vain to countermand by stealth his message to Iphigenia, and Achilles, angered at the use of his name for such an end, offers to save her when she arrives. She refuses, saying:

> 'Die not for me, nor slay thou any man,
> Let me be Hellas' saviour, if I may,'

and goes willingly to the sacrifice.

> '. . . But when King Agamemnon saw
> The maid for slaughter entering the grove,
> He heaved a groan, he turned his head away
> Weeping, and drew his robe before his eyes.'

The priest's knife was ready for the blow when the maiden vanished and in her place

> '. . . there lay a hind
> Most huge to see, and passing fair to view,
> With whose blood all the Goddess' altar ran.'

As related in the *Cypria* Artemis relented, snatched Iphigenia away, and carried her in a cloud to Tauris (in the modern Crimea), where she became a priestess of the goddess. Pliny has left a description of the scene as painted by the Greek artist Timanthes:

> 'Orators have sung the praises of his Iphigenia, who stands at the altar awaiting her doom. The artist has shown all present full of sorrow, and especially her uncle; but having exhausted all the characteristic features of sorrow, he adopted the device of veiling the features of the victim's father, feeling himself unable adequately to give expression to his feelings.'

The Pompeiian painting is, indeed, believed to be a free adaptation of the type set by Timanthes, although here the maiden is not standing but is being borne to the altar.

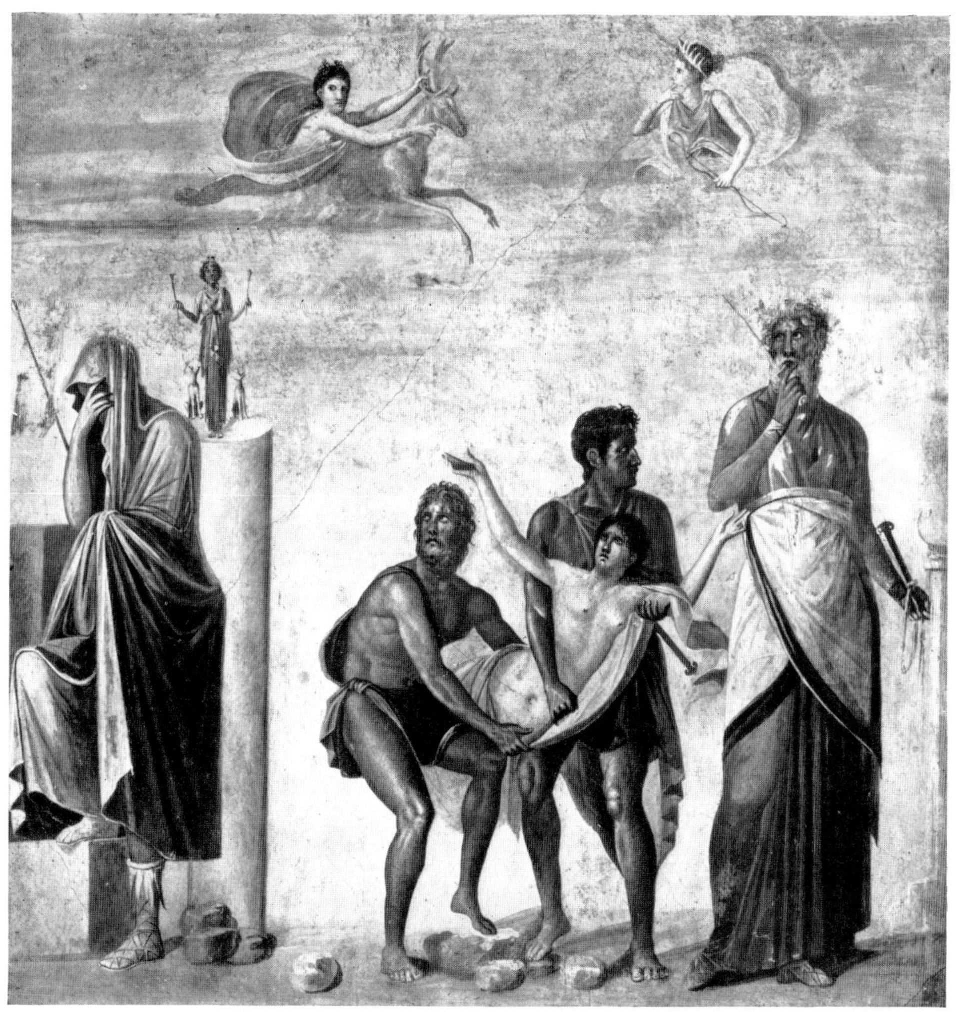

33. THE SACRIFICE OF IPHIGENIA AT AULIS. Roman wall painting from the House of the Tragic Poet at Pompeii, A.D. 63–79. Naples, National Museum, 9112. (Much repainted in the eighteenth century.)

Medieval romances and their sources differ even more than the ancient Greeks in describing what happened at Aulis. Dictys says that a pestilence afflicted the Greeks, which, they were told, was due to Agamemnon's slaughter of a beast sacred to Diana. Iphigenia was about to be sacrificed when a frightful storm delayed the ceremony and cast doubt upon its wisdom. A hind was found on the altar when the storm was over and the Greeks sacrificed it instead. Agamemnon, who had opposed the sacrifice of his daughter, was left in ignorance of her rescue, and she was sent to the king of the Scythians upon the advice of Achilles.

Dares simply says of the Greeks that 'tempests held them back' at Athens (not at Aulis) and that Calchas declared they 'should first return to Aulis [which he had not before mentioned] and sacrifice to Diana. They set out and reached Aulis.

34. THE SACRIFICE OF IPHIGENIA AT AULIS.
From a late fifteenth-century manuscript of Raoul Lefèvre's *Recueil*.
Paris, Bibliothèque Nationale, MS.fr.22552, fol.227v.

Here Agamemnon placated Diana.' Iphigenia is not mentioned, nor is there any explanation as to how Agamemnon appeased the goddess.

Benoit de Sainte-More and Guido delle Colonne, following Dares, omit the story of Iphigenia and say simply that Diana was offended by Agamemnon's failure to sacrifice to her before setting forth and that she relented when he did so. Lydgate tells the story of the substitution of the hind at the altar, claiming that he took it from Ovid. Lefèvre, however, says flatly that Agamemnon 'took his fair daughter Iphigenia, and in the presence of many great kings and princes sacrificed her unto the goddess Diana'. He may have taken his story directly from Ovid or indirectly from Boccaccio's *Genealogy of the Gods*, to which he refers several times in his romance. Ovid and Boccaccio tell two different forms of the legend—an actual sacrifice of Iphigenia and the substitution of the hind.

In the illustration from Lefèvre's romance Iphigenia, Agamemnon, and the temple of Diana are clearly labelled. Aulis is identified by an inscription beside the temple as the 'Isle of Andylle'.

35. THE SACRIFICE OF IPHIGENIA. Centre detail of a fresco, about 1757, by Giovanni Battista Tiepolo. See plate 36.

36. THE SACRIFICE OF IPHIGENIA. Fresco by Giovanni Battista Tiepolo (Italia

About 1757 Tiepolo decorated five rooms in the Villa Valmarana with subjects from famous poems. Three were from Greek and Latin classics; of the others, one shows scenes from Ariosto's *Orlando Furioso*, the other episodes from Tasso's *Gerusalemme Liberata*. One room is devoted to the *Iliad*; one has scenes from the *Aeneid*. The story of Iphigenia, on the walls and ceiling of the central room, was said by an eighteenth-century writer to have been taken from Ovid's *Metamorphoses*, but the frescoes suggest the emotion and suspense of Euripides rather than Ovid's delicate fantasy.

Tiepolo's brilliant presentation, with its broadly-treated figures, its grandiose architectural setting, and its enveloping flood of light, has a natural kinship to the heroic legends of Greece. The action fills the room as though it were a stage. The upraised eyes of the priest seem to behold not only the apparition of the hind in a cloud at the left but that of Diana in the nebulous ceiling above.

ut 1757. Vicenza, Villa Valmarana.

Leaving Aulis (Athens) the Greeks came to Tenedos, the port guarding the approach to Troy. 'Here,' says the summary of the *Cypria*, 'Achilles quarrels with Agamemnon because he is invited late', and here, too, according to Apollodorus' *Epitome*, Achilles killed Apollo's son, Tenes, thereby sealing his own doom. Dares' account of the action here is brief but gory: 'They came to Tenedos, and slew all who were there.' The romancers embroidered this assault into a full-fledged medieval attack, shown in Plate 37 as taking place directly from shipboard. As Raoul Lefèvre tells it:

'At this port was a passing strong castle and well peopled and full of great riches . . . . When they of the castle saw the Greeks they ran to arms and garnished the castle with good fighters. And the others issued out of the ships all armed . . . . Thus began the battle between them, right fierce and mortal, and there were enough slain and dead of both

37. THE GREEKS CAPTURE THE CASTLE AND PORT OF TENEDOS NEAR TROY.
From a fourteenth-century manuscript of the *Cronica Troyana*, a Spanish version of Benoit de Sainte-More's twelfth-century French romance.
Madrid, Escorial Library, MS h.I.6, fol.30.

parties, and many more of the Greeks than of the Trojans. But presently as the Greeks arrived in full strength the Trojans could no longer endure, but put themselves to flight, some to the castle and others to Troy. Then the Greeks besieged the castle round about, and assailed it on all sides. They that were within defended it passing well upon the walls, and slew many by shot and engines. But the Greeks put their engines all around the castle and set up their ladders to the walls, and went up on all sides . . . . And then the Greeks entered by force into the castle, and there slew all that they found, without sparing of man or woman.'

From Tenedos the Greeks went on to land at Troy. At first they were driven back. In this skirmish the Thessalian leader, Protesilaos, according to the *Iliad*, 'leapt from his ship, far first of all the Achaians' and was slain 'by a Dardanian man', usually said to be Hector. Protesilaos had left a newly-wedded wife, Laodamia, whose sorrow has been a favourite theme for poets through many centuries. Ovid chose her as one of the heroines whose love letters formed the theme of his *Heroides*. There Laodamia refers to a prophecy that marked for death the first 'to touch the soil of Troy', and begs her husband to be last to leave his ship.

38. MENELAUS AND ODYSSEUS DEMAND THE RETURN OF HELEN.
From a Corinthian column-krater, about 560 B.C.
Naples, Collection of Mario Astarita.

Soon after their arrival before Troy the Greeks sent an embassy to demand the return of Helen and the stolen treasure. The synopsis of the *Cypria* does not name the ambassadors: the *Iliad* and Bacchylides' fragmentary poem, *The Sons of Antenor or The Demanding Back of Helen*, say that they were Menelaus and Odysseus. Dares and the romancers call them Diomedes and Ulysses.

The vase painting shows Menelaus and Odysseus and their herald seated on the stair leading up from inside the city to the walls of Troy: facing them is Theano, priestess of Athena and wife of the Trojan prince, Antenor. She is attended by three women and a cavalcade of sons. The scene corresponds with what remains of Bacchylides' poem, in which Theano and her sons greet the Greeks while her husband hastens to prepare Priam and call the citizens of Troy for conference. The embassy, however, was unavailing, and the war began in earnest.

The scene in the tapestry (Plate 39) is very different. Here Priam, high on his throne and surrounded by his sons, including Hector and Paris, Deiphobus and Troilus, talks with Ulysses and Diomedes. The episode with Theano and her sons has disappeared. At the upper right is a separate scene which shows Achilles actively engaged during the conference in killing Teuthras king of Mysia, one of Troy's allies. Between this scene and Priam's throne rises a slender tree.

This tree was one of the marvels added to the story by romancers steeped in crusaders' stories of the exotic East and the Byzantine court. It might almost be an echo of a sight described in his *Antapodosis* by Liudprand of Cremona, ambassador from Tuscany to Byzantium in the tenth century:

'Before the emperor's seat stood a tree, made of bronze gilded over, whose branches were filled with birds, all made of gilded bronze, which uttered different cries, each according to its varying species.'

39. ULYSSES AND DIOMEDES DEMAND THE RETURN OF HELEN.
Franco-Flemish tapestry (Tournai), 1472–1474. Glasgow Art Gallery, Burrell Collection.

Lydgate's *Troy Book* describes the tree at length, with its

> '. . . rich branches and the leaves so fair,
> Twined each with other to make a pair,
> One leaf of gold, with one of silver sheen,
> And scattered through with stones both white and green.'

40. ACHILLES, LYING IN WAIT FOR TROILUS, SEES POLYXENA.
Attic black-figured hydria about 575–550 B.C. New York, Metropolitan Museum of Art, 45.11.2. Rogers Fund, 1945.

Early in the war Achilles killed Troilus, one of Priam's sons. The summary of the *Cypria* merely notes his death; other sources say that he was killed while exercising his horses near Apollo's temple.

Near the spring behind which Achilles lurks is Troilus' sister, Polyxena, with a water jar. No ancient Greek literature known today mentions Polyxena in this connection or describes Achilles' meeting with this princess whose fate was to be linked with his, but such an incident may have occurred in the lost *Cypria*.

Later writers changed the time of Troilus' death until almost the end of the war and connected it with Achilles' love for Polyxena. With Benoit de Sainte-More Troilus himself became the hero of a romance within romance, which was retold in varying forms by Boccaccio, Chaucer, and Shakespeare as the story of Troilus and Cressida.

THE ILIAD

41. ACHILLES [his name is inscribed]. From an Attic red-figured amphora, about 450–440 B.C. Rome, Vatican, H.487.

Achilles is the hero of Homer's *Iliad*, the only surviving early Greek epic centred on the action of the Trojan war. It tells of a bitter quarrel between Achilles and Agamemnon and its results; it covers only a few eventful weeks in the war's tenth year; and it ends before Troy's fall with the death of Hector, son of Priam, foremost among the Trojan heroes.

At the wedding feast of Peleus and Thetis the Fates had sung:

'There shall be born to you a son that knows not fear, Achilles, known to his enemies not by his back but by his stout breast.'

The *Iliad* seldom describes its heroes intimately: they live in action and in speech. To Homer Achilles was the 'brilliant', the 'swift-footed', but these epithets were often applied to others. The essential quality of this warrior-born is revealed by his decision in the light of what he knew concerning his own fate:

> '. . . my mother Thetis the goddess of the silver feet tells me
> I carry two sorts of destiny toward the day of my death. Either
> if I stay here and fight beside the city of the Trojans,
> my return home is gone, but my glory shall be everlasting;
> but if I return home to the beloved land of my fathers,
> the excellence of my glory is gone, but there will be a long life
> left for me, and my end in death will not come to me quickly.'

Unhesitatingly, except when consumed by anger and hurt pride, he chose death and glory. Even the pro-Trojan romancers could not fail to see Achilles as a hero. Lydgate wrote:

> 'And furthermore, to speak of Achilles,
> He was right fair and of great seemliness,
> with auburn hair, waving through its thickness,
> With blue-green eyes, wide open, bright, and large.
> Right true of word also, as I read,
> And no quarrel would he take on did he not understand
> That it was fully grounded upon right,
> And then he would acquit him like a knight.'

Raoul Lefèvre, no flatterer of Achilles, said that he had 'no equal among the Greeks'.

Nor has his glory faded. The vision of fearlessness, simple, unique, and fated, that inspired alike Homer and the Greek vase painter, lived still in the sonnet of Ernest Myers in the nineteenth century:

> 'Athwart the sunrise of our western day
> The form of great Achilles, high and clear,
> Stands forth in arms, wielding the Pelian spear.
> The sanguine tides of that immortal fray
> Swept on by gods, around him surge and sway.'

42. ATHENA RESTRAINING THE ANGER OF ACHILLES. Mosaic, first century A.D. Naples, National Museum, 9104.

After their fruitless embassy for the recovery of Helen the Greeks, according to the *Cypria*, attacked Troy. Failing to capture it by force they laid waste the surrounding countryside and neighbouring cities.

Given the impetuous nature of Achilles and the slow progress of the first nine years of the war under Agamemnon's leadership, it is not surprising that the *Iliad* should begin:

> 'Sing, goddess, the anger of Peleus' son, Achilleus.'

Once committed to the war, the hero's very devotion to glory at the cost of life made him impatient: as a prince royal and a fighter of renown he felt himself equal in position and superior in ability to Agamemnon. While the other Greeks had been waging indecisive actions against Troy, Achilles and his Myrmidons had captured neighbouring cities.

The situation was ripe for trouble. During one of his campaigns, the *Cypria* tells, Achilles had taken prisoner Chryseis, daughter of Chryses priest of Apollo. In the division of plunder the maiden had fallen to the share of Agamemnon, who refused her father's request for her return. In answer to the priest's petition Apollo sent upon the Greeks a pestilence so severe that a council was called to determine its cause. Achilles at once fixed the blame upon Agamemnon. Angrily Agamemnon agreed to release Chryseis, but demanded in her place Briseis, a maiden who had fallen to Achilles' share. Then, says the *Iliad*:

> '... ... ... the anger came on Peleus' son, and within
> his shaggy breast the heart was divided in two ways, pondering
> whether to draw from beside his thigh the sharp sword, driving
> away all those who stood between and kill the son of Atreus,
> or else to check the spleen within and keep down his anger.
> Now as he weighed in mind and spirit these two courses
> and was drawing from its scabbard the great sword, Athene descended
> from the sky. For Hera, the goddess of the white arms sent her,
> who loved both men equally in her heart and cared for them.
> The goddess standing behind Peleus' son caught him by the fair hair,
> appearing to him only, for no man of the others saw her.'

Achilles obeyed Athena's command and put up his sword, but although he surrendered Briseis he withdrew entirely from fighting, announcing to Agamemnon:

> '"... ... ... give me no more
> commands, since I for my part have no intention to obey you."'

43. ATHENA RESTRAINING THE ANGER OF ACHILLES. Wall painting, about 1757, by Giovanni Battista Tiepolo (Italian). Hall of the *Iliad*, Villa Valmarana, near Vicenza.

No such outburst of anger occurs in the Troy romances: as they tell the story, Achilles withdrew from battle later in the war because of his love for Priam's daughter, Polyxena, and his hope of winning her by making peace between Greeks and Trojans. Briseis, immediate cause of the trouble in the *Iliad*, disappears as such in the romances; under the names Briseida and Cressida she becomes the heroine of a new love story with the Trojan, Troilus.

Because of these wide differences in motivation an exact counterpart of the Roman painting would have been impossible in the Middle Ages. By Tiepolo's time, of course, the ancient motives had been re-established, and the Venetian artist presents Homer's story of the hero's wrath and Athena's forcible intervention; the boldness and sweep of his style, baroque tempered with neo-classic restraint, even evoke Homer's grandeur.

44. THE SURRENDER OF BRISEIS.
Roman wall painting from the House of the Tragic Poet, Pompeii, A.D. 63–79.
Naples, National Museum, 9105.

45. THE SURRENDER OF BRISEIS.
Marble relief, 1803, after a model by Bertel Thorwaldsen (Danish).
Copenhagen, Thorwaldsen Museum.

As Homer told this incident, Agamemnon

> 'Did not give up his anger and the first threat he made to Achilleus,
> but to Talthybios he gave his orders and Eurybates
> who were heralds and hard-working henchmen to him: "Go now
> to the shelter of Peleus' son Achilleus, to bring back
> Briseis of the fair cheeks leading her by the hand. And if he
> will not give her, I must come in person to take her
> with many men behind me, and it will be the worse for him."
> ... ...
> The man himself they found beside his shelter and his black ship
> sitting. And Achilleus took no joy at all when he saw them.
> These two terrified and in awe of the king stood waiting
> quietly, and did not speak a word at all nor question him.
> But he knew the whole matter in his own heart, and spoke first:
> "Welcome, heralds, messengers of Zeus and of mortals.
> Draw near. You are not to blame in my sight, but Agamemnon
> who sent the two of you here for the sake of the girl Briseis.
> Go then, illustrious Patroklos, and bring the girl forth
> and give her to these to be taken away. Yet let them be witnesses
> in the sight of the blessed gods, in the sight of mortal
> men, and of this cruel king, if ever hereafter
> There shall be need of me to beat back the shameful destruction."
> ... ...
> So he spoke, and Patroklos obeyed his beloved companion.
> He led forth from the hut Briseis of the fair cheeks and gave her
> to be taken away; and they walked back beside the ships of the Achaians,
> and the woman all unwilling went with them still.'

46. HECTOR PRINCE OF TROY. Detail from an Attic red-figured krater, about 490 B.C., showing the final encounter of Hector and Achilles. London, British Museum, E.468.

Chief antagonist of Achilles is Hector, Priam's eldest son and heir to his kingdom, 'loved by the gods best of all the mortals in Ilion'. He stands out among the Trojans as does Achilles among the Greeks. That hero's taunt to his fellows as he withdraws from fighting implies Hector's prowess:

> '"... stricken at heart though you be, you will be able
> to do nothing, when in their numbers before man-slaughtering Hektor
> they drop and die. And then you will eat out the heart within you
> in sorrow, that you did no honour to the best of the Achaians."'

In character the two were widely different. Achilles was impetuous, proud, and headstrong, taking no thought for his life because he considered it already lost through his choice of a glorious death. Hector, though renowned as a warrior, was reflective, one who weighed consequences, the responsibilities of his position, and the future of his people. To his kindliness Helen herself bore witness when she joined in the lament after his death:

> '"I have never heard a harsh saying from you, nor an insult.
> No, but when another, one of my lord's brothers or sisters, a fair-robed
> wife of some brother, would say a harsh word to me in the palace,
> or my lord's mother—but his father was gentle always, a father
> indeed—then you would speak and put them off and restrain them
> by your own gentleness of heart and your gentle words ..."'

In keeping with such a character and desirous of avoiding unnecessary slaughter, Hector, when Achilles' withdrawal seemed to afford an opportunity for ending the war, called for a single combat between Paris and Menelaus, bidding them

'"fight alone for the sake of Helen and all her possessions.
That one of them who wins and is proved stronger, let him
take the possessions fairly and the woman, and lead her homeward."'

In this combat Paris was overcome and according to the agreement his defeat should have ended the war, but the gods intervened. Aphrodite snatched away her favourite, so that the outcome seemed inconclusive, and Athena made it appear that the Trojans had broken their oath to keep peace during the contest. So the fighting began anew and Hector was left to rally his countrymen.

To the Middle Ages Hector was the ideal knight, the flower of chivalry. Yet they gave him, as they did Achilles and other heroes, a physical presence unknown to Homer. Dares set the pattern:

'Hector was fair and curly-haired; he lisped, was cross-eyed and bearded, swift-limbed and venerable in appearance, seemly in behaviour, war-like, great-spirited, clement to the citizens, fitting and worthy of love.'

Here, in contrast to the Homeric Hector, 'brilliant', 'bronze-helmed', 'glorious' —epithets applied impartially to many warriors—is a portrait instinct with life, even to incorporating physical defects.

The medieval admiration for Hector led to his inclusion as one of the three pagans in a popular list of Nine Heroes or Worthies. These Worthies are mentioned for the first time about 1310 in Jacques de Longuyon's *Vows of the Peacock*. De Longuyon says of Hector:

'Truly Hector was valiant beyond measure, for, as the poets recall to us, when King Menelaus came with violence to besiege noble King Priam in Troy because of Helen his wife, whom he loved greatly and whom Paris had stolen before the war, Hector took over the government of the city. At the sorties which were made by his advice he killed, I believe, nineteen kings in the defence of his body and more than a hundred emirs and counts. Later Achilles slew him very treacherously.'

The list comprised three pagans—Hector, Alexander the Great, and Julius Caesar; three Hebrews—Joshua, David, and Judas Maccabaeus; and three Christians—Arthur of Britain, Charlemagne, and the Crusader, Godfrey of Bouillon. Although the armorial devices of these heroes varied, Hector is often shown with the lion enthroned as in Plates 47–49.

The Heroes appeared as early as 1336 in a pageant at Arras; they were carved on the Rathaus at Cologne about the same time; were painted on a wall at Castle Runkelstein in the Tyrol about 1390; decorated a room in the Castle of La Manta in northern Italy about 1430; and one in the Castle of Valeria at Sion, Switzerland, later in the century. They were, indeed, among the most common of medieval decorative themes. The hall of Castle Manta is among the most imposing of remaining examples. At one end, next to the great fireplace, stands Hector, with Alexander beside him. Beneath Hector are Italo-French lines:

'I was born at Troy, the son of King Priam, I lived when Menelaus, of the Greek people, came to besiege Troy with a great army. There I killed thirty kings and fully three hundred others. Then Achilles killed me in villainous fashion, 1130 years before God was born.'

47. THE NINE HEROES: HECTOR AT THE EXTREME LEFT.
Illustration from a manuscript of *Le Chevalier Errant* by Tommaso, Duke of Saluzzo.
French, about 1390. Paris, Bibliothèque Nationale, MS.fr.12559, fol.125.

48. HECTOR AND ALEXANDER THE GREAT AMONG THE NINE HEROES.
Wall painting, French, c.1420–1430, at Castle Manta in Piedmont, North Italy.

49. HECTOR (OR ALEXANDER) AS ONE OF THE NINE HEROES. Part of a late fourteenth-century set of French tapestries, perhaps woven for Jean, Duke of Berry. New York, Metropolitan Museum of Art, The Cloisters Collection.

50. HECTOR'S FAREWELL TO ANDROMACHE BEFORE HIS BATTLE WITH AJAX.
Drawing, about 1815, by Felice Giani (Italian), illustrating the *Iliad*.
New York, Cooper Union Museum for the Arts of Decoration.

As the battle ebbed and flowed Hector went to the palace, sent Paris back to the fighting, from which Aphrodite had snatched him, then sought his own wife, Andromache. He found her accompanied by a nurse who carried their child, Astyanax. Andromache pleaded with her husband:

> ' "Please take pity upon me then, stay here on the rampart,
> that you may not leave your child an orphan, your wife a widow." '

He refused her plea, but gently, and held out

> '... ... ...his arms to his baby,
> who shrank back to his fair-girdled nurse's bosom
> screaming, and frightened at the aspect of his own father,
> terrified as he saw the bronze and the crest with its horse-hair
> nodding dreadfully, as he thought, from the peak of the helmet.
> Then his beloved father laughed out, and his honoured mother,
> and at once glorious Hektor lifted from his head the helmet
> and laid it in all its shining upon the ground. Then taking
> up his dear son tossed him about in his arms and kissed him.'

Giving the child to his wife he

> 'stroked her with his hand, and called her by name and spoke to her:
> "Poor Andromache! Why does your heart sorrow so much for me?
> No man is going to hurl me to Hades, unless it is fated,
> but as for fate, I think that no man yet has escaped it." '

Although Hector did not meet his death in the ensuing battle with Ajax, this is his last recorded meeting with Andromache according to the *Iliad*, from which Giani drew his theme.

Medieval romances transferred this farewell to the eve of Hector's fatal encounter with Achilles.

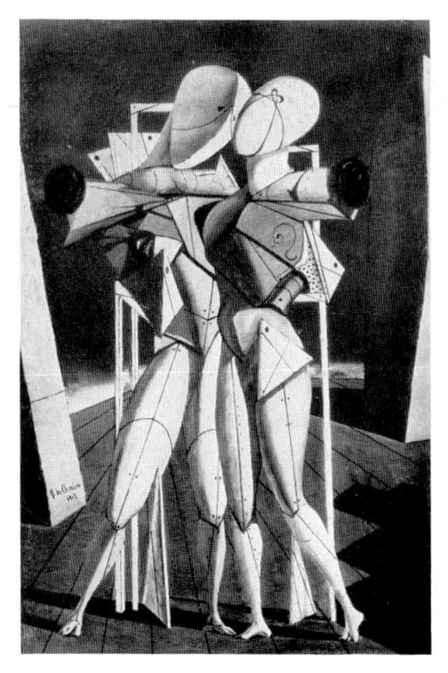

51–52. HECTOR AND ANDROMACHE.
Paintings, 1917 and 1924, by Giorgio de Chirico (Italian).
51: Milan, Collection of Gianni Mattioli. 52: Rome, Collection of Vittorio de Sica.

Only the name of these mannequin groups, belonging to the painter's early work, link them with the Trojan legend and the farewell of Hector and Andromache. The fact, however, that De Chirico gave the same title to several similar paintings evinces his unmistakable interest in the classic theme, an interest natural to an Italian artist who had spent his youth in Greece.

Here is no traditional scene of farewell; there is no child, no nurse, no beseeching Andromache. Nothing, indeed, could have been more foreign to the artist's conception than a literal representation: his purpose was to evoke an idea or a mood rather than to illustrate a specific scene. That the painting represents love shadowed by doom is self-evident.

De Chirico's Hector and Andromache series, dating from about 1916 to 1924, belongs on the whole to his cubistic period, although it has overtones of a short-lived metaphysical school which sought, by employing startling and incongruous combinations, to create a new reality. In all these Hector and Andromache paintings the figures are mannequins, but the modelling of the later examples is softer. The Trojan hero and his wife, faceless yet eloquent, stand in an armatured embrace, high upon the starkly-towered walls of 'earth's most famous town', a distant glow suggesting the fires that will soon engulf it.

53. THE COMBAT OF HECTOR AND AJAX IN THE PRESENCE OF ATHENA AND APOLLO. Attic red-figured kylix, about 475 B.C. Paris, Louvre, G.115.

To readers bred in the long tradition of romantic love, Hector's farewell to Andromache has seemed to portend his imminent death. In the *Iliad*, however, it simply furnishes a bright and tender interlude, providing an opportunity for the display of Hector's most human and appealing side. It is followed, not by a fatal encounter, but merely by a daylong contest with Ajax, son of Telamon, next to Achilles the mightiest among the Greeks. In the course of this combat, during which both men resort to hurling rocks, Ajax proves so much the stronger that Hector is thrown almost senseless to the ground. Apollo interposes on the Trojan's side and sets Hector on his feet again. The inconclusive battle continues until dusk, when heralds call a halt, and the two warriors part with expressions of mutual respect and admiration, Hector assuring Ajax that all will remember how

> 'These two fought each other in heart-consuming hate, then
> joined with each other in close friendship, before they were parted.'

Although neither champion has been defeated the Greeks immediately begin to build a fortified wall as protection for their ships.

54. THE COMBAT OF HECTOR AND AJAX DURING THE FIRST ATTEMPT TO BURN THE GREEK SHIPS. From a manuscript of Guido delle Colonne's *Historia*, North Italian, last quarter of the fourteenth century. London, British Museum, Add. MS.15477, fol.52.

Medieval romancers made little mention of the combat with Ajax immediately following Hector's farewell to Andromache—probably because they shifted the position of the parting scene. A contest with Ajax which they describe at greater length takes place later, when the Trojans had broken through the defences raised about the Greek ships and had begun to fire them. A rationalized ending to this battle and this attempt to burn the ships, invented seemingly by Dares, was generally followed in the romances. Hector, while fighting, discovered that Ajax was a kinsman, the son of Priam's sister Hesione, who had been given to Telamon when Hercules captured Troy. Classic sources do not call her the mother of Ajax, but in the romances the discovery of this relationship ends the combat, and Hector countermands the order to burn the ships. Later another and more serious attempt was made, in which over a hundred were burned.

In the manuscript illustration Hector, charging from the left, is followed by Paris with drawn bow. The names of the chief warriors are inscribed, Ajax being called Telamonius, 'son of Telamon'. At the right the Greeks flee, taking with them the wounded Diomedes. According to the romances, Hector killed Patroclus in an early stage of this battle.

55. THE BATTLE AT THE GREEK SHIPS. From a red-figured Etruscan amphora, early fifth century B.C. Munich, Museum für antike Kleinkunst, 3171.

After Achilles had broken with Agamemnon, Thetis had implored Zeus to allow the Trojans enough victory to prove her son's worth to the Greeks. Zeus had given the Trojans a chance to take the offensive; they had driven the Greeks back to their ships and were threatening these. When they saw the tide of battle turning so strongly against them, the Greeks sent ambassadors to Achilles begging him to return, offering him not only Briseis, but his choice among the spoils and one of Agamemnon's daughters as a bride. But he refused, saying angrily of Agamemnon's overtures:

> ' "I will join with him in no counsel, and in no action.
> He cheated me and he did me hurt. Let him not beguile me
> with words again. This is enough for him. Let him of his own will
> be damned, since Zeus of the counsels has taken his wits away from him." '

The Trojans, led by Hector, now broke down the gate of the rampart the Greeks had built to defend their ships and 'swarmed over the wall'. This struggle fills several books of the *Iliad*. Ajax stands out as a bulwark of the Greeks; Hector, of course, leads the Trojans; the gods take part, helping or hindering either side according to their own whims.

The vase painting was probably suggested by the description in the *Iliad's* fifteenth book, in which Ajax and his half-brother, Teucer, defend the vessels. Hector finally catches hold of the stem of one and calls for fire to kindle the fleet.

At the extreme right appears the hand of a Trojan bringing a torch. This is the turning point of the action: it is evident that, unless Achilles returns, the Greeks may lose even the ability to return home if defeated.

The battle at the ships which the *Iliad* told so stirringly and at such length was reduced in the romances to mere background action. All agreed, however, that Hector's withdrawal of the fire after his combat with Ajax was a fatal move, which destroyed the Trojans' hope of victory.

In the Pitti Palace fresco the *Iliad* was once more the inspiration for the scene. Here 'great-hearted Aias', on shipboard, wields 'a great pike for sea-fighting', while Hector calls:

> '"Bring fire, and give single voice to the clamour of battle.
> Now Zeus has given us a day worth all the rest of them:
> the ships' capture, the ships that came here in spite of the gods' will."'

And later in the struggle, as the painter indicates,

> 'Hektor stood up close to Aias and hacked at the ash spear
> with his great sword, striking behind the socket of the spearhead,
> and slashed it clean away, so that Telamonian Aias
> shook there in his hand a lopped spear, while far away from him
> the bronze spearhead fell echoing to the ground...'

56. THE BATTLE AT THE GREEK SHIPS. Fresco, 1819, by Francesco Sabatelli (Italian). Florence, Pitti Palace, Hall of the *Iliad*.

57. PATROCLUS TAKING LEAVE OF ACHILLES.
Attic red-figured stamnos by the Kleophrades painter, early fifth century B.C.
Rome, Villa Giulia, 26040.

Seeing the losing battle at the ships, Patroclus, Achilles' dearest companion, came to his friend and begged him to save the day by returning to battle. With his intervention the delayed action of the *Iliad* quickens its tempo.

Achilles still refused to fight but yielded to Patroclus' request that he be allowed to go out wearing his friend's armour so that the Trojans might believe Achilles had returned to combat. One condition Achilles made: 'When you have driven them from the ships, come back.'

So, armed with Achilles' sword, his 'well-fashioned helmet', and his 'great shield, huge and heavy', Patroclus led out the Myrmidons; the other Greeks followed and drove the Trojans from the ships. But Patroclus disregarded Achilles' command and pressed on to Troy. Hector, spurred by Apollo, 'drove his strong-footed horses straight for Patroclus'; both men leaped to the ground and began a long and bitter battle. Apollo's help turned the scale in the Trojan's favour and Hector thrust Patroclus through with his spear.

As 'death closed in upon him' the Greek warned his opponent:

> '"You yourself are not one who shall live long, but now already
> death and powerful destiny are standing beside you,
> to go down under the hands of Aiakos' great son, Achilleus."'

Here again the romances changed time and circumstances. They made no connection between the anger of Achilles and the death of Patroclus. According to Dares and his followers, Achilles was recovering from wounds early in the war when Patroclus, wearing his own armour, was slain by Hector. Dictys says that when Patroclus was killed, Achilles had withdrawn from battle because of his love for Polyxena. Dares' account was generally followed in the romances, hence Achilles had less cause to feel responsible for his friend's death and was not driven to such immediate action. In the lengthened time that elapsed between the slaying of Patroclus and that of Hector the romances inserted new incidents that reflected the spirit of their own times.

A bitter battle raged over the body of Patroclus, which Hector wished to throw to the dogs of Troy. Menelaus, in the *Iliad*, fought his way through the Trojans and stood guard over the corpse,

> 'and held the spear and the perfect circle of his shield before him,
> raging to cut down any man who might come forth against him.'

For a little while he was driven back, and Hector stripped from Patroclus' body the armour of Achilles and donned it himself. Then Ajax reached Menelaus' side and the two fought together until reinforcements came. Finally Menelaus

> '...dragged the body away from the Trojans among his companions,'

and, after more fighting, coupled with the intervention of Athena on the side of the Greeks and of Apollo on that of the Trojans, the Greeks reached their ships with their comrade's body.

58. THE FIGHT OVER THE BODY OF PATROCLUS. Roman relief. Mantua, Ducal Palace, Collection of Ancient Sculptures.

59. THE FIGHT OVER THE BODY OF PATROCLUS.
Fresco, 1538–1539, by Giulio Romano and helpers (Italian).
Mantua, Ducal Palace, Hall of Troy.

In this painting Giulio Romano made free use of the composition in the Roman sarcophagus relief shown in Plate 58. It is not certain whether at the time the fresco was painted this sarcophagus was in Mantua or in Rome, but in either case it was available for study. The group of Menelaus standing over the body of Patroclus appears in various Roman examples of sculpture in the round, including one in the Loggia dei Lanzi in Florence and the famous battered stump in Rome known for centuries as 'Pasquino', which served as a posting place for political lampoons or 'pasquinades'.

This battle scene is one of the comparatively rare examples of the use of an ancient presentation by a renaissance artist in precisely the same context. It is one of a series of frescoes in the Mantuan 'Hall of Troy', which makes no attempt to illustrate either pure epic or romance but covers the whole range of the war from the judgment of Paris to the building of the Trojan horse.

Before the fight for Patroclus' body was ended word of his friend's death was brought to Achilles. Almost beside himself with grief, the hero stood unarmed as he was before the ships and by his mere war cry put to flight the pursuing Trojans. Then the Greeks brought the body back, and Achilles led the mourning, vowing:

> '"I will not bury you till I bring to this place the armour
> and the head of Hektor, since he was your great-hearted murderer.
> Before your burning pyre I shall behead twelve glorious
> children of the Trojans, for my anger over your slaying.
> Until then you shall lie where you are in front of my curved ships."

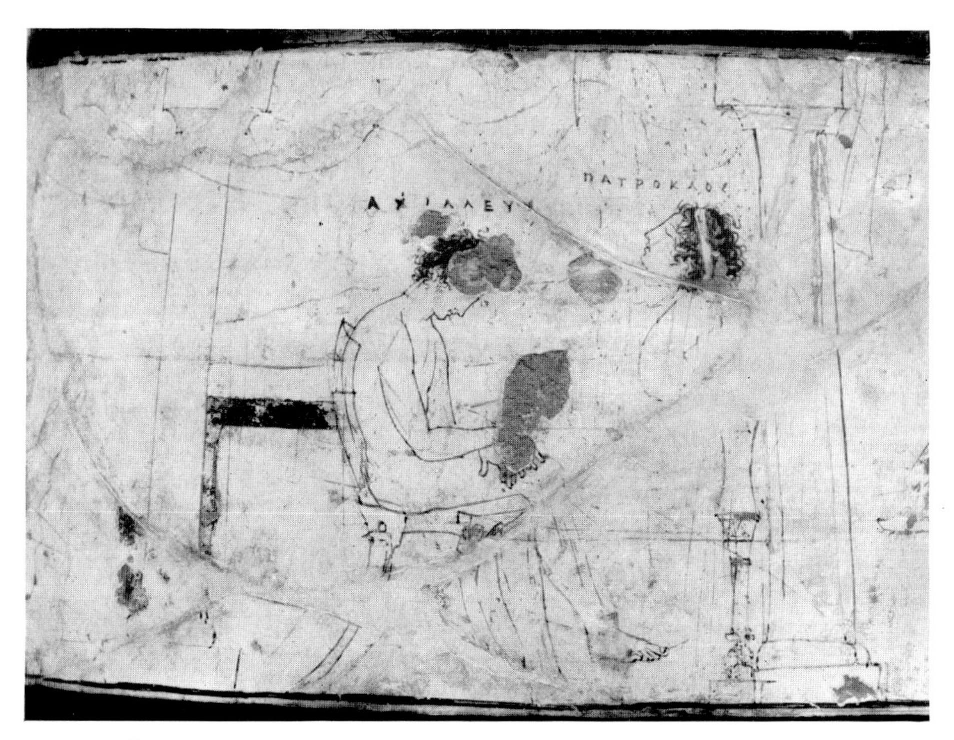

60. ACHILLES MOURNING OVER THE BODY OF PATROCLUS.
From an Attic white-ground lekythos, about 420 B.C. New York, Metropolitan Museum of Art 31.11.13, Rogers Fund, 1931.

> So speaking brilliant Achilleus gave orders to his companions
> to set a great cauldron across the fire, so that with all speed
> they could wash away the clotted blood from Patroklos—
> ... ...
> They washed the body and anointed it softly with olive oil
> and stopped the gashes in his body with stored-up unguents
> and laid him on a bed, and shrouded him in a thin sheet
> from head to foot, and covered that over with a white mantle.
> Then all night long, gathered about Achilleus of the swift feet,
> the Myrmidons mourned for Patroklos and lamented over him.'

While the Greeks mourned for Patroclus, Thetis hastened to Hephaestus, smith of the gods, who in one night made for her son armour far more magnificent than that which Hector had taken. At dawn she brought this armour to Achilles as he lay mourning by the body of Patroclus. Realizing that this was the gift and work of a god, Achilles roused himself and quickly made his peace with Agamemnon, who at once returned Briseis. Then he donned the shining armour, called for his war chariot, and set out for the battle despite the warning of his horse, Xanthos, that his own death was approaching.

As Patroclus, in the romances, was not wearing Achilles' armour, it was not taken by Hector; hence they omitted this entire sequence.

61. HEPHAESTUS MAKING ARMOUR FOR ACHILLES. Red-figured amphora, c.480 B.C. Boston, Museum of Fine Arts, 13.188.

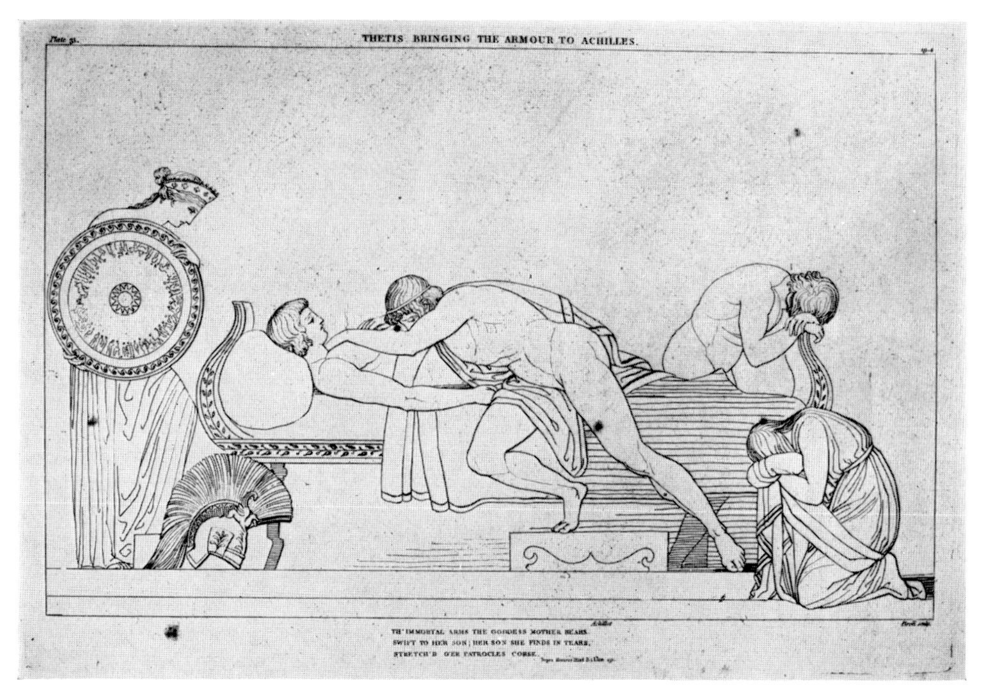

62. THETIS BRINGING ARMOUR TO ACHILLES AS HE MOURNS PATROCLUS.
Engraving by Piroli after a drawing by John Flaxman (English),
for an edition of the *Iliad*, 1793.

With the revival of classical studies the Homeric themes returned to art as well as literature. Flaxman's famous series of illustrations for the *Iliad* and the *Odyssey* follow the texts comparatively closely; his style, too, like that of many of his contemporaries, was strongly influenced by the linear drawing of Greek vases.

One of the *Iliad's* most exquisite descriptions is of the shield which Hephaestus made for Achilles at Thetis' request—a shield 'huge and heavy', upon which the god wrought the earth 'and the sky, and the sea's water', a city at peace, a city at war, and scenes of festival and harvest. Though the shield was meant for battle Homer emphasized the pursuits of peace—civic life in the market place, ploughing, harvesting, dancing, and the vintage festival in which

> 'Young girls and young men, in all their light-hearted innocence,
> carried the kind, sweet fruit away in their woven baskets,
> and in the midst a youth with a singing lyre played charmingly
> upon it for them, and sang the beautiful song for Linos
> in a light voice, and they followed him, and with singing and whistling
> and light dance-steps of their feet kept time to the music.'

This shield's panoramic life has kindled the imagination throughout the centuries. Vergil patterned his shield of Aeneas upon Homer's description, changing the decoration to fit Rome's martial history. Flaxman used it as the theme for a

63. THE SHIELD OF ACHILLES. Fragment of a Roman relief, first century A.D. Rome, Capitoline Museum.

delicate relief, *The Shield of Achilles*, exhibited in 1818. W.H. Auden's poem, *The Shield of Achilles*, composed after World War II, saw upon it no 'marble well-governed cities' or 'ritual pieties', but a waste of desolation and barbed wire.

The incidents on the shield above follow Homer's description in general. The fragment shows about half of the original composition. In the upper part is the city at peace, with a group gathered in the porticoed market place: in the lower, are the rural scenes, ploughing and harvesting. The sketchy nature of the work is due partly to the fact that the carving was little more than a guide for colouring, the whole having appeared originally as painting in relief.

64. A CENTAUR-ARCHER (SAGITTARY) AIDS THE TROJANS: HUPON IS KILLED: HECTOR AND ACHILLES MEET. Franco-Flemish tapestry (Tournai), after 1474. New York, Metropolitan Museum of Art, Fletcher Fund, 1952.

The *Iliad's* action moves swiftly after the death of Patroclus as Achilles, leaving his friend's body unburied in accordance with his vow, bends every effort to avenge him. Medieval romancers slowed the pace, transposing or adding incidents and changing or inventing characters. Three such changes appear in the tapestry: the slaying of 'Hupon the Great' in the upper part, the battle with the Sagittary in the centre, and the peaceful meeting of Achilles and Hector in the lower right.

Hupon was a character derived from Hipparchus or Hippothoös, king of Larissa, whom the *Iliad* mentions as a minor ally of the Trojans killed by Ajax in the battle over Patroclus' body. In the romances he has become 'great as a giant'.

The Sagittary or centaur-archer was introduced by the romances. Except for Cheiron the *Iliad* refers to centaurs only as 'beast men' and does not include them among the fighters. Neither Dares nor Dictys mentions them as Trojan allies. But in Benoit's romance a fighting centaur has been brought to Troy's aid from 'beyond the realm of the Amazons'. Just when or how he found his way into the romances is uncertain. The mounted archers of the East, riders who seemed as one with their horses, no doubt played a part in his origin. The Latin word for archer, *sagittarius*, of course contributed to the idea, for it meant not only an ordinary mounted archer but also the constellation, Sagittarius, represented by Babylonian, Greek, and Roman astronomers as a centaur with a bow. This figure, the ninth sign of the zodiac, was well known throughout the Middle Ages.

Raoul Lefèvre describes the sagittary as 'a marvellous beast that behind the middle was an horse and in front a man . . . . Hairy like a horse and had eyes red as a coal and shot right well with a bow. This beast made the Greeks sore afraid', so that they fell back to their tents, which appear here at the left.

The French inscription, which has been considerably damaged, reads when reconstructed: 'Achilles came impetuously into battle, where he killed a giant who fought with great bravery, a terrible man whose name was Hupon le Grand. The Sagittary, horrible and awful, killed Polienar in this combat. Diomedes, brave and mighty, slew the Sagittary.'

After the battle with the Sagittary the Greeks, according to the romances, asked for a long truce in order to bury their dead. During this truce occurred the meeting of Hector and Achilles, in which the romances emphasized chivalric curiosity concerning a brave adversary. The *Iliad's* strong motive for revenge was, of course, absent, for Achilles had no reason to feel responsible for the death of Patroclus at Hector's hand. As Lefèvre relates it:

'During the truce Hector went one day to the tents of the Greeks. And Achilles beheld him gladly because he had never seen him unarmed. And at the request of Achilles Hector went into his tent. And as they spoke together of many things Achilles said to Hector: "I have great pleasure to see thee unarmed, forasmuch as I had never seen thee before. But yet I shall have more pleasure when the day shall come that thou shalt die of my hand, which thing I most desire. For I know thee to be most strong, and I have often proved it unto the effusion of my blood, whereof I have great anger. And yet have I greater sorrow forasmuch as thou slewest Patroclus, him that I most loved in the world. Then thou mayest believe for certain that before this year be past his death shall be avenged upon thee by my hand."... Hector answered and said... "If thou think thyself so strong, make it so that all the barons of thine host promise and accord that we fight body against body. And if it happen that thou vanquish me, that my friends and I shall be banished out of this realm and we shall leave it to the Greeks. And thereof I shall leave good pledge. . . . And if it happen that I vanquish thee, make that all they of this host depart hence, and suffer us to live in peace." '

Agamemnon, hearing of this proposed combat, hastened to Achilles' tent to forbid it. In the lower right of the tapestry Achilles stands at the left, Hector at the right, while Agamemnon and Menelaus are behind. Parts of the figures are restorations: Hector, for instance, has been given typical Hapsburg features.

65. PRIAM AND HECUBA, FROM THE WALLS OF TROY, BEG HECTOR NOT TO FIGHT ACHILLES. From an Attic red-figured kylix, about 480 B.C.
Boston, Museum of Fine Arts, 98.933.

In the *Iliad* there is no room for peaceful dallying and chivalric admiration after Patroclus' death. Bent on vengeance, Achilles set forth in his new armour to lead his men into battle. The Greeks soon drove the Trojans back inside their city walls. Only Hector remained outside the gate, awaiting Achilles, who came sweeping across the plain, his armour shining like a star. From within the walls Priam called piteously to his son:

> ' "Hektor, beloved child, do not await the attack of this man
> alone, away from the others . . . .
> . . .   .
> Come then inside the wall, my child, so that you can rescue
> the Trojans and the women of Troy . . . ." '

Beside him stood Hecuba, bidding her son think of all her care for him in childhood:

> ' "Remember all these things, dear child, and from inside the wall
> beat off this grim man. Do not go out as champion against him.
> . . .   .
> So these two in tears and with much supplication called out
> to their dear son, but could not move the spirit in Hektor,
> but he awaited Achilleus as he came on, gigantic.' "

Yet as his enemy drew near Hector might have yielded to their prayers had it not been for his fear of being thought a coward, of having his fellows say:

> '"Hektor believed in his own strength and ruined his people",
> thus will they speak; and as for me, it would be much better
> at that time, to go against Achilleus and slay him, and come back
> or else be killed by him in glory in front of the city.'

As Hector's death draws near the romances make one of their most effective changes in the order of incidents. They combine the farewell to Andromache, which the *Iliad* places before the early combat with Ajax, with the scene near the end of the epic, in which the hero's parents plead with him not to fight. Then they place the combined action just before the fatal encounter with Achilles. It is rare to find the romances more dramatic than the *Iliad*, but from the modern point of view this change increases the suspense, quickens the action, and leads to the inevitable end. In keeping with the romantic interest in chivalric love, Andromache's part is stressed at greater length than that of Priam and Hecuba. Dares gives the main outline of the scene shown in the tapestry opposite. Lefèvre describes it in detail:

'. . . The night before, Andromache the wife of Hector, that had two fair sons by him, whereof one had to name Laomedon and the other Astromatas [Astyanax]. This Andromache saw that night a marvellous vision. And her seemed that if Hector went that day following to the battle he should be slain. And she . . . weeping said to him praying him that he would not go to the battle that day. Whereof Hector blamed his wife, saying that we should not believe nor give faith to dreams, and would not abide nor tarry therefore. When it was morning Andromache went unto King Priam and to the queen and told them the truth of her vision and prayed them with all her heart that they would do so much to Hector that he should not that day go to the battle. . . .

'And King Priam sent to Hector that he should keep him well that day from going to battle. Wherefore Hector was angry and said to his wife many words reproachable, because he knew that this came by her request. Howbeit, notwithstanding he armed himself. And when Andromache saw him armed she took her little children and fell down to the feet of her husband and prayed him humbly that he would take off his arms, but he would not do it. And then she said to him, "At the least, if ye will not have mercy on me, so have pity on your little children that I and they die not a bitter death, or that we shall be led in servitude and bondage to strange countries."

'At this point came to them the Queen Hecuba and the Queen Helen and the sisters of Hector, and they kneeled down before his feet and prayed him with weeping and tears that he would do off his harness and unarm him and come with them into the hall. But never would he do it for her prayers, but descended from the palace thus armed as he was and took his horse and would have gone to battle. But at the request of Andromache King Priam came running anon and took him by the bridle . . . and made him return. But in no wise would he unarm.'

The conflict eventually went against the Trojans. Hector entered it without more ado and presently confronted Achilles.

Though the epics gave Hector and Andromache only one son, later writers often spoke of two, known by various names. The romances, drawing on Dictys, called one by a form of the classic Astyanax and the other after his great-grandfather, Laomedon. In the tapestry both appear, but only Astyanax is named. The other

66. THE ARMING OF HECTOR: ANDROMACHE AND PRIAM PLEAD WITH HIM NOT TO FIGHT ACHILLES. Franco-Flemish tapestry (Tournai), 1472–1474. New York, Metropolitan Museum of Art, Fletcher Fund, 1939.

figures are inscribed—Hecuba, Helen, Polyxena, Andromache—except for one weeping woman whose actions and expression suggest Cassandra.

The French inscription reads:

'Andromache fearing the death of Hector, that in her dreams she had bewailed, upon her knees, with great lamentation, brought her children and besought him not to go out that day. Despite which Hector had himself armed for battle and mounted his horse.'

The presentation of the scene suggests the 'mansions' used in the setting of medieval drama as fixed points about which important actions centred. Such mansions, for instance, appear among the illustrations of a fifteenth-century manuscript of Milet's play, *The Destruction of Troy the Great.* A request to present this popular play in Tournai is dated 1472, the year in which a set of Troy tapestries was begun in that city for Charles the Bold, Duke of Burgundy.

According to the *Iliad* Hector waited outside the walls, debating whether to stand and fight or to offer the return of Helen. But his courage weakened when Achilles finally drew near:

> '... ... ...and he could no longer
> stand his ground there, but left the gates behind, and fled, frightened,
> and Peleus' son went after him in the confidence of his quick feet.
> As when a hawk in the mountains who moves lightest of things flying
> makes his effortless swoop for a trembling dove, but she slips away
> from beneath and flies and he shrill screaming close after her
> plunges for her again and again, heart furious to take her;
> so Achilleus went straight for him in fury, but Hektor
> fled away under the Trojan wall...
> ... ...
> But swift Achilleus kept unremittingly after Hektor,
> chasing him, as a dog in the mountains who has flushed from his covert
> a deer's fawn follows him through the folding ways and the valleys,
> and though the fawn crouched down under a bush and be hidden
> he keeps running and noses him out until he comes on him;
> so Hektor could not lose himself from the swift-footed Peleion.
> If ever he made a dash right on for the gates of Dardanos
> to get quickly under the strong-built bastions, endeavouring
> that they from above with missiles thrown might somehow defend him,
> each time Achilleus would get in front and force him to turn back
> into the plain, and himself kept his flying course next the city.
> As in a dream a man is not able to follow one who runs
> from him, nor can the runner escape, nor the other pursue him,
> so he could not run him down in his speed, nor the other get clear.
> How then could Hektor have escaped the death spirits, had not
> Apollo, for this last and uttermost time, stood by him
> close, and driven strength into him, and made his knees light?
> But brilliant Achilleus kept shaking his head at his own people
> and would not let them throw their bitter projectiles at Hektor
> for fear the thrower might win the glory, and himself come second.'

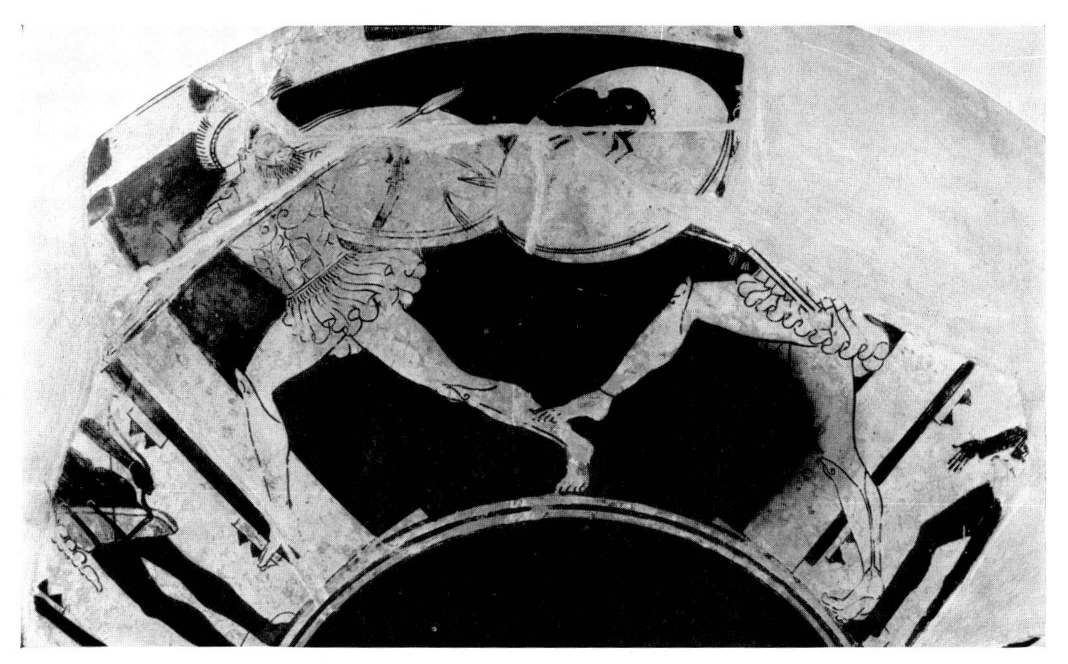

67. ACHILLES PURSUING HECTOR AROUND THE WALLS OF TROY.
From an Attic red-figured kylix, about 480 B.C. Boston, Museum of Fine Arts, 98.933.

68. ACHILLES PURSUING HECTOR AROUND THE WALLS OF TROY.
Lithograph, 1915, by Max Slevogt (German), New York,
Metropolitan Museum of Art, Dick Fund, 1926.

69. THE DEATH OF HECTOR. From an Attic red-figured hydria, fifth century B.C. Rome, Vatican.

Four times the two men circled the walls of Troy. Then even Apollo forsook the Trojan, and Athena, taking the shape of Hector's brother, Deiphobus, appeared beside him as though bringing aid. Encouraged by this support Hector stopped in his flight and challenged Achilles once more. Achilles flung his spear and missed, but Athena gave it back to him. Hector flung his in turn, but it glanced off Achilles' shield and out of Hector's reach. Turning to take a fresh spear from his brother Hector found no one there, knew that the gods had deceived him, and drew his sword. Once more Achilles cast a spear, and this time it found an opening in the armour taken from Patroclus, the place 'where the collar-bones hold the neck from the shoulders'. Mortally wounded Hector 'dropped in the dust', asking that his body be returned to his parents and prophesying that death would come to Achilles through Apollo.

> 'And the soul fluttering free of the limbs went down into Death's house
> mourning her destiny, leaving youth and manhood behind her.
> Now though he was a dead man brilliant Achilleus spoke to him:
> "Die: and I will take my own death at whatever time
> Zeus and the rest of the immortals choose to accomplish it." '

Dares followed the classical account fairly closely, saying that Achilles, though wounded by Hector, 'began nevertheless to pursue him, nor did he cease until he killed him'. Dictys, however, says that Hector had set out to meet the Amazon Penthesilea when Achilles ambushed him.

In the romances, of course, the pursuit about the walls disappears: the Middle Ages had no mind to show their hero fleeing. Bent upon glorifying Hector and vilifying Achilles, the romancers maintained that the Greek had killed the Trojan

70. THE DEATH OF HECTOR.
Illustration from a manuscript of Benoit de Sainte-More's *Roman de Troie*, French, 1264.
Collection of 'Huis Bergh' at 's-Heerenberg, Holland.

treacherously. According to Benoit, Hector had slain a Greek and, wishing to take his armour as a prize, seized the helmet with his right hand to drag it off, leaving his right side exposed. Achilles, seeing this, thrust him through with his spear. This is the action shown in the upper band of the manuscript illustration above: in its lower band, the Trojans carry their dead hero home.

71. ACHILLES DRAGGING HECTOR'S BODY.
Attic black-figured lekythos, early fifth century B.C.
New York, Metropolitan Museum of Art, 25.70.2, Fletcher Fund, 1925.

Achilles stripped the armour from Hector and then, despite the hero's dying plea, fastened the body by the heels to his chariot and dragged it, head down in the dust, to the Greek ships. (Vergil says he dragged it three times about the walls of Troy.) From the battlements Priam and Hecuba and the other Trojans watched in horror; Andromache, hearing the tumult, ran to the walls, fainted at the sight, and then, recovering, joined

> '... ... ...the women of Troy in mourning
> "Hektor, I grieve for you. You and I were born to a single
> destiny, you in Troy in the house of Priam, and I
> in Thebe, underneath the timbered mountain of Plakos."'

Among the Greeks rejoicing over Hector's death mingled with sorrow for Patroclus, whose body still lay unburied awaiting the completion of Achilles' vengeance. But the spirit of Patroclus, caring only for the peace denied to those unburied, appeared to Achilles that night, beseeching him piteously:

> ' "... ... ...Bury me
> as quickly as may be, let me pass through the gates of Hades.
> The souls, the images of dead men, hold me at a distance,
> and will not let me cross the river and mingle among them,
> but I wander as I am by Hades' house of the wide gates." '

Then Achilles cried out to his friend

> '...and with his own arms reached for him, but could not
> take him, but the spirit went underground, like vapour,
> with a thin cry, and Achilleus started awake, staring.'

72. ACHILLES AND THE SHADE OF PATROCLUS. Drawing, 1790's, illustrating the *Iliad* by John Flaxman (English). New York, Metropolitan Museum of Art, Rogers Fund, 1918.

Obedient to the wishes of Patroclus, Achilles hastened preparations for the funeral rites. The Myrmidons cut timber for the pyre and laid upon it the body of their dead companion. Then, in accordance with custom,

> 'They covered all the corpse under the locks of their hair, which they cut off
> and dropped on him, and behind them brilliant Achilleus held the head
> sorrowing, for this was his true friend he escorted toward Hades.'

Then, companioned only by close mourners and the Greek leaders, Achilles sacrificed

> '. . . twelve noble sons of the great-hearted Trojans
> with the stroke of bronze, and evil were the thoughts in his heart against them,
> and let loose the iron fury of the fire to feed on them.
> Then he groaned, and called by name on his beloved companion:
> "Good-bye, Patroklos, I hail you even in the house of the death god
> For all that I promised you in time past I am accomplishing.
> Here are twelve noble sons of the great-hearted Trojans
> whom the fire feeds on, all, as it feeds on you. But I will not
> give Hektor, Priam's son, to the fire, but the dogs to feast on." '

73. ACHILLES SLAYING TROJAN CAPTIVES AT THE FUNERAL OF PATROCLUS. Detail of an Etruscan painting from the François tomb at Vulci, early third century B.C. Rome, Torlonia Collection.

The Etruscan painting shows this scene with all the dramatic intensity and boldness characteristic of this enigmatic people, in whose art Greece and the Orient met.

The names of the characters are inscribed. At the left is the shade of Patroclus, the head outlined against the splendid wings of Vanth, an Etruscan goddess of the Otherworld. Achilles, magnificently virile, plunges his sword into a captive, while just beyond another Etruscan deity, Charun (daemonic equivalent of the Greek Charon), waits to conduct the shade to Hades. In contrast to the warm-toned bodies of the others this sinister, scowling figure has flesh of livid blue. At the right Ajax, son of Telamon, brings forward another Trojan to the sacrifice.

After the funeral rites of Patroclus and their attendant games, Achilles continued his revenge. Thrice each day for twelve days he dragged the body of Hector about Patroclus' tomb, but Apollo preserved it from mutilation or decay and finally interceded with Zeus. The king of the gods sent Thetis to Achilles commanding him to 'accept ransom for the body', and a message to Priam bidding him approach Achilles with gifts.

74. PRIAM RANSOMING HECTOR'S BODY. Attic red-figured skyphos, about 480 B.C. Vienna, Kunsthistorisches Museum.

In the ensuing scene between the old father and the slayer of his son, Achilles emerges at his best, compassionate, and conscious that he is given to ungovernable anger. Priam

> '. . .caught the knees of Achilleus in his arms, and kissed the hands
> that were dangerous and manslaughtering and had killed so many
> of his sons . . .'

and begged for the body of Hector. His words

> '. . . stirred in the other a passion of grieving
> for his own father. He took the old man's hand and pushed him
> gently away, and the two remembered, as Priam sat huddled
> at the feet of Achilleus and wept close for manslaughtering Hektor

and Achilleus wept now for his own father, now again
for Patroklos. The sound of their mourning moved in the house. Then
... ...
he rose from his chair, and took the old man by the hand, and set him
on his feet again, in pity for the grey head and the grey beard,
and spoke to him and addressed him in winged words: "Ah, unlucky,
... ...
How could you dare to come alone to the ships of the Achaians
and before my eyes, when I am one who have killed in such numbers
such brave sons of yours? The heart in you is iron. Come, then,
and sit down upon this chair, and you and I will even let
our sorrows lie still in the heart for all our grieving."
... ...
In answer to him again spoke aged Priam the godlike:
"Do not, beloved of Zeus, make me sit on a chair while Hektor
lies yet forlorn among the shelters; rather with all speed
give him back, so my eyes may behold him, and accept the ransom."
... ...
Then looking darkly at him spoke swift-footed Achilleus:
"No longer stir me up, old sir. I myself am minded
To give Hektor back to you." . . .'

Then Achilles

'Called out to his serving-maids to wash the body and anoint it
all over; but take it first aside, since otherwise Priam
might see his son and in the heart's sorrow not hold in his anger
at the sight, and the deep heart in Achilleus be shaken to anger;
that he might not kill Priam and be guilty before the god's orders.'

75. PRIAM RANSOMING HECTOR'S BODY. Relief, 1815, by Bertel Thorwaldsen (Danish). Copenhagen, Thorwaldsen Museum.

The *Iliad* inspired Thorwaldsen's relief as it had done the Greek vase painter more than two thousand years before. Medieval romances could have no place for this scene, since they did not admit the mishandling of Hector's body.

76. THE FUNERAL OF HECTOR. Franco-Flemish tapestry (Tournai), 1472–1474. Glasgow Art Gallery, Burrell Collection.

In the *Iliad* the Trojans burn the body of Hector, and after they have quenched the fire with wine, gather the ashes into a golden casket and bury it beneath a grave-barrow of heavy stones. On this note of lonely austerity the epic ends:

'Such was their burial of Hektor, breaker of horses.'

Medieval romancers, bred in a different tradition and familiar with the princely effigies of their churches, devised a funeral appropriate to their own time. Raoul Lefèvre described precisely such a scene as that in the tapestry above.

Priam and his counsellors considered 'how they might keep the body of Hector without corruption and without burial'. In the great temple of Apollo, Priam 'had made by their counsel, a rich sepulchre upon four pillars of gold lifted up on high, upon which was made a rich tabernacle of gold and of precious stones. And on the four corners of the tabernacle were four images of gold that had semblance of angels. And above the tabernacle there was a great image of gold that was made after the semblance of Hector and had the visage turned towards the Greeks and held a naked sword and seemed to menace the Greeks. And there was in the midst of the tabernacle a place empty, where the masters put the body of Hector in flesh and bones, clad in his best garments and robes. It stood upon its feet and might endure for a long time in that wise without corruption because of certain science that the masters had set on the summit or top of the head of Hector, that is to say a vessel that had a hole in the bottom. This vessel was full of fine balm that distilled and dropped down to a place above his head and so spread down in all the members of his body . . . . And all the people that would see Hector they saw him verily as he had been in life. To this sepulchre the same masters made a lamp of fine gold burning continually without going out or quenching. And afterward they made an enclosure so that no man should approach or go into this tabernacle without licence or leave. And in this temple King Priam ordained and set great plenty of priests to pray to the god without ceasing for his son Hector, and he gave them good rents.'

Behind Hector's effigy medieval priests are shown reading Christian services within a Gothic enclosure. Gothic arches and carvings enrich the throne-like structure upon which sits the figure with drawn sword. Tall candles burn before it and below are grouped the royal family's mourners: Paris, Priam, Troilus, Hecuba, Polyxena, Andromache, and Helen.

THE FALL OF TROY

With Hector's death the fall of Troy and the doom of Achilles grew near. The action between Hector's funeral and the city's capture formed the theme of three lost, somewhat overlapping, epics. The first of these, the *Aethiopis*, continues the story of Achilles and ends with his death. As in the *Iliad* he is impetuous and violent, but the romantic and exotic played a larger part in his character and adventures than in the older epic. Penthesilea, queen of the Amazons, is a heroine such as the *Iliad* never knew: both she and Memnon, king of the Ethiopians, for whom the epic is named, come from far-off, mysterious places to fight as Troy's allies.

The *Iliad* had mentioned 'the Amazons who fought men in battle', and Helen had referred to them slightingly as 'the Amazon women, men's equals', but they were not included among the warriors who fought at Troy. The author of the *Aethiopis*, however, composing a sequel, felt free to emphasize these warrior-women who kept themselves unencumbered by either husbands or male children and had all the allure of the unknown. Proclus' summary of the *Aethiopis* introduces its heroine tersely:

'The Amazon Penthesileia, the daughter of Ares and of Thracian race, comes to aid the Trojans.' Her fate is treated with equal brevity: 'and after showing great prowess [she] is killed by Achilles and buried by the Trojans. Achilles then slays

77. ACHILLES CATCHES PENTHESILEA AS SHE FALLS FROM HER HORSE. From a red-figured Apulian krater, fourth century B.C. Collection of Landgrave Philip of Hesse, Schloss Adolphseck.

78. ACHILLES SUPPORTING THE BODY OF PENTHESILEA.
Original model, 1837, for a marble relief by Bertel Thorwaldsen (Danish).
Copenhagen, Thorwaldsen Museum.

Thersites [a foul-mouthed Greek] for abusing and reviling him' because of his love for Penthesileia.

In the vase painting Achilles, like the Greeks of Homer's time, is shown fighting on foot but catching Penthesilea as she falls from her horse after he had mortally wounded her. Although early Greek literature does not describe the Amazons as fighting mounted, they are so shown in vase paintings as early as the sixth century B.C., presumably because they came from a land noted for its horsemen and would have been forced to travel long distances overland to Troy.

The story that Penthesilea's beauty smote Achilles with remorse after he had killed her was widespread in late classical literature. The *Aethiopis* may, indeed, have developed it much more fully than we know. A passage in one of Propertius' Latin elegies takes knowledge of the incident for granted when referring to 'Penthesilea . . . whose bright beauty conquered the conquering hero, when the helm of gold laid bare her brow.' Quintus of Smyrna expanded the story in the romantic mood of the fourth century after Christ:

'The warriors gazed, and in their hearts they prayed
That fair and sweet like her their wives might seem,
Laid on the bed of love, when home they won.
Yea, and Achilles' very heart was wrung
With love's remorse to have slain a thing so sweet,
Who might have borne her home, his queenly bride,
To chariot-glorious Phthia; for she was
Flawless, a very daughter of the Gods,
Divinely tall, and most divinely fair.'

Dictys followed the classical tradition of her death at Achilles' hand but Dares said that she was killed after Achilles' death by his son, Neoptolemus or Pyrrhus. Medieval romances followed Dares' pattern: not until the Renaissance was this poignant episode retold in its ancient setting. The medieval versions omitted the story of Achilles' love for the Amazon and concentrated their romantic emphasis upon the Trojan princess Polyxena as heroine.

Another love, not mentioned in the *Aethiopis*, dominated the close of Achilles' life according to later writers such as Hyginus, Philostratus, Dictys, and Dares. Early authors do not say how Achilles met and loved Polyxena, Priam's daughter. Dictys

79. ACHILLES SEES POLYXENA AT HECTOR'S TOMB. Illustration by Jean Mielot from a manuscript of Christine de Pisan's *Épître d'Othéa*, 1461. Brussels, Bibliothèque Royale, MS.fr.9392, fol.98v.

mentions two occasions for their meeting: first, when Hecuba went with her daughters to Apollo's temple outside the walls of Troy, and second, when Polyxena accompanied Priam to Achilles' tent to ask for Hector's body. The latter is the occasion mentioned by Philostratus. Dares, who rejected the idea of the capture and ransom of the Trojan hero's body, says that Achilles first saw the maiden on the anniversary of Hector's death when she went with her family to visit his tomb at Apollo's temple. Medieval romances, which stressed the Greek hero's love for Polyxena, followed Dares' account. Raoul Lefèvre gives a typical version:

'Achilles had great desire to go to Troy to see the city and the feast of the anniversary of Hector, whom he had slain. And so he went all unarmed unto the temple of Apollo where was the sepulchre of Hector. . . . There was the Queen Hecuba and Polyxena her daughter, that was passing fair, with a great number of ladies.' Then Achilles . . . 'said to himself that he had never seen so fair a woman, nor better formed nor made, and withal she was one of the most noble women of the world. Then was Achilles shot with the dart of love, that struck him to the heart so marvellously that he could not cease to behold her, and the more he beheld her the more he desired her.'

In the illustration from Christine de Pisan's moralized account of the meeting, the temple has been transformed into a Christian chapel, where Hector's kin kneel in medieval mourning garb below the statue of the armed Apollo upon the altar. Christine draws from the old story the moral that the good knight should avoid all strange loves.

Soon after Penthesilea's death, the *Aethiopis* relates, Memnon, king of Ethiopia and son of Eos the dawn goddess, arrived to aid the Trojans. He too was slain by Achilles, who then, inflamed by victory, pursued the fleeing troops and 'rushing into the city with them is killed by Paris and Apollo'. Some said that Apollo alone shot the bolt, others that it was Paris, and still others that Apollo assumed the Trojan's form. Achilles had incurred Apollo's wrath by slaying the god's son, Tenes, at Tenedos; from the lips of the dying Hector in the *Iliad*, the Greek had heard the prophecy of his own death

' ". . . . . . on that day when Paris and Phoibos Apollo
destroy you in the Skaian gates, for all your valour." '

Hyginus says that the arrow struck Achilles' heel, the only spot left vulnerable when Thetis had dipped him in the River Styx in infancy; according to Apollodorus, 'Achilles was shot with an arrow in the ankle by Alexander and Apollo.' Although both these accounts belong to the second century A.D., a vase painting of the sixth century B.C. shows the hero's body with the arrow through the heel.

The *Aethiopis* tells of a fierce contest for Achilles' body, which Ajax son of Telamon finally carried to the Greek ships while Odysseus held off the Trojans. The Greeks built a funeral pyre but 'Thetis, arriving with the Muses and her sisters, bewails her son, whom she afterward catches away from the pyre and transports to the White Island.' The hero's comrades then raised a sepulchral mound and held the usual funeral games. The White Island, according to Pausanias, was in the Black Sea, opposite the Danube's mouth. There, he said, Achilles abode with Patroclus, Ajax, and other friends, and 'Helen was wedded to Achilles.' Philostratus gave the same account of the hero's bride and final dwelling place, while Apollodorus

80. THE DEATH OF ACHILLES: AJAX RESCUES HIS BODY: MENELAUS KILLS AMASOS AN ETHIOPIAN FOLLOWER OF MEMNON. Attic black-figured amphora, sixth century B.C. Philadelphia, University Museum, MS 3442.

81. A MEDIEVAL PICTURE OF ACHILLES' DEATH: HE IS KILLED BY PARIS IN APOLLO'S TEMPLE. Detail from a drawing related to a series of 15th-century tapestry designs. Paris, Louvre.

said that Achilles dwelt with Medea in the Isles of the Blest. The *Odyssey*, however, declares that the body of Achilles was burned, his ashes mingled with those of Patroclus in a golden urn, and buried. Odysseus, visiting the Otherworld, finds the hero's shade striding restlessly 'past the streams of Oceanus...past the rock Leucas, past the gates of the sun and the land of dreams', in 'the mead of asphodels, where the spirits dwell, phantoms of men who have done with toils.'

Achilles' death as related in Dictys, Dares, and the romances, and even in such a late classic work as Philostratus' *Heroicus*, was very different from the story told in the *Aethiopis*. It came about, they said, because of his love for Polyxena, and through treachery rather than in battle.

He had withdrawn from fighting not, as in the *Iliad*, because of anger with Agamemnon, but because he wished to end the war and wed Polyxena. It is at this point that the romancers bring in the embassy from Agamemnon begging him to return to battle. He refuses, but allows his Myrmidons to fight without him. The Trojans slaughter them in such numbers that he comes back to avenge them. It is at this late period, rather than at the beginning of the war as in the *Cypria*, that Achilles kills Troilus.

The death of Troilus spurs Hecuba to revenge. She summons Achilles to meet her in the temple of Apollo, supposedly to discuss his marriage, but arranges with Paris to kill him there (Plate 81). According to Lefèvre:

> 'As soon as Achilles heard the messenger speak that came from the Queen Hecuba, the fool, being evil-counselled, took with him the son of Duke Nestor and both went unto the temple of Apollo. And as soon as they were come Paris and his knights ran upon him, and Paris cast at him three darts wherewith he hurt him sore. Achilles drew out his sword, that had no more armour, and wrapped his arm in his mantle, and smote in among the knights right fiercely and slew seven of them. But finally the son of Duke Nestor, Archilogus, and Achilles both were slain within the temple.'

Neither Dares nor the romancers mention the legend of the hero's vulnerable heel, although some authors say that he was wounded in the soles of his feet as he knelt in prayer at the god's shrine.

Troilus, whose death precipitated that of Achilles according to Dares, Dictys, and medieval versions, was a much more important figure in the romances than in surviving classical literature. The *Iliad* barely mentions him. The fragments of the *Cypria* say that Achilles killed him early in the war. He plays a conspicuous part in the Middle Ages and in the Renaissance largely because he was the lover of Cressida. This heroine appears in the *Iliad* as Chryseis, whom Agamemnon returns to her father because of Apollo's wrath. No known ancient author connects her with Troilus.

In the course of centuries the name of Chryseis became confused with that of Briseis, whom Agamemnon took from Achilles. Benoit, who called her Briseïde, tells the first known version of her love for Troilus and her desertion of him for the Greek Diomedes. Benoit states the theme followed in later versions: 'Greatly was she loved, and greatly did she love, but her heart was not constant.' In this romance she becomes the daughter of Calchas, whom Dares had called a renegade Trojan. Agamemnon, grateful to him for information concerning Troy, arranges to have her sent to the Greek camp, where she forgets Troilus and takes Diomedes as her lover. Guido tells much the same story.

82. TROILUS AND OTHER TROJANS DELIVER BRISEÏDE (Cressida) TO THE GREEKS. From a manuscript of Benoit's *Roman*, Italian, second half of the fourteenth century. Venice, Biblioteca Marciana, MS.fr.17, fol.105.

From Benoit and Guido, Boccaccio drew his Italian poem, *Il Filostrato* (The One Prostrated by Love). Here, for the first time, the loves of the Trojan and the Greek for the inconstant heroine, whom Boccaccio calls Criseida, was the theme of an independent work, not a mere incident in a long romance. Boccaccio dwelt on the love of Troilus and Criseida before she went to the Greek camp and on the Trojan's grief at her unfaithfulness. He changed many details, such as the character of her kinsman, Pandarus, who acts as the go-between and whose name has become a synonym for procurer. He also changed the circumstances of her leaving Troy, having her exchanged for the Trojan Antenor, whom the Greeks had captured. Troilus and his companions accompanied her, and Diomedes, who had brought Antenor to meet them, began his suit almost at once. This is shown in the scene above.

About fifty years after Boccaccio's poem Chaucer retold the story, more compassionately, in his *Troilus and Criseyde*. The outcome remains the same, but the blame is laid, not on the heroine but on the common frailty of human love.

Benoit, Guido, Boccaccio, and Chaucer mention the death of Troilus at Achilles' hand: they are silent as to the fate of Cressida. Late in the fourteenth century the Scot, Robert Henryson, composed an ending for her story in his *Testament of Cressid*. Cast off by Diomedes, she became a leper; Troilus discovered her in this plight, befriended her, and finally gave her honourable burial.

By Shakespeare's time the once love-torn heroine had become a wanton. His *Troilus and Cressida* closes fittingly with cynical quips by Pandarus.

83. ODYSSEUS GIVES ACHILLES' SON HIS FATHER'S ARMS. Attic red-figured kylix by Douris, about 490 B.C. Vienna, Kunsthistorisches Museum, N.3695.

The summary of the *Aethiopis* ends with strife between Ajax and Odysseus for the arms of Achilles: an old commentator adds that Ajax killed himself. The story is expanded in the synopsis of the *Little Iliad*, next in chronological sequence of the lost epics. The Greeks, advised by Athena, awarded the arms to Odysseus, rating cunning above strength, whereupon Ajax slew himself. Eventually the arms were given to Achilles' son, whom Deïdamia, daughter of the king of Scyros, had borne. This youth, Neoptolemus or Pyrrhus, was brought up at his grandfather's court, but after Achilles' death the Greeks learned from Hector's brother, Helenus, whom they had captured, that they could not win the war without the young man. According to the *Little Iliad*, 'Odysseus brings Neoptolemus from Scyros and gives him his father's arms.'

The romances kept the incident of the arming of Achilles' son, whom they consistently called Pyrrhus, but changed the context and omitted the suicide of Ajax. In the detail from the tapestry, opposite, Ajax and Agamemnon, within a sumptuous tent, clothe Pyrrhus in medieval armour.

84. AJAX AND AGAMEMNON ARM THE SON OF ACHILLES. Detail of a late-fifteenth-century Franco-Flemish tapestry. London, Victoria and Albert Museum.

85. THE THEFT OF THE PALLADIUM: DIOMEDES HAS TAKEN THE IMAGE FROM ATHENA'S ALTAR. Red-figured Apulian stemless cup by the Diomed painter, early fourth century B.C. Oxford, Ashmolean Museum.

In addition to bringing Achilles' son to Troy, Helenus, the captive Trojan soothsayer, also told the Greeks that they must obtain the Palladium, an image of Pallas Athena that had fallen from heaven and was kept in Athena's temple in Troy. While it remained in the city Troy could not be taken. According to the *Little Iliad*, Odysseus carried 'the Palladium out of Troy with the help of Diomedes.' Other accounts stressed the role of Diomedes, some saying that it was really he who had stolen the image, having stood on the shoulders of Odysseus to scale the city wall. He had then refused to draw up his companion, and Odysseus in revenge lurked in the darkness to kill him as he returned. The moonlight, however, gleamed upon Odysseus' sword and Diomedes beat him off.

The burlesque scene, in which Odysseus holds the image (Plate 86), was probably inspired by one of the farces dealing with mythological subjects which were

86. BURLESQUE ON THE THEFT OF THE PALLADIUM. Red-figured Apulian oïnochoe, fourth century B.C. London, British Museum, F.366.

widely popular among the Greek-speaking people of South Italy. Odysseus was a favourite comic character of such productions.

The Greeks were also told that they must have the arrows of Hercules. These belonged to their comrade Philoctetes, wounded on the way to Troy and left behind on an island because of the wound's smell. He was brought to the army, but still the city did not fall.

In the romances the opportunity for stealing the Palladium is arranged by the Trojan princes, Antenor and Aeneas, under pretence of a peace conference with the Greeks. They also use this conference to make favourable terms for themselves. Antenor's name was associated even in the *Iliad* with fondness for the Greeks; the story of his actual treachery is considerably later. Lycophron's *Alexandra* (about 320–after 283 B.C.) says that he released the Greek warriors from the wooden horse and gave the signal for the rest to attack.

The attitude of Aeneas was full of contradictions even in ancient literature. The *Iliad* refers to him as

> '... ... ... forever angry with brilliant Priam
> because great as he was he did him no honour among his people.'

Dionysius of Halicarnassus, quoting an earlier source, says that Aeneas betrayed Troy because he was jealous of the honour shown to Paris. For Vergil, of course, he was the national hero; there is no hint of treachery in the *Aeneid*. Dares and Dictys agree that he and Antenor called a conference with the Greeks late in the war, but their treatment then diverges. According to Dictys Antenor alone carried out active negotiations and stole the Palladium; Dares omitted the story of the Palladium but had Aeneas help both in plans to betray the city and in actually opening the gates. According to him the Greek conspirator 'told Antenor and Aeneas, and the others with whom it had been arranged, to lead all their men to the Scaean gate and open it during the night, to show a light and introduce the army. Antenor and Aeneas were ready at the gate by night; they took in Neoptolemus, threw open the gate to the army, made a light, and asked that the protection of flight be given to themselves and their folk.'

The medieval attitude toward Aeneas was curiously ambivalent. On the one hand the romances, taking over the story of the stolen Palladium, managed subtly to implicate Aeneas in treacherous acts. Guido and Lefèvre, for instance, do not have him actually share in the theft, but he plots with Antenor the conference which gave the opportunity. On the other hand the wide admiration for Vergil and for Aeneas as the traditional colonizer of Italy demanded that he be considered completely honourable.

The tapestry opposite follows in general the accounts of Guido and Lefèvre, but introduces Aeneas. The conference scene appears at the left, Priam standing by an altar and image of Jupiter. His name is inscribed on his sleeve; most of the others have their names upon their hats. Opposite Priam is Ulysses, gesticulating eloquently; farther back are Diomedes and Aeneas. The latter looks up sideways from under his downswept brim, his parted lips seeming to convey a surreptitious message to Diomedes. A little farther to the right is Antenor.

The extreme right is divided into two scenes. Above, inside Minerva's temple, Antenor bribes Theano, metamorphosed into a priest, to give him the Palladium. In the background Aeneas and an unnamed man hold the image in a Gothic shrine. Below is a scene in the temple of Apollo, where an eagle carries the Trojan sacrifice to the Greek ships, a phenomenon naturally interpreted by Cassandra as an evil omen.

87. MEDIEVAL VERSION OF THE THEFT OF THE PALLADIUM: ULYSSES AND DIOMEDES DISCUSS PEACE WITH PRIAM: ANTENOR ARRANGES FOR THE THEFT: AN EAGLE SNATCHES THE TROJAN SACRIFICE. Right side of a late-fifteenth-century Franco-Flemish tapestry. Madrid, Collection of the Duke of Alba.

As to the Palladium's ultimate fate, accounts vary. A number of ancient writers, including Dionysius of Halicarnassus, say that Aeneas saved the true image when Troy fell; that it remained hidden in the city; and that the Greeks were given a copy. According to accepted Roman tradition Aeneas brought it to Italy and it eventually came to rest in the temple of Vesta which his descendants built in the Roman Forum.

88. ATHENA BUILDING THE TROJAN HORSE. Attic red-figured kylix, about 470–460 B.C. Florence, Museo Archeologico.

The theft of the Palladium did not immediately bring about Troy's fall, so the Greeks looked for a method of stealthy penetration. According to classical accounts they constructed the famous wooden horse, which has come down as a symbol of attack from within. The *Little Iliad* says: 'Epeius, by Athena's instruction, builds the wooden horse. . . . Then after putting their best men into the wooden horse and burning their huts, the main body of the Hellenes sail to Tenedos. The Trojans, supposing their troubles over, destroy a part of their city wall and take the wooden horse into their city and feast as though they had conquered the Hellenes.' In the vase painting here Athena herself shapes the gigantic horse.

As the *Iliad* ends before the death of Achilles and the fall of Troy, it says nothing about the horse. The *Odyssey*, however, describes it. At a banquet in the palace of

Alcinoüs, Odysseus asks the royal bard to sing

'of the building of the horse of wood, which Epeius made with Athena's help, the horse which once Odysseus led up into the citadel as a thing of guile, when he had filled it with the men who sacked Ilios.'

Vergil's description in the *Aeneid* is even more familiar:

'Broken in war and thrust back by the fates, the Danaan chiefs . . . build by Pallas' divine art, a horse of mountainous bulk, and interweave its ribs with planks of fir. They feign it as a votive offering; this rumour goes abroad. Here, within its dark sides, they stealthily enclose the choicest of their stalwart men and deep in the paunch fill the huge cavern with armed soldiery.'

The wooden horse was a favourite subject of ancient sculptors. Pausanias, in the second century A.D., spoke of a statue given by the citizens of Argos to Delphi: 'a bronze horse supposed to be the wooden horse of Troy'. He also noted that on the Athenian Acropolis 'there is a horse called Wooden set up in bronze. That the work of Epeius was a contrivance to make a breach in the Trojan wall is known to everybody. . . . But legend says of the horse that it contained the most valiant of the Greeks, and the design of the bronze figure fits in well with this story.'

89. THE BUILDING OF THE TROJAN HORSE. Painting by Giovanni Battista Tiepolo (Italian), about 1760. Hartford, Wadsworth Atheneum.

'The Trojans were suspicious of the wooden horse,' says the synopsis of the *Sack of Ilium*, 'and standing round it debated what they ought to do. Some thought they ought to hurl it down from the rocks, others to burn it up, while others said they ought to dedicate it to Athena. At last this third opinion prevailed. Then they turned to mirth and feasting, believing the war was at an end. But at this very time two serpents appeared and destroyed Laocoön and one of his two sons, a portent

90. LAOCOÖN SACRIFICING: THE SERPENTS ENCIRCLE HIM AND HIS SONS.
Illustration from the *Aeneid*, II. 191–198. Vatican Vergil, fifth century A.D.
Rome, Vatican, cod.vat.lat.3225, fol.18v.

which so alarmed the followers of Aeneas that they withdrew to Ida.' The Phaeacian minstrel in the *Odyssey* tells much the same version of the horse's reception but does not mention Laocoön or the serpents.

In the *Aeneid* Vergil tells the story of Laocoön more fully and somewhat differently. As Apollo's priest, Laocoön warns his Trojan countrymen against the horse, using the phrase, now proverbial, 'I fear the Greeks bearing gifts', and hurls his spear at its side. The Trojans are about to destroy it when the Greek Sinon is brought in, pretending to be a deserter. He says that the horse was made to appease Athena for the theft of the Palladium, that the Greeks are leaving, and that if the offering is taken into the city Troy will become immensely powerful. At this moment

'a pair of serpents with endless coils are breasting the sea and side by side making for the shore. Their bosoms rise amid the surge, and their crests, blood-red, overtop the waves; the rest of them skims the main behind and their huge backs curve in many a fold; we hear the sound sent from foaming seas. . . . Pale at the sight, we scatter. They in unswerving course fare towards Laocoön; and first each serpent enfolds in its embrace the youthful bodies of his two sons and with its fangs feeds upon the hapless limbs. Then himself too, as he comes to their aid, weapons in hand, they seize and bind in mighty folds; and now, twice encircling his waist, twice winding their scaly backs around his throat, they tower above with head and lofty necks. He the while strains his hands to burst the knots, his fillets steeped in gore and black venom; the while he lifts to heaven hideous cries, like the bellowings of a wounded bull that has fled from the altar.'

91. LAOCOÖN. Marble group, about 50 B.C. Probably a Roman copy of an earlier work. Rome, Vatican.

Vergil's description of the death of Laocoön and his sons is the classic version in literature; the marble group is its counterpart in art. Shortly before his death in A.D. 79 the Elder Pliny wrote of it: 'The Laocoön, which stands in the Palace of the Emperor Titus, a work to be preferred to all that the arts of painting and sculpture have produced. Out of one block of stone the consummate artists, Agesandros, Polydoros, and Athenodoros of Rhodes made, after careful planning, Laocoön, his sons, and the snakes marvellously entwined about them.' Buried for centuries after Rome's decline, the copy illustrated here was discovered by chance in 1506 above the ruins of Nero's Golden House and was recognized immediately from Pliny's description.

92. LAOCOÖN (a view of Toledo in the distance). Painting, about 1601–1606, by El Greco (Spanish). Washington, National Gallery of Art, Samuel H. Kress Collection.

Though the Middle Ages were familiar with Vergil, the story of Laocoön, despite its picturesque quality, does not appear in the romances. This was due, no doubt, to the fact that he was not mentioned by either Dictys or Dares; nevertheless it seems strange that Benoit, Guido, and Lefèvre should all have omitted the incident.

The Trojans, convinced that the serpents had been sent to punish Laocoön because he had hurled his spear at the horse, prepared to make amends to Athena for slighting her offering. Vergil continues the story of how they brought the horse within the walls:

' "Draw the image to her house," all cry, "and supplicate her godhead." We part the walls and lay bare the city's battlement. All gird themselves for the work; under the feet they place gliding wheels, and about the neck stretch hempen bands. The fateful engine climbs our walls, big with arms. Around it boys and unwedded girls chant holy songs and delight to touch the cable with their hands. Up it moves, and glides threatening into the city's midst. O Motherland! O Ilium, home of the gods, and ye Dardan battlements, famed in war! Four times at the gate's very threshold it halted, and four times from its paunch the armour clashed; yet we press on, heedless and blind with frenzy, and set the ill-omened monster on our hallowed citadel . . . . Meanwhile the sky revolves and night rushes from the ocean, wrapping in its mighty shade earth and heaven and the wiles of the Myrmidons.'

According to a fragment from the *Little Iliad* it was the Greek Sinon, emerging from the horse 'when it was midnight, and the clear moon was rising', who gave the signal for his countrymen to return from Tenedos to the attack. Vergil, who has Sinon brought in as a pretended deserter, has him open the horse, but says that it was Helen who, 'feigning a solemn dance . . . held a mighty torch and called the Danaans'.

93. THE WOODEN HORSE BROUGHT INTO TROY.
Roman wall painting from Pompeii, second half of the first century A.D.
Naples, National Museum, 9040.

The figure with outstretched arm at the upper left in this painting may be Helen beckoning with her torch; below, the fateful horse is being dragged toward a tall sacred column and statue of Athena. The effect of moonlight is admirably suggested in this work of nineteen centuries ago. Contrasted masses of light and shade form the composition; the moonlit surfaces shine broadly in the enveloping dark; details are lost in the illusion of light-filled landscape.

The Middle Ages changed the Trojan horse from wood to bronze, or, as Caxton phrased it, a 'horse of brass'.

The change came about gradually. Dictys mentioned briefly that the horse was made of wood. Dares reduced it to a horse's head above the Scaean gate, through which the Greeks entered by night. Benoit implied that his audience knew the material but did not specify it. So far as is known Guido delle Colonne was the first to say that the Greeks made 'a horse of bronze, *equm ererum*, big enough to hold a thousand men'. With but few exceptions later romancers followed Guido.

Benoit's lack of explicit description gave open invitation to change and elaboration, and stories of marvellous works in metal had long been filtering in from the

94. THE TROJAN HORSE, A 'HORSE OF BRASS', WITHIN THE WALLS OF TROY.
Left side of a late-fifteenth-century Franco-Flemish tapestry.
Zamora, Cathedral Museum.

East. The late Greek romances of Alexander the Great were filled with eastern marvels, such as brazen elephants which served as engines of war. Though *The Thousand and One Nights* as we know it is later than Guido's work, the Third Kalendar's Tale, in which a brazen horse and rider admit travellers to the City of Brass was probably current much earlier. As far north as Britain, Geoffrey of Monmouth, writing before Guido's time, had included among Merlin's prophecies a brazen horse and rider which should guard London. These marvels doubtless owed much to the actual mechanical devices in metal to be seen in the East and at the Byzantine Court.

Guido, a Sicilian writing in Messina, was in a position to be familiar with such tales, for the Saracens' influence was strong in the land that they had held for more than two and a half centuries. And there was a strong local interest as well in one of the then surviving 'wonders' of nearby Naples—a bronze horse, probably Roman work, which was popularly believed to have been made by Vergil in his medieval guise of magician. Conrad of Querfurt, Bishop of Hildesheim, mentioned it in a letter written during a visit to Italy in 1194–1196, and tradition says that it survived until 1322. Then, according to one legend, it was destroyed by the veterinarians of the city because it prevented horses from injuring their backs, and so interfered with business. Another account says that it was removed by the priests because it fostered superstition. In the eighteenth century an attempt was made to identify one of the colossal bronze horse heads in the National Museum at Naples with the remains of this statue.

In the Zamora tapestry opposite, the horse, gaily caparisoned with brocade as for a tournament, has disgorged the warriors who were hidden within it. Behind it is the gap in the wall made to drag it into the city. Far at the left sits Helen, her name woven into her headdress, looking out across the sea.

The Old French inscription at the upper left reads *le grant cheval darain*, 'the great horse of brass.'

Though Dares had omitted the story of the horse, the accounts of Dictys and Vergil gave it an important part in the romances. Most of these followed Dictys rather than Vergil in saying that the Trojans allowed the Greeks to drag the horse into the city as a gift to Athena, although, when the gate proved too small, they broke down their own wall to admit it. Dictys treated the horse merely as a device for destroying part of the wall and making easy entry for the Greek forces by night, but the romances followed the Vergilian tradition of using it as a means of stealthy penetration. 'In this horse,' says Lefèvre, 'was a subtle man named Sinon that had the keys of the horse for to open it when the Trojans were asleep and resting them in the night. And as soon as they issued out of the horse they gave a token of fire to them that were in the fields. . .' Then Sinon 'went out and lit his fire,' whereupon the rest of the Greeks 'entered into the city by the gate that was broken to bring in the horse of brass. And the thousand knights issued out and where they found the Trojans they slew them in their houses where they slept. . . . Thus entered the Greeks into the city, and slew men and women and children without sparing any, and took all that they found in their houses. They slew so many that ere it was day they had slain more than twenty thousand.'

Within the city walls that night Helen awaited her fate. Paris was dead, killed not long after he had slain Achilles, and his place had been taken by his brother Deiphobus. Most ancient authors agreed with the statement in the *Odyssey* that her 'heart already turned toward going home again'. She had, to be sure, almost betrayed the Greeks within the wooden horse by walking about it in the darkness and calling to each of the men concealed in the voice of his own wife. But Menelaus himself explains that this action must have been due to the prompting of some god 'who sought to bring the Trojans honour'. Vergil represented her as torn by doubts and fears and taking refuge in Vesta's temple when the assault came. But according to Tryphiodorus' *Taking of Ilios*: 'all night long fair Helen herself . . . displayed from her chamber to her friends her golden torch.'

The toilet of Helen appears in Greek vase painting and on the engraved backs of Etruscan mirrors. In these she is being prepared by attendants for conquest—

95. THE TROJAN HORSE DISGORGES ITS BURDEN. Illustration from a late-fifteenth-century manuscript of Raoul Lefèvre's *Recueil*. Paris, Bibliothèque Nationale, MS.fr.22552, fol.276v.

96. THE TOILET OF HELEN. Painting, 1914, by Bryson Burroughs (American). Baltimore, Collection of Mrs. Bryson Burroughs.

probably that of Paris. The Helen hymned by the chorus of Euripides' *Trojan Women* might well have used all her cosmetic arts as means to increase her safety on that fatal night. The women of this chorus had watched her care for beauty throughout the weary years of war. When Troy had fallen and the Greeks were setting sail for home, they prayed that storms might overwhelm both men and ships:

> 'And, God, may Helen be there,
> With mirror of gold,
> Decking her face so fair,
> Girl-like; and hear, and stare,
> And turn death-cold:
> Never, ah, never more
> The hearth of her home to see;
> Nor sands of the Spartan shore,
> Nor tombs where her fathers be.'

With a sly humour that would have delighted this chorus, Burroughs painted his Helen, preparing to captivate the victors, while outside her window Troy burns.

The synopsis of the *Sack of Ilium* makes but little mention of the long awaited meeting of Helen and Menelaus at Troy's fall: 'Menelaus finds Helen and takes her to the ships, after killing Deiphobus.' The *Little Iliad*, however, says that he

97. THE MEETING OF MENELAUS AND HELEN. From an Attic black-figured neck-amphora, about 550 B.C. New York, Metropolitan Museum of Art, 56.171.18. Fletcher Fund, 1956.

first drew his sword to kill her, but catching sight of her breast unveiled, he cast the sword away. Neither mentions where Menelaus found his wife. Among later accounts some say that she was in her chamber with Deiphobus, some that she was hidden in the palace, and Vergil that she had taken refuge in Vesta's temple.

Menelaus set sail with Helen for Greece and, after being driven out of the way by storms, as related in the *Odyssey* and the *Returns*, reached home, where the two lived in peace, married their daughter Hermione to Achilles' son Neoptolemus, and entertained Telemachus, Odysseus' son, voyaging in search of his father.

According to a prophecy in the *Odyssey*, Menelaus was not to die but to be transported to the Elysian Fields because he had married Helen and was 'counted son-in-law of Zeus'. Pausanias tells two different legends of Helen. One relates that

98. THE MEETING OF MENELAUS AND HELEN AT THE FALL OF TROY. Attic red-figured skyphos, signed by Hieron, about 480 B.C. Boston, Museum of Fine Arts, 13.186.

Menelaus died and after his death Helen was driven from Sparta and took refuge in Rhodes with its queen, Polyxo, whom she believed to be her friend. But Polyxo's husband had been killed in the war with Troy and she held Helen responsible for his death. 'So,' says Pausanias, 'when Helen was bathing, the queen sent some handmaidens in the guise of Furies, who seized her and hanged her upon a tree. Hence there is in Rhodes a sanctuary of Helen of the Tree.' Yet in the same chapter he notes that in the White Isle 'Helen was wedded to Achilles'.

Besides this tradition of Helen, Waster of Cities, there was another legend which reduced the long war to emptiness. First told, perhaps, by Stesichorus in the sixth century B.C., this account furnished the theme of Euripides' *Helen*. According to it Helen had never gone to Troy but had been carried by the gods to Egypt while Paris stole a phantom in her place. Menelaus, according to Euripides, arrives in Egypt on his homeward way. The phantom he has brought from Troy vanishes; he is reunited with his wife; and he learns that through the ten weary years of war:

> '. . . Helen, by Simois crimsoned water,
> Was a breath, was a battle-cry—nought besides.'

The play ends happily enough with the pronouncement of Helen's brother Castor and Pollux:

> 'To wanderer Menelaus Heaven's doom
> Appoints for home the Island of the Blest.'

99. THE RETURN AND RECONCILIATION OF MENELAUS AND HELEN. Illustration from *Le Livre des Estoires dou Commencement dou Monde*, Neapolitan, 1350–1360. London, British Museum, Royal MS.20, D.I, fol.181r.

Raoul Lefèvre echoes the sentiment of most of the romances when he reports considerable enmity towards Helen after the capture of Troy. Ajax Telamon, Lefèvre says, was in favour of burning her, 'for whom so much hurt and evil was come and that so many worthy kings and princes had died for. And there was a great murmur at this, so that only with great pain did Agamemnon, Ulysses, and Menelaus save her. But Ulysses with his fair language said so much to them of divers things that they were content that Helen should have no harm.'

The fourteenth-century minstrels' romance, *The Siege and Battle of Troy*, tells the story differently, saying nothing of Greek enmity. The 'earls and barons' of Menelaus

> 'Fetched Helen the Queen out of the tower,
> And brought her to the king her lord,
> Either kissed other and were accord.'

In Lydgate's *Troy Book* admiring crowds accompany Menelaus when he sets out

> 'With his queen, the goodly fair Helen
> And because she was so famous and so fair,
> Great was the press and marvellous the repair
> From every part her beauty to behold,
> For whose sake Troy, with walls still far from old
> Had been destroyed, that noble, royal town
> And many a man full worthy of renown,

Had lost his life—that no man can gainsay—
And all for Helen, the wife of Menelay,
When a thing's done, it may then be no other.'

In the manuscript illustration the Greek ships sail homeward at the left; at the right, Menelaus and Helen arrive at home and talk together in an upper chamber.

The *Little Iliad* and the *Sack of Ilium* both told of the fall of Troy and the deaths of Priam and of Hector's little son, Astyanax. According to the *Sack of Ilium* 'Neoptolemus kills Priam who had fled to the altar of Zeus Herceius [Zeus of the Household Altar].' Accounts of the death of Astyanax vary. The *Sack of Ilium* says that Odysseus hurled him from the city wall; the *Little Iliad* has Neoptolemus strike the boy with his sword. In Euripides' *Trojan Women* Neoptolemus throws the child from the walls some time after Priam's death. Vase paintings often combine the death of the old king and that of his grandson at the hands of Neoptolemus.

Below Neoptolemus forces Priam toward the altar, while with his other hand he swings Astyanax above his head. At the left Ajax the Lesser assaults Cassandra.

100. NEOPTOLEMUS KILLING PRIAM AND ASTYANAX. From an Attic red-figured calyx-krater, about 465 B.C. Boston, Museum of Fine Arts, 59.178.

101. PYRRHUS (Neoptolemus) KILLING PRIAM.
Fifteenth-century illustration by Apollonio di Giovanni in a manuscript of the *Aeneid*.
Florence, Biblioteca Riccardiana, MS.492, fol.86v.

As Vergil tells the story, when Priam saw the foe at his doors he threw 'his long-disused armour about his aged, trembling shoulders', girded on his sword, and rushed to join the conflict. Hecuba, however, who had already gathered her daughters about the household altar for sanctuary, 'drew the aged man to her and placed him on the holy seat, saying, . . . "this altar will guard us all, or thou wilt die with us." '

At this moment Pyrrhus burst into the courtyard and killed Polites, one of Priam's sons, before his eyes. Thereupon Priam 'hurled his weak and harmless spear' at Pyrrhus, who dragged him 'to the very altar-stones, . . . raised high the flashing sword and buried it to the hilt in his side.'

In the manuscript illustration Pyrrhus stabs Priam as he bends over Polites, while Menelaus looks on. At the right Hecuba, robed in rich brocade, rushes toward her husband, her arms upflung in horror.

The fate of the Trojan women after their city's fall has furnished themes to poets and artists innumerable throughout the centuries. The brief remaining summaries of the lost epics outline the histories of some, notably of Polyxena, Hecuba, Andromache, and Cassandra: no doubt they were treated more fully in the epics themselves.

Polyxena, almost without exception, has been portrayed as the innocent victim of passions beyond her control. The synopsis of the *Sack of Ilium* gives the bare fact that the Greeks 'sacrifice Polyxena at the tomb of Achilles', but does not say why the deed was done. Euripides' tragedies emphasize the emotional reactions of the characters. In his *Hecuba* the shade of Achilles appears above his grave demanding her sacrifice as a condition for raising the spell that holds the Greek ships from going home. Hecuba implies that he demands the maiden to avenge his death at the hand of Paris, though ' . . . never aught of harm wrought she to him.' Like her

102. THE SACRIFICE OF POLYXENA. Attic black-figured amphora, sixth century B.C. London, British Museum, 97.7–27.2.

Greek counterpart Iphigenia, Polyxena goes proudly to her fate, addressing her slayers:

> 'O Argives, ye which laid my city low,
> Free-willed I die: on my flesh let no man
> Lay hand: unflinchingly will I yield my neck.
> But by the gods, let me stand free, the while
> Ye slay, that I may die free; for I shame
> Slave to be called in Hades, who am royal.'

Awed by her bearing the Greeks vie with each other to give her honourable burial.

In Ovid's *Metamorphoses* Achilles demands the Trojan princess that his tomb 'may not lack its fitting honour' when the living divide the spoils of Troy; but in Seneca's *Trojan Women* he asks for Polyxena's death 'that in the Elysian Fields he may wed her'. Philostratus' *Life of Apollonius* gives a more romantic version: Polyxena seeks out Achilles' tomb and there kills herself that she may be his bride in the other world.

The maiden's fate moved Pausanias so deeply that, describing her death as shown in Polygnotos' painting of the Sack of Troy at Athens, he wrote, 'Homer did well to omit so savage a deed.' Of this painting, or the Polyxena in a similar scene by Polygnotos at Delphi, an anonymous Greek poet wrote, '. . . in her eyes lies all the history of the Trojan War.'

In the tapestry opposite, events following Troy's capture appear in medieval guise. Pyrrhus kills Priam in a temple with Gothic windows; its statue of Apollo, except for the sun above the shrine, might represent a Christian saint. Polyxena kneels upon Achilles' tomb, flat-topped like those that cover many a crusader's grave.

The tapestry follows closely the story told by Guido and Lefèvre, although its Latin and French inscriptions are, like modern captions, freely condensed to serve their purpose. Pyrrhus, as Lefèvre tells it, kills Polyxena because 'she was the cause of the death of his father'. Neither Lefèvre nor Guido says that Achilles demanded her death, but that the gods decreed it because Apollo's temple had been polluted by Achilles' blood when he was slain there for her sake.

Between Pyrrhus and Apollo's temple appear Andromache and Cassandra, conducted, according to the inscriptions on the tapestry and later romances, by Ajax son of Telamon. Below them Hecuba, maddened by horror, is biting one of the Greeks. This incident is an echo of an old legend, preserved in the romances. According to Euripides' *Hecuba* and other ancient sources, the unhappy Trojan queen was transformed into a dog; Ovid does not mention this change of form, but he says that she bit the stones and barked; Quintus Smyrnaeus says that she was changed first to a dog and then to stone.

At the extreme right are the author or narrator and assistants, surrounded by books. The French inscription at the upper right reads: 'Thus ends the unhappy tale of the city worthy of high renown, Troy the great.'

103. PYRRHUS SLAYS PRIAM AND SACRIFICES POLYXENA. Right side of a late-fifteenth-century Franco-Flemish tapestry. Zamora, Cathedral Museum.

Cassandra took refuge in Athena's temple when the city fell. There, according to ancient accounts, she was attacked by 'Ajax the Lesser, son of Oïleus'. In dragging her away, says the *Sack of Ilium*, he tore with her the image of the goddess, which so frightened the Greeks that they almost stoned him. The *Odyssey* relates the punishment that overtook him: he lost both ship and life on his homeward way. Cassandra was given to Agamemnon and with him met the tragic end celebrated by Greek dramatists.

Later writers changed the story considerably. Dares says that Cassandra and Andromache took refuge in the temple but makes no mention of Ajax: both were later freed and went with Helenus to the Chersonesus. Dictys, closer to ancient tradition, says that Ajax the Lesser found the women in the temple and took them away but did them no harm. Cassandra was then given to Agamemnon but did not accompany him to his home.

104. AJAX SON OF OÏLEUS SEIZES CASSANDRA AT THE ALTAR OF ATHENA.
From an Attic red-figured neck-amphora, about 450 B.C. New York, Metropolitan Museum of Art, 56.171.41. Fletcher Fund, 1956.

Benoit, as in the manuscript page opposite, followed Dictys in having Ajax the Lesser find the two women and take them from the temple. His story bridges the gap between the classic version and that of the later romancers, which completely confused the two Ajaxes. In many of them it was the son of Telamon who took the women from the temple, but the son of Oïleus who was shipwrecked, though not drowned, on his homeward way.

The end of the son of Telamon was also different in the romances: he did not kill himself because of his failure to win Achilles' arms, but was found dead in bed after Troy's capture. His death was blamed on the enmity of Greek leaders, especially Ulysses.

105. AJAX SON OF OÏLEUS FINDS CASSANDRA AND ANDROMACHE IN MINERVA'S TEMPLE AND TAKES THEM AWAY: BELOW, TROY IS LEVELLED TO THE GROUND. From a manuscript of Benoit's *Roman*, Italian, second half of the fourteenth century. Venice, Biblioteca Marciana, MS.fr.17, fol.204.

106. THE CAPTIVE ANDROMACHE. Painting, 1888, by Sir Frederick Leighton (English). Manchester, City Art Gallery.

After Troy fell 'the bright son of bold Achilles led the wife of Hector to the hollow ships' says a fragment of the *Little Iliad*; the summary of the *Sack of Ilium* is even more concise: 'Neoptolemus takes Andromache as his prize.' Two of Euripides' plays, *The Trojan Women* and *Andromache*, deal partially or wholly with her fate. In the former she comes on the stage with her young son Astyanax, only to find that the Greeks have ordered him to be thrown from the walls of Troy.

Various sources tell Andromache's story. She was taken to Epirus, where she became the slave of Neoptolemus and had a son by him. During his absence she barely escaped death at the hands of his wife, Hermione, daughter of Menelaus and Helen; this is the plot developed in Euripides' *Andromache*. According to Vergil and others she eventually married Helenus, the only son of Priam and Hecuba to survive the war, and with him founded a 'little Troy' in Epirus, which Aeneas visited on his way to Italy. Dares says that she, Cassandra, and Helenus, with other Trojans, escaped captivity, but the romances, following Dictys, tell much the same story as the Greek dramatists of Andromache's captivity and Hermione's jealousy.

In Leighton's painting Andromache stands forlorn among the other women who have gone to draw water from the spring, presumably near the palace of Neoptolemus. The Royal Academy's first publication of the painting in *Royal Academy Pictures*, 1888, stated that the scene was suggested by Hector's farewell in the *Iliad* and quoted Mrs. Browning's translation of this passage in which the hero has a prophetic glimpse of his wife as a captive drawing 'the water of Greek wells' while

> '... ... ... some standing by
> Marking thy tears fall, shall say, "This is she,
> The wife of that same Hector who fought best
> Of all the Trojans when all fought for Troy." '

THE ORESTEIA

107. THE MURDER OF AGAMEMNON.
From a Greek bronze shield band, second half of the sixth century B.C.
Olympia Museum.

Agamemnon, according to old versions of the tale, took Cassandra with him to Mycenae, where his wife Clytemnestra, Helen's sister, awaited him. Believing him responsible for the death of their daughter Iphigenia, infatuated with his cousin, Aegisthus, and jealous of Cassandra, Clytemnestra planned her husband's death. The details of his murder vary considerably. According to the summary of the *Returns* he was slain by Clytemnestra and Aegisthus together; the *Odyssey* says that Aegisthus stabbed him at the feast held in honour of his return and Cassandra shared his fate. ' "Saddest of all," the shade of Agamemnon tells Odysseus, "I heard the cry of Priam's daughter, whom crafty Clytemnestra slew beside me." ' Sophocles and Euripides call Agamemnon's murder the work of both. In Aeschylus' *Agamemnon* the queen assumes the responsibility, proclaiming proudly to the elders of the city how she had entangled her husband in a robe and stabbed him:

> ' "Thus have I wrought the deed—deny it I will not. Round him, like as to catch a haul of fish, I cast a net impassable—a fatal wealth of robe—so that he should neither escape nor ward off doom. Twice I smote him . . . Once he had fallen, I dealt him yet a third stroke." '

On the shield band (Plate 107) Clytemnestra stabs her husband in the back while Aegisthus grips him around the neck. Medieval romances say that Aegisthus, with the connivance of Clytemnestra, killed Agamemnon in his bed on the night of his return, as shown in the manuscript illustration from a German version of Guido.

108. CLYTEMNESTRA AND AEGISTHUS KILL AGAMEMNON. From a manuscript of a German version of Guido's *Historia*, Rhenish, fifteenth century. Munich, Bavarian State Library. Cod.lat.61, fol.179.

109. CLYTEMNESTRA KILLS CASSANDRA. Bronze relief from the Argive Heraeum near Mycenae. Greek, seventh century B.C. Athens, National Museum.

Clytemnestra herself stabs her rival in this relief. There are no inscriptions, but no other incident seems to fit this action, the *Odyssey's* version of Cassandra's end.

Medieval romancers followed Dictys' story of Cassandra, in which she did not accompany Agamemnon to his home but was last seen on the shores of Troy, lamenting her dead kin and prophesying disaster for the Greeks. They had demanded that she tell them how they would fare on their homeward way, and she foretold pains and perils before they should reach their own country, and, especially, that Agamemnon would meet death at the hands of his own family. Then she disappears from the pages of romance except for a brief mention by Guido and later writers, who say that Clytemnestra received a letter informing her that Agamemnon had wedded one of Priam's daughters (unnamed) and meant to bring her home as queen. This letter, however, is treated as a falsehood, devised by an enemy to compass Agamemnon's death.

With the Renaissance the classic story was revived, receiving considerable attention from Boccaccio both in the *Genealogy of the Gods* and *De Claris Mulieribus*, and passing into later handbooks of mythology. Cassandra's death, however, seems not to have been a popular theme in art in any period.

Clytemnestra marries Aegisthus but punishment eventually overtakes the guilty pair. Orestes, Agamemnon's young son, who had been sent by his sister Electra to be brought up safely in another land, was commanded by Apollo to avenge his father's death. With his comrade Pylades he came back to Mycenae and, aided by Electra, killed them both. But in fulfilling the obligation of vengeance, he had incurred the guilt of matricide.

This situation of divided loyalties and perplexing problems furnished themes for Aeschylus, Sophocles, and Euripides. The only remaining example of the normal Greek trilogy upon a related theme is Aeschylus' *Oresteia*, three plays dealing with Agamemnon and his family. The first, *Agamemnon*, tells of that hero's death at his wife's hand. In the second, the *Choëphori* (Libation-Bearers), Orestes kills first Aegisthus and then his mother at Apollo's command. Immediately seized by the Furies of remorse, he flees for help to the shrine of Apollo at Delphi. The third play, the *Eumenides* (Furies), opens at Delphi, where the god counsels the fugitive to go to Athens. The scene then shifts to that city, where the court of the Areopagus tries his case, and, by the deciding vote of Athena, acquits him. The Furies are reconciled by her judgment and the play ends on a note of absolution by means of law.

Sophocles treats the theme of vengeance in his *Electra*. The emphasis is laid so strongly here upon the death of Aegisthus, which is placed at the end, after that of Clytemnestra, that the matricide seems less horrible. The dramatist regards Apollo's command as justification for the act; Orestes feels no remorse, there are, therefore, no Furies, and no need for absolution. At the end the chorus declares that the curse of blood-guilt, which has lain upon Agamemnon's family for generations, has now been lifted.

Euripides deals with the theme twice—once in his *Electra* and later in his *Orestes*, separate plays rather than parts of a trilogy. Both present searching but compassionate studies of human suffering mounting to frenzied intensity. In the first brother and sister together kill their mother and Aegisthus, Electra playing a much more vengeful part than in the works of Aeschylus and Sophocles. Orestes is bidden to go to Delphi and Electra into exile, but neither obeys the command. In the *Orestes* both are still in the palace of Mycenae, driven so near to madness that they are prepared to slaughter everyone there. Then Apollo intervenes again, bids Orestes marry his sister to Pylades and himself go to Athens for trial. So far as is known Euripides wrote no play centred about the trial, but in his *Iphigenia in Tauris* Orestes tells his long-lost sister that he had been acquitted at Athens but was still haunted by the Furies. This play is in the nature of a sequel, relating the journey to Tauris, which finally brings peace to the tormented hero.

110. ORESTES KILLS AEGISTHUS. Attic red-figured stamnos, early fifth century B.C. Berlin, Staatliche Museen, 2184.

The Greek vase painting shows Orestes plunging his sword into Aegisthus' breast. Behind her brother Electra raises a weapon to strike, while Clytemnestra stretches out imploring arms above Aegisthus' head.

The romance version of Orestes' vengeance has none of the torment and haunting remorse which the Greek dramatists gave the story. At the feast held when he was knighted Orestes asked the king who has sheltered him to help avenge his father and recover his land—the latter motive seems fully as important as vengeance. He set forth with a band of knights and reached Mycenae, which refused to surrender. It was eventually obliged to yield, however, and Orestes captured his mother. He killed and mutilated her and, as Guido tells it, 'had her drawn naked outside the city for the dogs to eat.' Aegisthus, who returned with aid, he also captured, dragged through the city, and hanged.

Menelaus, arriving a little later, disapproved of Orestes' vengeance upon Clytemnestra, perhaps because she was his sister-in-law. He charged Orestes with being unfit to rule and assembled the Greek nobles at Athens to consider the case

III. A MEDIEVAL VERSION OF THE VENGEANCE OF ORESTES.
From a manuscript of a German version of Guido's *Historia*, Rhenish, fifteenth century. Munich, Bavarian State Library, Cod.lat.61, fol.183.

—a feudal version of the trial before the Athenian court of the Areopagus. Orestes, however, answered not as a Christian knight, but as a pagan warrior, 'the gods willed it'. The duke of Athens offered to defend him at arms against anyone who chose to press the charge. None accepted, and the story ends on a note of reconciliation. As in Greek legend 'Orestes took Hermione, the daughter of Menelaus and Helen, as his wife.'

Hermione, according to classic authors, was the wife of both Orestes and Neoptolemus (Pyrrhus); which was her first husband varied in different versions of the tale. The romances met this problem by having Pyrrhus steal her from Orestes after their marriage, whereupon Orestes slew him or caused him to be killed and reclaimed Hermione.

112. IPHIGENIA, ORESTES AND PYLADES AT THE TEMPLE OF ARTEMIS IN TAURIS. Roman wall painting in the House of Pinarius Cerialis, Pompeii, A.D. 63–79.

The story of Cassandra and Agamemnon leads almost imperceptibly into that of Agamemnon's daughter Iphigenia, and Orestes' further history.

The painting shows the scene between brother and sister in a stage setting for Euripides' *Iphigenia in Tauris.* Iphigenia and her attendants are in the centre, Orestes and Pylades at the right, and Thoas, king of Tauris, at the left. According to Euripides, Orestes' next step after the acquittal at Athens, which had failed to bring him peace of mind, was to go, at Apollo's bidding, to the savage land of Tauris and from there bring an image of Artemis which had fallen from heaven. This deed, the god promised, would satisfy the Furies.

With Pylades, now Electra's husband, Orestes set out and reached the distant land to which his sister had been carried from Aulis at the beginning of the war. Here in Tauris she had been obliged to consecrate for sacrifice to Artemis all strangers landing on its shores. When the two Greeks were brought before her she told them that she could save one if he would carry a message back to Greece begging her brother to rescue her. The friends strove to save each other and in the course of the discussion brother and sister learned each other's identities. Iphigenia helped to steal the image on the pretext of cleansing it from their pollution. The three fled to Orestes' ship, but it was driven back to shore and Thoas ordered the Greeks to be slain. Athena, however, appeared in mid-air above the stage, ordered

113. A COLONNADE IN TAURIS LOOKING OUT TO SEA. Setting for Act I of Gluck's opera, *Iphigénie en Tauride*, as produced in Stockholm at the Royal Opera in 1785. Painted by Jacob Mörch from a sketch by J. D. Dugourc.

Thoas to let them all depart in peace, and bade Orestes build a temple to Artemis on his return, in which Iphigenia would serve as priestess. The curse that had driven four generations of Orestes' family to murder their kin was finally lifted, and all united in obeying the goddess of wisdom and justice.

The story of Iphigenia, omitted or scamped in medieval romances, became immensely popular in the drama and opera of the seventeenth and eighteenth centuries. Racine's play, *Iphigénie en Aulide*, produced in Paris in 1674, used a variant of the old tradition of two Iphigenias. Agamemnon is simply told that Diana demands the sacrifice of 'a maiden of Helen's blood, Iphigenia.' As his daughter is Helen's niece everything points to her. But Achilles, summoned on pretext of marriage, brings with him Eriphyle, a captive maiden who loves him and whose jealousy plays an important part. She betrays Agamemnon's plan to send Achilles and Iphigenia away secretly. Calchas then discloses that Eriphyle is the daughter of Helen and Theseus and her true name is Iphigenia. Eriphyle kills herself, Diana's terms are met, and Iphigenia and Achilles look forward to marriage.

Gluck's opera, *Iphigénie en Tauride*, was produced in Paris in 1779, the same year as Goethe's prose *Iphigenie* at Ettersburg. Here, as in Euripides' play, Orestes and Pylades strive to save each other. Pylades, released to try to rally the scattered Greek forces, is delayed. As the knife is raised for his sacrifice Orestes exclaims: 'Thus thou too didst pass away, Iphigenia my sweet sister.' These words bring recognition. Pylades arrives with aid, Thoas is killed, and all escape without either divine intervention or moral triumph.

Besides Gluck's two operas there were at least thirty settings for Iphigenia in Aulis between 1632 and 1819 and over fifteen for Iphigenia in Tauris between 1704 and 1817.

In 1779 Goethe produced his prose version of *Iphigenie auf Tauris* at the court theatre at Ettersburg, he himself playing the part of Orestes. The play was given its final verse form in 1787. The classic serenity that pervades this drama is not simply the Greek acceptance of fate; the play presents clearly the contrast between the pagan attitude and that of eighteenth-century humanitarian ethics. Euripides' Iphigenia deceives the barbarian Thoas as a matter of course; a happy ending is reached only by Athena's intervention. Goethe's Iphigenia has found Thoas kind, tells him the whole story, and wins his consent to depart in peace.

With the homecoming of Orestes and Iphigenia the last of Atreus' blood found rest. Most of the Greeks who fought at Troy were dead or back at home: the Trojans had embarked on long and perilous wanderings. The adventures of one Greek and one Trojan have their own epics. To the Greeks the *Odyssey* was the supreme treatment of the wanderings of Odysseus after the war: other legends were grouped about him, but the adventures they related did not parallel Homer's. Aeneas prince of Troy was a familiar figure in literature as well as legend by Vergil's time; in the *Aeneid* the poet established the canon of the hero's deeds and of his connection with Rome.

THE ODYSSEY

114. ODYSSEUS. Carnelian ringstone (impression). Roman. New York, Metropolitan Museum of Art, 41.160.766. Bequest of William Gedney Beatty, 1941.

Odysseus is shown here disguised as a beggar for his return to Ithaca; the pointed cap and beggar's staff are his distinguishing characteristics in ancient art.

Odysseus alone among the Greeks who fought at Troy has an epic of his own dealing with the adventures that befell him during the ten years between the war's end and his re-establishment in his own home at Ithaca. The lost epic of the *Returns*, which told the histories of many heroes on their homeward way, was written later than the *Odyssey*: judging from its synopsis, it omitted the adventures of Odysseus because they had already been told. Another epic of Odysseus' later life, the *Telegonia*, is also preserved only in Proclus' brief summary and in a few references. In the *Odyssey* as in the *Iliad* Odysseus is represented as prudent and ingenious but courageous; later legend, fed by popular burlesques, tended to show him as deceitful and somewhat cowardly.

The *Odyssey* opens with an assembly of the gods on Olympus in the tenth year after Odysseus has left Troy. Athena protests to Zeus that the nymph Calypso, on whose mythical island of Ogygia the hero was shipwrecked seven years before, will not let him go. Zeus promises to send Hermes to Calypso bidding her let Odysseus depart; Athena herself goes in disguise to Ithaca to encourage the hero's son, Telemachus, to rid his mother of the suitors who are trying to force her to choose a husband from among them. Telemachus commands them to depart; when they refuse, he starts out himself in search of his father. He obtains some news of him from the wise chieftain Nestor at Pylos and then goes on to Sparta, where Menelaus tells him that he has heard Odysseus is a captive in Ogygia, and describes to him the fall of Troy. Athena then advises Telemachus to return home secretly, as the suitors are plotting to kill him. These events fill the first four books of the *Odyssey*. The fifth tells of Odysseus' departure from Ogygia; the next seven are devoted to his arrival at the land of the Phaeacians and his tale of his adventures since the fall of Troy. The last twelve books tell of his return to Ithaca, of the situation he finds there, of the action against the suitors, and of his reunion with Penelope, his wife. Many of the places left vague and mythical in Homer's account of his hero's wanderings were early identified by Greek mariners and colonists and later by Italians with spots in or near southern Italy.

Medieval romances devoted comparatively little space to the adventures of Ulysses (Odysseus) after the war was over and made few radical changes in the structure of the ancient story. Medieval illustrations of these scenes, therefore, are fewer than those from other portions of the Trojan legend, although selected incidents lent themselves extremely well to moralized versions. The characters were, of course, represented in contemporary costume and setting.

115. ULYSSES. Roman statuette. Rome, Vatican.

This typical representation of Ulysses, with beard and pointed cap, probably formed part of a group in which the hero offered wine to the giant Polyphemus.

116. ULYSSES. Franco-Flemish tapestry, 1480–1483. Boston, Museum of Fine Arts.

In this late medieval representation the Greek hero, youthful and beardless, stands on his ship, one hand on a hunting leopard. The inscription across his chest reads 'eloquent Ulysses'. This tapestry and its companion opposite are believed to come from a set devoted to famous women such as Penelope, Dido, the Roman heroines Lucretia and Virginia, and Judith of the Apocrypha.

117. PENELOPE. Franco-Flemish tapestry, 1480–1483. Boston, Museum of Fine Arts.

In her palace at Ithaca Penelope, in brocaded dress and elaborate jewels, sits at the loom on which, for three years, she wove a funeral robe for her husband's father, using it as a pretext for delaying her choice among her many suitors and unravelling at night what she had done during the day. The inscription records her determination: 'I, Penelope, shall be the wife of Ulysses forever.'

118. 'PENELOPE GRIEVING FOR ODYSSEUS'. Roman copy of a Greek statue, considerably restored. Rome, Vatican.

119. PENELOPE. Painting, 1917, by Carlo Carrà (Italian). Milan, Collection of Carlo Frua de Angeli.

The mourning woman, or Penelope, illustrated opposite, in the vase painting on Plate 142 and the relief on Plate 147, is a familiar figure in ancient art. Sometimes it represents an undoubted Penelope; at other times it may have been part of a grave monument. Carrà's Penelope states the theme in a terminology wholly modern. He has interpreted the figure in geometric forms which belong partly to his cubistic period and partly to endeavours of the Italian metaphysical group to create enigmatic moods by novel contrasts and juxtapositions. It combines 'the romantic appeal of the remote in time with a new' stylistic expression.

120. ODYSSEUS ON THE ISLAND OF CALYPSO.
Bronze cheek-piece of a helmet, Greek, fourth century B.C.
Berlin, Staatliche Museen.

Hermes, coming as the messenger from Zeus to bid Calypso let Odysseus go, found the nymph singing at her loom in a vine-hung grotto. 'But brave Odysseus he did not find within; for he sat weeping on the shore, where, as of old, with tears and groans and griefs racking his heart, he watched the barren sea and poured forth tears.' He could think only of his home beyond this sea, because 'the nymph pleased him no more'.

121. CALYPSO'S ISLAND. Painting, 1928, by Bryson Burroughs (American). Baltimore, Collection of Mrs. Bryson Burroughs.

Obedient to the command of Zeus, Calypso aided Odysseus in building a raft and brought him cloth for sails. He set out hopefully on his journey home, but was soon wrecked by the wrath of Poseidon, whose gigantic son, the Cyclops Polyphemus, he had blinded on his way to Ogygia. A mighty swimmer, Odysseus cast off his encumbering robes and struggled through the stormy waves to the nearest coast, where he found the mouth of a stream that gave easy access to land. Staggering exhausted out of the water he hid himself under a heap of leaves among the bushes, for fear he might have been cast on some savage shore, and fell into a heavy sleep.

122. ODYSSEUS, ATHENA, NAUSICAÄ, AND A HANDMAID.
Attic red-figured amphora, fifth century B.C. Munich, Museum für antike Kleinkunst.

The shore upon which Odysseus had been cast was that of Scheria, land of the Phaeacians, a mythical kingdom long identified with the island of Corfù off the northwest coast of Greece. There Odysseus' protecting deity, Athena, set afoot a plan to make him welcome. Appearing in a dream to Nausicaä, daughter of its king, Alcinoüs, in the form of one of her friends, she urged her to gather her maids and 'go a-washing at the dawn of day'.

So, early in the morning, Nausicaä had the mule cart harnessed, 'the high one with good wheels'. Her maids filled it with the family's clothing and her mother added all the things necessary for a pleasant picnic.

When the washing had been done in the river and the clothes spread to dry along the shore, the princess and her maids bathed in the clear stream, ate their lunch, and began to play ball. Athena caused Nausicaä to miss her aim so that the ball fell into a deep pool. The maidens screamed and Odysseus awoke. Holding before

123. NAUSICAÄ'S MAIDENS WASH THE CLOTHES.
Reverse of the amphora shown opposite.

him a spray of leaves and standing aloof, he appealed for help. The maidens fled in fright from the unkempt stranger, but Nausicaä stayed to hear his story. Then she called for food and drink and clothing, and told him to follow her and her maidens as they returned home, but at a distance for fear gossip might say: 'What tall and handsome stranger is following Nausicaä? Where did she find him? A husband he will be, her very own. Some castaway, perhaps, she rescued from his vessel, some foreigner.'

Athena does not appear in this scene as the *Odyssey* tells it; when she meets Odysseus a little later she is disguised as a humble maid who gives the final directions for reaching the palace. The vase painter shows her, perhaps to suggest her watchful care, perhaps to present two scenes in one. Neither does he show Nausicaä standing steadfast as Homer says, but turning to flee. Unlike her maidens, however, she looks over her shoulder at the stranger as though about to turn toward him.

124. ODYSSEUS AND NAUSICAÄ. Painting, dated 1609, by Pieter Lastman (Dutch). Brunswick, Ducal Museum.

The Dutch painter's rendering of this scene is just such a combination of marine, landscape, and still-life, with a classical flavour, as appealed strongly to the patrons of seventeenth-century Holland. There is nothing in the least Greek about the picture, though there is a suggestion of generalized antique drapery in the robe of the maiden kneeling at the right. Nausicaä is a sturdy and determined Dutch girl. Attention is centred on a theme dear to the Netherlandish painters of the period —an elaborate still-life of glass and metal tableware and of fruits and pastries spread upon a cloth in the foreground. At the right a music book and a lute case add to the wealth of contemporary detail.

At the palace of Alcinoüs, which Homer furnished with all the splendours of an Aegean civilization gone long before his time, Odysseus was received with hospitality, feasted, and given a bed spread with purple. In the morning Alcinoüs summoned his chief men to hear the stranger's story. Before the feast began the king's bard sang a song of Troy which moved Odysseus to tears: he took up the tale and related what had happened since he had left the ruined city.

After sacking the country of the Siconians he had come to the land of the Lotus-eaters where some of his men ate of this 'honeyed fruit', fell into a dreamy inaction, forgetting all their past and wishing only to stay and 'feed on lotus'. These men Odysseus had brought to the ships by force and bound them fast.

Next they came to the land of the Cyclopes, savage one-eyed giants. Odysseus left most of his ships at a nearby island, and, mooring his own vessel close to the cave of the immense Polyphemus, Poseidon's son, went with twelve of his men to seek provisions. Not content with the cheeses and kids in the giant's cave he waited, in the hope of obtaining more, until Polyphemus returned from shepherding his flocks. But when the Greeks asked for hospitality in the name of the gods, Polyphemus retorted that he paid the gods no heed and promptly killed two of Odysseus' crew for his supper. In the morning he repeated this performance for breakfast, and then left with his flock, blocking the doorway of the cave with a great stone that only he could move. During the day the imprisoned men made their plans, and Odysseus had them sharpen a great stake. When the giant had eaten two more men that evening Odysseus handed him a cup of powerful wine. After its third filling Polyphemus began to ask more about these strangers. Odysseus told him that his name was No-man and was promised, in return for the wine, that he would be eaten last. When the giant had sunk into a drunken sleep the Greeks heated the sharp stake red hot and put out the one eye in the middle of his forehead. His cries

125. THE BLINDING OF POLYPHEMUS. Attic black-figured kylix, sixth century B.C. Paris, Bibliothèque Nationale.

126. THE BLINDING OF POLYPHEMUS. Illustration by Jean Mielot from a manuscript of Christine de Pisan's *Épître d'Othéa*, French or Flemish, 1461. Brussels, Bibliothèque Royale, MS.fr.9392, fol.22v.

brought his fellow Cyclopes to the door, but when he cried that No-man was murdering him they declared that what no man did must be the act of Zeus and left without entering the cave.

The story of Polyphemus was stressed very little in the Troy romances. Dares' *History* stopped with the fall of Troy and the departure of the Greeks and of Aeneas. Dictys gave a very brief account of Polyphemus in which this character was not a giant, did not quarrel with Odysseus, and was not blinded. Benoit de Sainte-More and Guido delle Colonne told the incident briefly, saying that Polyphemus was a mighty warrior whose sister one of Ulysses' companions stole. In the ensuing conflict Ulysses put out, not one single eye but one of two. On the authority of Ovid Lydgate reverted to the one-eyed giant, but Raoul Lefèvre omitted the Polyphemus story entirely.

Christine de Pisan, who seldom took her material from the Troy romances, used the classic version of a giant with one eye, which she doubtless knew from the standard Latin or from a moralized Ovid. The illustrator of her *Epistles* showed the giant in medieval costume and had trouble suggesting the one eye in the middle of the forehead. The moral Christine drew from this incident was that a young knight should avoid sloth lest he lose the eye of his understanding and therefore his honour.

Toward morning Polyphemus rolled the great stone away from the cave's door, setting himself beside it to feel his flock in case some of the strangers tried to escape among them. But the wily Odysseus was ready for this: he had tied each of his remaining men under the belly of a ram, with another ram on each side to act as guard. Himself he could not tie, so he clung by his hands to the long, shaggy wool of the largest in the flock. This hampered the ram so that he left the cave last of all and Polyphemus, noticing this, said:

'"What, my pet ram! Why do you move across the cave hindmost of all the flock? Till now you never lagged behind. . . Ah, but you miss your master's eye, which a villain has put out. . . If only you could sympathize and get the power of speech to say where he is skulking from my rage, then should that brain of his be knocked about the cave and dashed upon the ground."'

127. ODYSSEUS AND HIS COMPANIONS ESCAPING FROM THE CAVE OF POLYPHEMUS. Painting, 1802, by Henry Fuseli (Swiss). Private Collection.

128. ODYSSEUS ESCAPING FROM THE CAVE OF POLYPHEMUS UNDER A RAM.
From an Attic black-figured kylix, sixth century B.C.
London, British Museum, No.407.

Quickly Odysseus gathered his men in his waiting ship and set sail. When he had gone to the farthest limit of hailing distance from the shore he called back in derision, whereupon Polyphemus tore off the top of a high hill and flung it in the direction of the voice. The Greeks begged their leader not to anger the giant

129. POLYPHEMUS HURLING A ROCK AT THE SHIP OF ODYSSEUS.
Detail of a Roman wall painting from Boscotrecase, first century A.D.
New York, Metropolitan Museum of Art, 20.192.17. Rogers Fund, 1920.

further, but he taunted the Cyclops again and again and finally gave his true name. Then Polyphemus prayed to his father Poseidon, lord of the sea:

' "If I am truly thine, and thou art called my father, vouchsafe no coming home to this Odysseus, spoiler of cities, Laertes' son, whose home is Ithaca. Yet if it be his lot to see his friends once more, and reach his stately house and native land, late let him come, in evil plight, with loss of all his crew, on the vessel of a stranger, and may he at home find trouble." '

And Poseidon heard the giant's prayer and heeded it, so that Odysseus, although he reached his home at last, was the only man left alive from all his ships.

The Roman painting from which Plate 129 was taken was based, not on the *Odyssey*, but on the story of Polyphemus' hopeless love for the beautiful nymph Galatea. Its source may have been *The Cyclops*, a poem written by the Greek Philoxenus in the late fifth or early fourth century B.C., in which Dionysius, tyrant of Syracuse, was satirized as the stupid giant. Philoxenus is said to have represented himself as the clever hero Odysseus. Ovid's *Metamorphoses* tells both the story of Odysseus and Polyphemus and that of the giant's love for Galatea, but only a passing allusion connects them. The detail of the painting opposite shows Polyphemus hurling a rock at Odysseus' ship. The dominant figures in the complete composition are those of Galatea and the giant wooing her by playing the syrinx.

The interest in Turner's painting, of course, is not in the myth but in the landscape. The writhing Cyclops high at the left might be but another cloud about to vanish before the sunrise, while the gay ships are more like barques in holiday guise than the vessels of weary wanderers.

130. ULYSSES DERIDING POLYPHEMUS. Painting, 1829, by J. M. W. Turner (English). London, National Gallery.

131. ODYSSEUS AND HIS MEN ATTACKED BY THE LAESTRYGONIANS.
Graeco-Roman wall painting, first century B.C. Rome, Vatican Library.

After escaping from the Cyclops Odysseus came to the land of Aeolus, who controlled the winds. To speed the hero on his way Aeolus gave him a bag in which were imprisoned all the unfavourable winds, while he loosed the wind that would carry the ships to Ithaca. But, within sight of home, Odysseus fell asleep at the helm, and his companions, thinking that the sack contained gold and silver, opened it. The winds rushed out and blew them off their course, and Aeolus refused to help again. Presently they came to the country of the Laestrygonians, cannibal giants, who sank all the ships except that of Odysseus, which was prudently anchored outside the harbour, and killed their crews.

The paintings illustrated here are part of a series showing the adventures of Odysseus. They have a continuous landscape background, painted in a loose, almost impressionistic style, the scenes divided by red pilasters to give the effect of looking out through windows to a wide sea and fantastic, fairy-tale lands conceived in the mood of the *Odyssey*.

In the picture above the Laestrygonians are attacking Odysseus' companions, one giant even dashing into the water after a Greek. In that opposite, they hurl rocks and tree trunks at the Greek ships. Soon there arose 'the dreadful din of dying men and crashing ships'. Quickly Odysseus drew his sword and cut the

132. THE LAESTRYGONIANS DESTROY THE SHIPS OF ODYSSEUS' COMPANIONS. Graeco-Roman wall painting, first century B.C. Rome, Vatican Library.

cable that held his own vessel to the shore. Falling heartily to their oars, his men 'tossed up the water in terror for their lives...but all the other ships went down together there.'

From the shores of the Laestrygonians Odysseus and his remaining ship came to the island of Aeaea, where dwelt Circe, daughter of the Sun. Half the crew went ahead to Circe's house, 'built of smooth stone upon commanding ground.' Later tradition identified this with the heights of Monte Circeo on the Italian shore north of Terracina, a steep-cliffed peninsula which may once have been an island, as ancient writers state. All about the palace were animals that 'stood erect, wagging their long tails, fawning'. These had once been men, robbed of their human shapes by Circe's magic. The enchantress sat within, singing sweetly while she tended 'her great imperishable loom'. Suddenly she opened her door and invited the strangers to enter. All accepted eagerly except their leader Eurylochus. Having made her guests comfortable on couches and chairs she gave them a refreshing draught and, when they had drunk it, touched them with a wand. At once 'they took on the heads of swine, the voice, the bristles, and even the shape, yet was their reason as sound as heretofore'. This report Eurylochus brought to Odysseus, who set out heavy-hearted to try for their rescue. On his way he was

133. CARICATURE OF CIRCE HANDING ODYSSEUS THE DRUGGED CUP.
Boeotian black-figured skyphos, fourth century B.C.
Oxford, Ashmolean Museum.

134. ODYSSEUS AND HIS COMPANIONS AT THE HOUSE OF CIRCE.
From an Attic red-figured krater, about 440 B.C. New York, Metropolitan Museum of Art, 41.83. Gift of Amelia E. White, 1941.

met by Hermes, who gave him the herb moly, a potent counter-charm, and told him that thus armed he might safely drink and then, when Circe touched him with her wand, draw his sword.

135. ODYSSEUS AT THE HOUSE OF CIRCE. Graeco-Roman wall painting, first century B.C. Rome, Vatican Library.

Odysseus kept on to Circe's palace and called before her gate. She led him within and placed him on 'a silver-studded chair, beautiful, richly wrought...and she prepared a potion in a golden cup...but put therein a drug, with wicked purpose in her heart.' Then she struck him with her wand and cried, ' "Off to the sty, and lie there with your fellows!" ' As she spoke Odysseus drew his sword, and the enchantress fell upon her knees, begging for mercy. Then, having supplied him with all comforts, she led him to the sty and there anointed his comrades with a counter-charm. The hair fell from them 'and once more they were men, men younger than before, much fairer too, and taller to behold.' Circe made all welcome, and for a year they stayed in her halls and feasted with no harm, except that one of their number, Elpenor, fell from the palace roof overcome with sleep and wine.

In the wall painting above Odysseus has arrived at Circe's house 'of smooth stone', bent on rescuing his comrades. The enchantress welcomes him, holding open 'the shining doors'. The scene with the kneeling woman, at the right, has been interpreted as Circe begging for mercy after Odysseus has resisted her magic.

According to Christine de Pisan's moralized version of the story:

'Circe was a queen, whose realm was upon the sea of Italy, and she was a great enchantress and knew much of sorcery and witchcraft. And Ulysses, who went to sea after the destruction of Troy, as he thought to have returned to his own country through many great and perilous torments, arrived at a haven of the same land. He sent to the queen his knights to see whether he might safely find haven in her land or no. Circe received his knights full gently, and with courtesy had made for them a potion, full delicious to drink, but the potion had such strength that suddenly all the knights were changed into swine.

'Circe may be understood in many ways. It may be understood to be a land or a country where knights were kept in foul and villainous prison, and also she may be likened to a lady full of wantonness and idleness, who keeps by her many knights bearing arms, such as the people of Ulysses. . . And therefore it is said to the good knight that he shall not sojourn at such a place. Circe's swine may be taken for hypocrisy, which the good man should avoid above all things. Saint Gregory sayeth in his *Moralia* that the life of hypocrites is but a false vision and an imagined fantasy.'

136. ULYSSES AND HIS COMPANIONS AT CIRCE'S PALACE. Illustration by Jean Mielot from Christine de Pisan's *Épître d'Othéa*, French or Flemish, 1461. Brussels, Bibliothèque Royale, MS.fr.9392, fol.5.

137. CIRCE AND HER LOVERS IN A LANDSCAPE. Painting by Dosso Dossi (Italian), early sixteenth century. Washington, National Gallery of Art, Samuel H. Kress Collection.

Dosso Dossi's Circe bears the impress of the romantic epics of the Renaissance. As a painter at the court of Alfonso d'Este at Ferrara, he was familiar with the *Orlando Furioso*, completed there by the duke's favoured poet, Ariosto. The *Orlando* blended elements of chivalric romance with those of classical lore: its enchantress, Alcina, was a composite of the Greek Circe and the sinister Morgan le Fay of Arthurian legend. The painting's title is traditional, but whether it represents Ariosto's rather than Homer's enchantress is of no moment—one is the direct descendant of the other. Unlike her Greek prototype, however, Alcina needed no drugged cup. She

> '. . . made the ready fish obey
> By simple words and by mere magic lore,'

as does this sorceress, reciting her spell from a tablet with cryptic signs, while a book of cabalistic diagrams lies open at her feet. Like Ariosto's Alcina, too, she has transformed her lovers not only into beasts but into birds, fountains, and rocks, 'olive, palm, or cedar, firs or bays.' The deer, the lion, the dogs, the busy spoonbill —all may once have been men. So also may have been the very elements of the landscape, the sheltering trees or the pool at the enchantress' feet.

138. THE WINE OF CIRCE. Watercolour 1863–1869, by Edward Burne-Jones (English). Collection of the Marquess of Normanby.

Three centuries later, for Burne-Jones' *Wine of Circe*, Rossetti wrote a descriptive sonnet characteristic of the close connection made by the English Pre-Raphaelite painters between the arts of poetry and painting:

> 'Dusk-haired and gold-robed o'er the golden wine
> She stoops, wherein, distilled of death and shame,
> Sink the black drops; while, lit with fragrant flame,
> Round her spread board the golden sunflowers shine.'

When Odysseus and his companions left Circe's isle after a happy year, the enchantress told him that his future way would not be easy; to discover his best course he must first consult the prophet Teiresias in Hades, abode of the dead. When he had reached its portal and moored his ship, he must dig a pit and sacrifice a ram and a black ewe, letting their blood fill the trench. The spirits of the dead would then flock about him to drink, for only blood could give them a passing sense of life. But no matter how they pleaded he must not let them drink until Teiresias had told him his true course.

Following Circe's direction, Odysseus reached Hades, beyond the earth's limits, where 'deadly night is spread abroad'. The first spirit he saw there was that of young Elpenor, who was still unburied and therefore unable to rest among the dead. On the vase opposite Elpenor rises from the reeds, while Odysseus sits, sword in hand, to keep the spirits from drinking the sacrificial blood. Hermes, not mentioned in the *Odyssey's* description, stands on the shore.

The shades of the dead thronged about Odysseus to drink the blood but he kept them away resolutely until Teiresias appeared, even though he recognized among them the spirit of his mother. Teiresias, having drunk, told Odysseus that he would encounter many perils and finally win through to Ithaca alone; that when he reached home he would be obliged to slay his faithful wife's unwelcome suitors; and finally would go a-journeying once more to meet 'death from the sea' in a hale old age.

When Teiresias had gone the other shades came and drank, first among them those of many noble women of bygone days. After them came the shade of Achilles, who asked for news of his son and of his father, Peleus. But the spirit of Ajax held aloof, angry still that Odysseus had received the armour of Achilles.

Medieval romances, bent on removing pagan elements, omitted this visit to a spirit world. Benoit substituted a brief mention of an oracle which gave Odysseus information about the spirits; Guido, more sceptical, said that the oracle's answers were reliable 'except as to what becomes of the souls of the dead.'

139. ODYSSEUS IN HADES.
From an Attic red-figured pelike, second half of the fifth century B.C.
Boston, Museum of Fine Arts, 34.79.

140. ODYSSEUS IN HADES. Graeco-Roman wall painting, first century B.C. Rome, Vatican Library.

In the painting above the ship of Odysseus is moored at the left; the entrance to Hades is in the centre, through an arched rocky cavern. The two large reclining figures near the centre are probably the deities of the rivers Acheron and Cocytus. In the dimly lighted land of Hades Odysseus talks with Teiresias, while about them stand the waiting shades.

Returning from Hades, Odysseus stopped once more at Circe's isle, buried the body of Elpenor, and then took leave of the enchantress, who warned him of perils yet to come. First he must pass the island of the Sirens, part woman and part bird, whose songs were so compelling that all who heard them cast themselves into the sea in the hope of reaching that isle and perished in the waters. Odysseus, following Circe's instructions, filled his men's ears with wax and had himself bound to the mast, bidding his companions keep him there no matter how he might beg to be released. When he heard the Sirens' song he struggled mightily, but the bonds held, the men could not hear, and all passed safely. Tradition associates the Sirens' dwelling with the steep, rocky Galli islands near Positano on the Amalfi coast.

Next they passed through a narrow channel between the cave of Scylla, a

141. ODYSSEUS AND THE SIRENS.
From an Attic red-figured stamnos by the Siren Painter, 475–450 B.C.
London, British Museum, No.3440.

monster with six snaky heads, and Charybdis, a frightful whirlpool. The vessels escaped the whirlpool, but Scylla snatched six of the screw. This perilous spot was later identified with the Straits of Messina.

Teiresias and Circe had warned Odysseus to respect the cattle of the sun god, pastured on an island near Scylla's cave. He would have passed it by but his men pleaded for rest. Held there by adverse winds the men grew hungry, and one day, in Odysseus' absence, they killed some of the cattle. The ship put to sea once more —for the last time. A frightful storm broke it to pieces and all perished except Odysseus, who improvised a raft and made his way to Calypso's island of Ogygia, which he had left after his long sojourn only to be cast on the Phaeacian shore. Here ends the story of his adventures as he told them to King Alcinoüs.

The tale roused the Phaeacians' sympathies; they gave Odysseus rich gifts and sent him the next day by one of their own ships to Ithaca. There is no parting scene in the *Odyssey* between the hero and Nausicaä at the time of his sailing from the land to which she had been the first to welcome him. She appears for the last time as Odysseus goes to the banquet at which he related his adventures, and says simply:

' "Stranger, farewell! When you are once again in your own land, remember me, and how before all others it is to me that you owe the saving of your life." '

When the Phaeacian ship reached Ithaca Odysseus was asleep. The sailors carried him ashore, left his gifts with him and sailed away. But Poseidon, remembering the blinding of his son Polyphemus, was so angry at their rescue of the Greek that, when the ship had almost reached home, he turned it into a great rock opposite the harbour mouth.

Absent from Ithaca for twenty years, Odysseus, when he awoke, did not at first recognize his own land. Athena, however, appeared to him in disguise, told him where he was, and warned him that more than a hundred suitors had quartered themselves in his home, where they were wasting his property and insisting that his wife choose one of them as a husband. To ensure his safety and make it easier for him to avenge himself on them the goddess then transformed him into a beggar, with bleared eyes and shrivelled flesh; as such he sought shelter with his faithful swineherd, Eumaeus, who received him kindly though without recognition.

Meanwhile Telemachus had also returned to Ithaca and soon arrived at the home of Eumaeus to learn how matters stood at the palace. The swineherd sent to tell Penelope of her son's arrival and to warn her that his life was in danger. Athena then bade Odysseus reveal himself to Telemachus and, for a little while, restored him to his proper aspect. Father and son took counsel together and decided that

142. TELEMACHUS AND PENELOPE.
Drawing after an Attic red-figured skyphos, second half of the fifth century B.C.
Chiusi, Museum.

143. TELEMACHUS AND PENELOPE.
Painting, about 1509, by Pintoricchio (Italian), fresco transferred to canvas.
London, National Gallery.

Telemachus should go to the palace and mingle with the suitors, while Odysseus should follow as a beggar.

No scene in the *Odyssey* describes exactly such a private conversation between Telemachus and Penelope as that shown on the Greek vase painting opposite, but it is a natural incident for any artist to illustrate. The patterned cloth, set up on a tapestry loom, suggests Penelope's device for putting off the suitors, though they had long since discovered her trick of pulling out her work at night and had forced her to complete it. Now she was faced with a decision and was obliged to find some other plan.

Pintoricchio shows, not a simple conversation between mother and son, but a sixteenth-century scene in which a brisk young man, accompanied by several others, rushes into the room where Penelope sits at her loom. In the doorway stands Odysseus in his beggar's garb. Through the open window are retrospective glimpses of the adventures he will presently relate (Plate 144). In the foreground rides his ship, long since destroyed, with Odysseus tied to the mast and in the sea about it Sirens, who, in Mediterranean lands, became mermaids with two tails. Beyond is the island of Circe, where she changed his men into swine.

144. PENELOPE AT HER LOOM. Detail from Plate 143.

Arriving at the palace with a seer whom he had befriended on his voyage and brought with him to Ithaca, Telemachus told Penelope the story he had learned from Menelaus—that Odysseus was still alive, but marooned upon an island. The seer, however, declared that the hero was much nearer home and would not be long delayed, but this Penelope could not believe.

Then the swineherd came, bringing with him Odysseus in his beggar's guise. In the palace courtyard they found Odysseus' dog, who had not been full grown when his master left for Troy.

'Here,' says the *Odyssey*, 'lay the dog, this Argos, full of fleas. Yet even now, seeing Odysseus near, he wagged his tail and dropped both ears, but toward his master he had not strength to move. Odysseus turned aside and wiped away a tear, swiftly concealing from Eumaeus what he did.' Odysseus followed Eumaeus into the hall. 'But upon Argos fell the doom of darksome death when he beheld Odysseus, twenty years away.'

145. ODYSSEUS RECOGNIZED BY HIS DOG ARGOS. Roman sarcophagus relief, second century A.D. Naples, Museum of San Martino.

Within the banqueting hall Odysseus made the round of the suitors, begging from each to learn what kind of men they were. All were as stingy as they were greedy, and one threw a footstool at the beggar's head. This roused the others to remonstrance and grieved Penelope greatly when it came to her ears. She sent for the beggar, to ask whether he might have heard anything of Odysseus in his wanderings. He, however, saying that he feared the suitors, asked her to wait until evening to speak with him.

146. EURYKLEIA WASHING THE FEET OF ODYSSEUS IN THE PRESENCE OF PENELOPE AND TELEMACHUS. Greek terracotta relief, first half of the fifth century B.C. New York, Metropolitan Museum of Art, 25.78.26. Fletcher Fund, 1925.

When the suitors had departed for the night Odysseus and Telemachus removed all weapons from the hall; then, his son having gone to bed, Odysseus awaited the coming of Penelope.

When Penelope came to the hall the beggar gave her a fictitious account of having seen Odysseus in Crete and assured her that he would be home before the year's end. Penelope still doubted but was moved to tears, and asked the old nurse, Eurykleia, to bathe the stranger's feet. It occurred to Odysseus then that Eurykleia had done this often in past years and might well remember a scar left by a wild boar's tusk. And so, indeed, she did, and said softly: 'You really are Odysseus, my dear child, and I never knew you till I had handled my master o'er and o'er.' But Odysseus stopped her quickly, for he was not yet ready to be recognized.

147. THE RETURN OF ODYSSEUS. Greek terraccotta relief, about 460 B.C.
New York, Metropolitan Museum of Art, 30.11.9. Fletcher Fund, 1930.

Penelope, meanwhile, told of a dream she had the night before in which an eagle killed her geese and warned her that he was in reality her husband come 'to bring a ghastly doom on all the suitors.' The beggar felt that the dream's meaning was clear, but Penelope still doubted, because 'two gates there are for unsubstantial dreams, one made of horn and one of ivory,' and only those that passed through the gate of horn were true.

Then she spoke of her plan for choosing among the suitors on the morrow. She would have twelve axes set in a row in the great hall, and the man who could shoot an arrow through the rings in the heads of all twelve should be her husband.

As is common in Greek art, the relief opposite does not represent the scene literally, for Telemachus is here, though the *Odyssey* says that he had gone to rest.

The second relief is even more generalized: it shows a group in which all who have been faithful to Odysseus are gathered about the sorrowing Penelope. Odysseus in beggar's guise stands before her; immediately behind her is Telemachus; the old man at the extreme left is Laertes, Odysseus' father; the swineherd Eumaeus is seated on the ground.

The night brought Penelope and Odysseus only a troubled sleep. When morning came the suitors returned and again began to feast, still in quarrelsome mood, demanding that Penelope choose a husband among them at once.

148. ODYSSEUS SLAYING THE SUITORS. Attic red-figured skyphos, about 450 B.C. Berlin, Antiquarium.

Now Athena had put into Penelope's mind the idea of requiring the suitors to use the great bow of Odysseus for their trial of skill in shooting. She brought it into the hall and addressed them:

' "Well then, my suitors,—since before you stands your prize,—I offer you the mighty bow of prince Odysseus; and whoever with his hands shall lightliest bend the bow and shoot through all twelve axes, him I will follow and forsake this home." '

Telemachus set up the axes and tried the bow. Three times he failed to bend it; at the fourth he might have succeeded, but Odysseus shook his head. Then all the suitors took their turns, but could not bend the bow that Odysseus had handled so easily long ago. Meanwhile Odysseus, in the courtyard, had revealed himself to Eumaeus and a faithful herdsman; then, returning to the hall, he asked permission to try the bow. The suitors refused haughtily. Penelope intervened, but Telemachus sent her to her chamber, where Athena wrapped her in deep sleep. Telemachus

149. THE SUITORS SLAIN BY ODYSSEUS.
Reverse of the skyphos shown opposite.

then told Odysseus to try the bow, and moved to his father's side, armed with sword and spear. Odysseus sent the arrow through all twelve axes; next he threw off his rags and addressed the suitors:

' "So the dread ordeal ends! Now to another mark I turn. . . . " '

He aimed an arrow at the throat of the suitor who had thrown the footstool and pierced him through and through.

Then, turning on the angry and bewildered suitors, Odysseus declared himself as Penelope's husband and lord of Ithaca. The frightened men, who had only their swords, tried alternately to flee or to rush him, but the merciless arrows mowed them down, and Telemachus brought more arms to use when the arrows were gone. The suitors too found arms but Athena deflected their spears, and soon none were left alive except two members of the household staff who had obeyed their commands unwillingly.

150. ODYSSEUS AND PENELOPE. Roman wall painting, first century A.D. Pompeii, Macellum (Covered Market).

Eurykleia waked Penelope with the news of Odysseus' return and the suitors' deaths. Dazed, Penelope came into the hall where she saw Odysseus sitting 'by a tall pillar, looking down, waiting to hear if his stately wife would speak when she should look his way.' Odysseus saw that she needed time to grasp what had happened, and bade the household go on as usual. Then he once more took his seat in the hall and Penelope made her decisive test of his identity. She bade Eurykleia have moved out for him the great bed from the bridal chamber. None but she herself, her maid, and Odysseus knew that a growing tree had been built into this bed, so that it was impossible to move. Angrily Odysseus demanded who had dared to cut down that tree—and Penelope cast herself into his arms. Long hours they talked and when Odysseus said he had been promised death from the

151. ODYSSEUS SLAYING THE SUITORS. Pen and watercolour drawing for the *Odyssey*, dated 1802, by Henry Fuseli (Swiss). Zürich, Art Museum.

152. PENELOPE AND ODYSSEUS EMBRACE. Drawing by Primaticcio (Italian), mid-sixteenth century, for the Odysseus series at Fontainebleau, now destroyed. Stockholm, National Museum.

sea in a hale old age, Penelope, out of long experience with sorrow, answered him:

'"If gods can make old age the better time, then there is hope there will be rest from trouble."'

The last book of the *Odyssey* is devoted to clearing up the situation regarding the suitors' kin. First, however, Hermes conducts the spirits of the slain to the Underworld, where they meet the heroes who had died at Troy and tell them of Odysseus' homecoming. Odysseus goes to the home of his father, Laertes, and there the avenging kin of the dead men attack the household. But Athena appears in the guise of Mentor, the wise old man to whom Odysseus had entrusted the education of Telemachus, and makes peace between the foes 'for all coming time'.

153–154. PENELOPE'S NIGHTS; ULYSSES AND PENELOPE. Lithographs by Honoré Daumier (French), in *Charivari*, April 24 and June 26, 1842. From the series *Histoire Ancienne*. New York, Metropolitan Museum of Art. Bequest of Howard Carter, 1949.

Odysseus, a popular figure in Greek burlesque as early as the fourth century B.C., appears in several of Daumier's satiric series on *Ancient History*, directed against the pseudo-classicism of his time. In the first illustration Penelope has fallen asleep over an embroidery frame instead of a tapestry loom, while

> 'Her absent husband's well-loved face
> Forever burned, star-like, before her eyes
> But to weave her plot and her tapestry for three years
> She needed the subtlest of threads.'

The second picture parallels humorously the *Odyssey's* last reference to its hero on the reunion night, when, his long story over, 'pleasant sleep fell on him, easing his limbs.' As for Penelope, 'No sleep fell on her eyelids till he had told her all.'

> 'Chastely reclining on their modest bed
> The noble couple were at last together,
> And when Ulysses snored, from his beguiling mouth
> Penelope snatched a kiss in loving theft.'

The *Odyssey* ends on a note of reconciliation, but Odysseus' fate was not yet fulfilled. The last of the lost epics, the *Telegonia*, named from Telegonus, the hero's son by Circe, tells of Odysseus' later life and of his death that finally came from the sea.

The *Telegonia*, according to Proclus' summary, is 'in two books by Eugammon of Cyrene, which contain the following matters. The suitors of Penelope are buried by their kinsmen, and Odysseus, after sacrificing to the Nymphs, sails to Elis to inspect his herds. He is entertained there by Polyxenus and receives a mixing bowl as a gift; the story of Trophonius and Agamedes and Augeas then follows. He next sails back to Ithaca and performs the sacrifices ordered by Teiresias, and then goes to Thesprotis, where he marries Callidice, Queen of the Thesprotians. A war then breaks out between the Thesprotians, led by Odysseus, and the Brygi. Ares routs the army of Odysseus and Athena engages with Ares, until Apollo separates them. After the death of Callidice Polypoetes, the son of Odysseus [and Callidice] succeeds to the kingdom, while Odysseus himself returns to Ithaca. In the meantime Telegonus, while travelling in search of his father, lands at Ithaca and ravages the island: Odysseus comes out to defend his country but is killed by his son unwittingly. Telegonus, on learning his mistake, transports his father's body with Penelope and Telemachus to his mother's island, where Circe makes them immortal, and Telegonus marries Penelope, and Telemachus Circe.'

Dictys told of Odysseus' death at the hand of Telegonus, but without the oddly mixed marriages, and passed it on to medieval romance with the tale of a wedding more adapted to the taste of the new time—that of Telemachus and Nausicaä.

At the close of the seventeenth century Fénelon's *Telemachus* introduced an entirely new sequence of adventures, based on Telemachus' search for his father as told in the *Odyssey*, but expanded into a romance of wanderings even wider than those of Odysseus himself.

155. TELEMACHUS AND MENTOR FEASTED BY CALYPSO AND HER NYMPHS. Brussels tapestry, eighteenth century, based on Fénelon's *Telemachus*. Austrian National Collections.

Telemachus, the first books of which appeared in 1699, was one of the most significant variations on a Homeric theme since the emergence of medieval romances. It was essentially an eighteenth-century conception, basically didactic and critical in harmony with current tastes. It owed much of its wide popularity to the general belief that it was a satire on the French court.

The tapestry illustrated overleaf in Plate 155 shows a scene which takes place early in the first book. Telemachus, conducted by Minerva in the guise of Mentor, has been shipwrecked on Calypso's isle not long after his father's departure, and finds the nymph still unconsoled. She brings him 'a tunic of the finest wool, whiter than snow, and a purple robe embroidered with gold.' His pleasure in these is, of course, rebuked by Mentor. Then in Calypso's grotto her nymphs set before them a feast of game, 'served up with elegance. Wine, more richly flavoured than nectar, was poured from large silver vases, and sparkled in cups of gold that were wreathed with flowers; and baskets were heaped with all the variety of fruit that is promised by spring and bestowed by autumn.'

Eventually Telemachus becomes enamoured of one of the nymphs, Eucharis, and so rouses Calypso's jealousy that he and Mentor are obliged to throw themselves into the sea and swim to a nearby vessel. They begin their wanderings again, to an accompaniment of precepts and advice suggested by the governments of every land they see. Finally Minerva reveals herself in her true form and Telemachus arrives in Ithaca to find his father 'under the friendly roof of his faithful Eumaeus.'

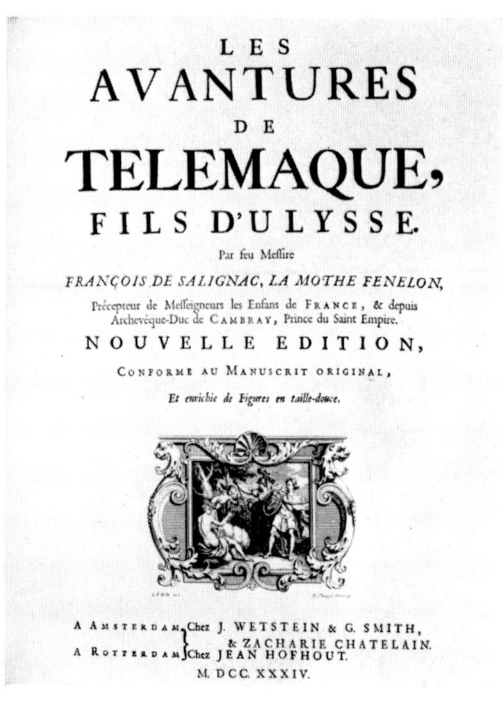

LES
AVANTURES
DE
TELEMAQUE,
FILS D'ULYSSE.
Par feu Messire
FRANÇOIS DE SALIGNAC, LA MOTHE FENELON,
Précepteur de Messeigneurs les Enfans de FRANCE, & depuis Archevêque-Duc de CAMBRAY, Prince du Saint Empire.
NOUVELLE EDITION,
CONFORME AU MANUSCRIT ORIGINAL,
Et enrichie de Figures en taille-douce.

A AMSTERDAM, Chez J. WETSTEIN & G. SMITH, & ZACHARIE CHATELAIN.
A ROTTERDAM, Chez JEAN HOFHOUT.
M. DCC. XXXIV.

156. TITLE PAGE OF AN EDITION OF FÉNELON'S TELEMACHUS, Amsterdam, 1734. New York, Metropolitan Museum of Art. Dick Fund, 1946.

THE AENEID

'Arms and the man I sing, who forced by Fate,
And haughty Juno's unrelenting hate,
Expelled and exiled left the Trojan shore.
Long labours, both by sea and land, he bore,
And in the doubtful war, before he won
The Latin realm, and built the destined town:
His banished gods restored to rites divine,
And settled sure succession in his line,
From whence the race of Alban fathers come,
And the long glories of majestic Rome.'

So, in the *Aeneid's* opening lines, Vergil states the purpose of his epic.

The *Iliad* had predicted a bright future for Aeneas—he should be

'... ... ... lord over the Trojans
and his sons' sons, and those who are born of their seed hereafter.'

Later writers differed as to whether his descendants ruled over a new Troy in Asia Minor or sought a new land. There was still the tradition that Aeneas had betrayed his city, but this was passed over lightly because of his part in founding Rome. Before Vergil's day the emphasis had shifted from Troy to Italy: Aeneas had settled Lavinium, Rome's forerunner, tradition said, and had established there the worship of his ancestral gods. His son Ascanius founded Alba Longa; Alba Longa colonized Rome; and from Rome sprang not only Italy but the great Empire to which medieval men looked back as to a Golden Age.

The very seriousness of Vergil's purpose weighs somewhat against the attractiveness of his hero by the standards of today. A man burdened with such responsibilities as Aeneas could not rival the picturesque individuality of Hector or Achilles. Aeneas had to preserve both his own life and the lives of his companions to achieve his destiny: not for him was the immortality of a glorious death, but rather the establishment of an enduring state. The quality essential for this was the Roman *pietas*, the acceptance and fulfilment of duty toward gods and men. If, in the course of this duty, individuals suffered, their sacrifice was necessary. Aeneas himself was permitted to see little of his accomplishment: his reward was that he made possible the prophesied destiny:

'... Rome, 'tis thine alone, with awful sway,
To rule mankind, and make the world obey,
Disposing peace and war thy own majestic way;
To tame the proud, the fettered slave to free:
These are imperial arts, and worthy thee.'

Vergil saw the consolidation of Roman power in Julius Caesar's hands and the early years of Augustus' reign, which marked the beginning of the long Roman peace. He died before the Senate had decreed the great Altar in the emperor's honour (Plate 157), but not before he had seen in Augustus a second Aeneas, to whose genius the *Aeneid* pays tribute.

157. AENEAS SACRIFICING TO THE TROJAN GODS IN ITALY.
Roman relief, 13–9 B.C. from the Altar of Peace, Rome.

The Italian achievements of the Trojan hero, though celebrated in the Aeneas romances of the twelfth century, played little part in the main stream of the Troy romances proper. Perhaps the very familiarity of Vergil throughout the Middle Ages contributed to this omission. The romances themselves counselled those who wished more knowledge of Aeneas after the fall of Troy to 'read Vergil in the *Aeneid*.'

The *Aeneid* opens with a storm. In their seventh year of wandering Aeneas and his Trojans have drawn near the north coast of Africa. Seeing them so close to Italy Juno remembered the slight put upon her by Paris, and that Aeneas was the son of her successful rival, Venus. She remembered, too, a prophecy that 'time to come should see the Trojan race' overthrow Carthage, a city she held dear. Quickly she made her way to Aeolus, god of the winds, who let loose a tempest at her request. As the waves threatened to engulf the ships

> 'Struck with unusual fright, the Trojan chief,
> With lifted hands and eyes, invokes relief.'

158. THE SHIPS OF AENEAS TOSSED BY STORM.
From a manuscript of the *Aeneid*, fifth century A.D.
Rome, Vatican Library, cod.lat.vat.3867, fol.77. The Codex Romanus.

159. NEPTUNE STILLS THE TEMPEST: THE SHIP OF AENEAS ARRIVES AT THE SHORE OF CARTHAGE: AENEAS AND ACHATES TALK WITH VENUS. Right half of a cassone panel, about 1460, by Apollonio di Giovanni (Italian). New Haven, Yale University Art Gallery, Jarves Collection.

Neptune, noting the unauthorized storm, reproved Aeolus for interfering with his rule of the ocean and calmed the waters:

'The god himself with ready trident stands,
And opes the deep, and spreads the moving sands;
Then heaves them off the shoals—where'er he guides
His finny coursers, and in triumph rides,
The waves unruffle, and the sea subsides.'

The Trojans, driven upon the African coast, set out to explore it: Aeneas and his faithful companion Achates climbed a hill to reconnoitre. There they were met by Venus in the guise of a huntress, who told them that they should proceed to nearby Carthage, where the widowed Dido, Queen of Tyre, fleeing from her husband's murderer, was building a new city. She assured them that their men and ships were safe, then disappeared.

In the cassone detail above Neptune, in fantastic costume, trident in hand, rides 'high on his chariot' to still the sea. Behind him the ships of Aeneas have reached the shore, while at the extreme right Venus talks with Aeneas and Achates.

160. DETAIL FROM PLATE 159.

161. THE MEETING OF DIDO AND AENEAS. Illustration from a manuscript of the *Aeneid*, about 1460, by Apollonio di Giovanni (Italian). Florence, Biblioteca Riccardiana, N.492, fol.72v.

Aeneas and Achates made their way into the city, where they found Dido's workmen building to Juno a golden shrine on whose walls were painted

> 'Whatever did unhappy Troy befall—
> The wars that fame around the world had blown.'

Among these painted scenes Aeneas saw Achilles in his chariot, Hector's body dragged about Troy's wall, Penthesilea in battle, even himself fighting 'amidst the Grecian train'.

As he marvelled at these paintings Dido entered with majestic walk. A throng gathered about her, among whom Aeneas saw leaders from some of the ships that he had believed lost. They asked the queen for hospitality, and Aeneas, approaching, added his request to theirs. Dido welcomed them graciously, declaring that her own woes had taught her to pity those of others. Sending food to the Trojan crews, she invited Aeneas and his companions to a banquet at her palace.

In the manuscript illustration Dido stands within Juno's temple talking with the Trojan leaders, while Aeneas and Achates approach from the right. The chariot of Achilles appears painted upon the temple wall, and the Trojan horse on wheels as it was drawn into the city. Outside, at the right, the workmen are busy building the temple wall.

Aeneas sent Achates to the ships to bring his young son Ascanius to the feast. Venus, fearing that Dido might prove treacherous towards Aeneas and his

162. DIDO AND AENEAS FEASTING. Illustration from a manuscript of the *Aeneid*, about 1460, by Apollonio di Giovanni (Italian). Florence, Biblioteca Riccardiana, N.492, fol.75.

men, bade her son Cupid, god of love, assume the Trojan boy's form and stir passion in the queen's breast. She then wrapped the real Ascanius in a deep sleep and no one at the banquet dreamed that it was the god of love himself whom the queen caressed.

When the banquet was over the minstrel sang to the guests, and Dido then asked Aeneas to tell of Troy's fall and his own wanderings:

> ' "The Grecian strategems, the town betrayed:
> The fatal issue of so long a war,
> Your flight, your wanderings, and your woes, declare;
> For, since on every sea, on every coast,
> Your men have been distressed, your navy tossed,
> Seven times the sun has either tropic viewed,
> The winter banished, and the spring renewed." '

From this point on through the next two books the *Aeneid* follows the pattern of the *Odyssey*, telling Aeneas' earlier adventures as a story within a story and presenting the best-known of all descriptions of the fall of Troy.

At Dido's feast Aeneas begins his story with the scenes he saw as he made his way toward his home, after vainly trying to save Cassandra and Priam. The enamel opposite presents these scenes almost literally. Helen sits in Vesta's shrine, the busy gods are clearly labelled. Venus counsels Aeneas, Neptune brandishes a

163. THE FALL OF TROY AS RELATED BY AENEAS. Limoges enamel, 1525–1530, based on a woodcut in the Grüninger Vergil, Strassburg, 1502. New York, Metropolitan Museum of Art, Gift of Henry Walters, 1925.

trident resembling a three-tongued torch. Juno encourages the Greeks sailing in from Tenedos, and Pallas hovers above a falling tower. Jove is represented as the Christian's Hand of God emerging from the clouds to scatter lightning upon the doomed city. At the left is a scene not described in the *Aeneid.* A bearded man throws up his arms from a flaming tower, while behind him a child is hurled to death. In Vergil's epic Priam already lay dead. Soon, continued Aeneas,

> 'The graceless Helen in the porch I spied
> of Vesta's temple; there she lurked alone;
> Muffled she sate, and what she could, unknown,

But, by the flames that cast their blaze around,
That common bane of Greece and Troy I found.
For Ilium burnt, she dreads the Trojan sword;
More dreads the vengeance of her injured lord.'

Enraged that she should live among the general slaughter he determined to kill her, but Venus, appearing suddenly, bade him care for his own family:

' "Look if your helpless father yet survive,
Or if Ascanius or Creüsa live.
Around your house the greedy Grecians err;
And these had perished in the nightly war,
But for my presence and protecting care.
Not Helen's face, nor Paris, was in fault;
But by the gods was this destruction brought.
Now cast your eyes around, while I dissolve
The mists and films that mortal eyes involve,
Purge from your sight the dross, and make you see
The shape of each avenging deity.
Enlightened thus, my just commands fulfil,
Nor fear obedience to your mother's will.
Where yon disordered heap of ruin lies,
Stones rent from stones,—where clouds of dust arise,—
Amid that smother, Neptune holds his place,
Below the wall's foundation drives his mace,
And heaves the building from the solid base.
Look, where, in arms, imperial Juno stands
Full in the Scaean gate, with loud commands,
Urging on shore the tardy Grecian bands.
See! Pallas, of her snaky buckler proud,
Bestrides the tower, refulgent through the cloud:
See! Jove new courage to the foe supplies,
And arms against the town the partial deities.' "

Greek accounts of Aeneas' flight from Troy vary. *The Sack of Ilium* and *The Roman Antiquities* of Dionysius of Halicarnassus say that he saved his entire family by taking them to Mount Ida before the city fell. Dionysius also says that he remained there with his followers for some time, while his son, Ascanius, went back to Troy to aid a returning band of refugees among the ruins—perhaps an echo of the humble settlement which excavations have revealed above the Homeric city. Eventually Aeneas, Ascanius, and the others set forth on their wanderings. Xenophon and Apollodorus mention only the saving of Aeneas' father, Anchises, stressing the fact that it was this filial act and the rescue of the Trojan household gods that gave him his reputation for piety. The hero's wife, Creüsa, is described by Pausanias as among the captive Trojan women in Polygnotos' painting at Delphi.

Comparatively few ancient representations of the flight show Creüsa, Aeneas, Anchises, and Ascanius together. On the vase shown opposite the woman preceding Aeneas and Anchises suggests Aphrodite leading them to safety rather than a wife accompanying her husband.

164. AENEAS CARRYING ANCHISES FROM TROY. Attic black-figured neck-amphora, about 500 B.C. New York, Metropolitan Museum of Art, 56.171.26. Fletcher Fund, 1956.

165. CARICATURE OF AENEAS RESCUING ANCHISES AND ASCANIUS FROM TROY. Roman wall painting from Herculaneum, first century A.D. Naples, National Museum, 9089.

In the *Aeneid* the flight began with Aeneas carrying Anchises and leading Ascanius, while Creüsa followed. But in the darkness, as he told Dido:

> ' " Alas! I lost Creüsa: hard to tell
> If by her fatal destiny she fell,
> Or weary sate, or wandered with affright;
> But she was lost for ever from my sight. " '

The Romans themselves must occasionally have grown tired of the term 'pious Aeneas': the caricature, which may represent characters from a mime, was evidently directed at an overblown legend of filial piety. The hero, his father, and his son are a cross between monkeys and dogs. The box carried by Anchises probably contains the household gods whose rescue contributed to the legend.

166. RAPHAEL'S ALLUSION TO AENEAS AND ANCHISES. Detail from the fresco of the Fire in the Borgo, designed by Raphael and executed by assistants, in the *Stanze dell'Incendio* in the Vatican, 1514–1517.

Vasari describes these figures in his *Life of Raphael Sanzio* written in 1550: 'On the other side, after the manner of Vergil's story of Anchises being carried by Aeneas, is shown an old sick man overcome by his infirmity and the flames of the fire; and in the figure of the young man are seen courage and strength and great effort.'

167. THE BURNING OF TROY. Painting, about 1600–1603, by Adam Elsheimer (German). Munich, Alte Pinakothek.

Here the flames of burning Troy light up the crumbling walls and the death-dealing horse; in their eerie light the struggling Trojans seem like sufferers in some grotesque Underworld. In the left foreground Aeneas, in classical costume, carries Anchises on his back. Behind him follows a Trojan in sixteenth-century garb: contrary to Vergil's description the boy Ascanius does not hold his father's hand but walks in front holding a torch. The woman with outstretched arm leading the way is sometimes identified as Creüsa; perhaps, like the figure on the Greek vase, she may be Venus in human guise.

Elsheimer painted this typical night scene, with its profusion of small figures picked out in strong contrasts of light and shade, after he had settled in Rome and had come under the strong classical influence of renaissance Italy. The overall effect, however, is similar to the work of such Flemish artists as Bosch, painter of devil-populated fantasies, or of Jan Brueghel's vision of the Underworld.

The romances of Troy say little about the escape of Aeneas and his family from Troy, beyond the fact that he rescued his father, generally referring their readers to Vergil for further information.

Soon after leaving Troy Aeneas and his company arrived at Delos, where they consulted Apollo's oracle as to their destination. As usual it replied ambiguously: 'Seek out your ancient mother; here shall the house of Aeneas sway all regions.' Anchises then remembered that the Trojans were said to have come from Crete. To Crete they sailed and established a settlement, but sickness broke out and crops

168. AENEAS AND HIS COMPANIONS SIGHT ITALY; ANCHISES OFFERS THANKS. Limoges enamel, 1525–1530, based on a woodcut in the Grüninger Vergil of 1502. New York, Metropolitan Museum of Art. Gift of J. Pierpont Morgan, 1925.

failed. Then the gods of Troy appeared to Aeneas in a dream and told him he must seek a land which some called Hesperia, or the West, but others Italy. This had been the Trojan's true homeland.

They set sail, stopping on their way at the island of the Harpies, creatures with the bodies of birds and the heads of women. These stole the Trojans' food and, when driven off, predicted

> ' "Fierce famine is your lot—for this misdeed,
> Reduced to grind the plates on which you feed." '

After leaving the Harpies' island the Trojans found in Epirus, on the northwestern shore of Greece, a settlement ruled by Priam's son Helenus, now married to Hector's widow, Andromache. Here they were welcomed warmly and loaded with gifts. Leaving Epirus they crossed the Ionian Sea toward the heel of Apulia and arrived in sight of another shore, which they greeted with the joyous shout of 'Italy!' A haven opened before them, and they saw a temple on the Heights of Minerva—perhaps the village of Castro which stands above a small rocky bay with ancient fortifications traditionally known as *Castrum Minervae*. They offered prayers to the goddess as the first deity to welcome them, and then Anchises, standing on the vessel's stern, made an offering to the gods of sea and land and wind for safe and quick arrival at their new home.

But they were not to reach their goal so easily. To avoid Scylla and Charybdis they sailed southward, as Helenus had advised, along the coast of Sicily instead of through the Straits of Messina, and then skirted the island's southern and western shores. In the course of their voyage they came to the land of the Cyclopes, where they rescued a Greek who had been left behind when Odysseus' company had escaped so narrowly, and had a glimpse of the gigantic, blinded Polyphemus. Then, as they halted at Drepanum on Sicily's northwestern tip, Anchises died, 'spent with old age', and Aeneas prepared for the final stage of his journey, up Italy's west coast toward the site of Rome. It was at this moment that Juno called forth the storm that cast the Trojans on the shore of Africa. Here, with a reference to Dido's hospitality, Aeneas ends the story of his adventures.

The enamel shown in Plate 168 crowds together places actually far apart. Scylla and Charybdis are marked in the foreground; beyond, is the coast of Italy. But Minerva's temple, eastward across the Gulf of Tarento, here seems close beside the Sicilian shore.

While Aeneas told his tale the passion awakened by Cupid had grown in Dido's breast. She had vowed to remain forever faithful to her husband's memory, and she still held this a binding vow. To her sister Anna, however, she confided that not since her husband's death had she felt this touch of 'the former flame'. Anna counselled her to consider how great a kingdom might arise if Carthage were upheld by Trojan arms, and advised her to delay the sailing of Aeneas.

Seeing the queen so fast in the toils of love, Juno, planning to prevent Aeneas, at any cost, from reaching Italy, decided that the Trojans would achieve less glory if they remained in Carthage. Accordingly she proposed to Venus that they should work together and arrange a marriage between their favourites, and took steps toward this end.

The next day, when the queen, Aeneas, Ascanius, and the court went hunting in a forest, Juno summoned a storm which poured 'hail, and thunder, and tempestuous rain'. Aeneas and the queen took shelter in the same cave and yielded to love.

> 'From this ill-omen'd hour, in time arose
> Debate and death, and all succeeding woes.
> The queen, whom sense of honour could not move,
> No longer made a secret of her love
> But called it marriage, by that specious name
> To veil the crime, and sanctify the shame.'

169. DIDO AND AENEAS RIDE OUT TO HUNT. Detail from a mosaic pavement of the fourth century A.D., found in 1946 in the ruins of the cold bath of a Roman house at Low Ham, Somerset, England, and installed in the Great Hall of Taunton Castle, Somerset County Museum.

170. DIDO AND AENEAS TAKE SHELTER FROM THE STORM.
From a manuscript of the *Aeneid*, fifth century A.D. Rome, Vatican Library, cod.vat.lat.3867, fol.106. The Codex Romanus.

171. DIDO AND AENEAS RIDE OUT TO HUNT AND TAKE SHELTER FROM THE STORM UNDER A TREE. Illustration from a thirteenth-century German manuscript of Heinrich von Veldecke's twelfth-century German romance, *Eneide*. Berlin, State Library, cod.germ.fol.282, XI.

The manuscript illustration shows the change made in the setting of the forest scene in Heinrich von Veldecke's adaptation of the *Roman d'Enéas*. Instead of a cave, as in the French version, the two take refuge under a tree which spreads its branches like a roof to give shelter from the 'fearful storm'. Here Aeneas wrapped the queen in his cloak to warm her and found himself sharing her passion. In the upper band of the illustration Dido and Aeneas ride out to hunt, Dido accompanied by one of the toy lapdogs which play such delightful parts in medieval romance.

172. DIDO AND AENEAS TAKE SHELTER FROM THE STORM IN A CAVE.
Seventeenth-century Flemish tapestry in the Austrian National Collections.

The tapestry, based on the *Aeneid*, shows the entrance to the cave and interprets the scene in a typically baroque manner, employing rollicking Cupids to direct a realistic storm.

In Dido Vergil created one of the world's most human heroines of passionate and essentially tragic love: a woman torn between a vow of fidelity and the force of a passion denied so long that her nature had rebelled. For such a woman, whose fate it was to cross the imperial destiny of Rome, there could be no happy ending. The poet may have had in mind, some think, the Medea of Apollonius Rhodius' *Argonautica*; he may also have pondered the fate of that other woman from the African shore whose death was still fresh in Roman minds—Cleopatra, dead by her own hand after her defeat at Actium.

The rumour that a successful suitor had won Dido's love reached the king of Libya, an unsuccessful suitor. He complained to Jupiter who, seeing Aeneas dallying contentedly, sent Hermes to remind him that Carthage was not his destined goal:

> ' "What means thy lingering in the Libyan land?
> If glory cannot move a mind so mean,
> Nor future praise from flitting pleasure wean,
> Regard the fortunes of thy rising heir:
> The promised crown let young Ascanius wear,
> To whom the Ausonian sceptre, and the state
> Of Rome's imperial name, is owed by Fate." '

Aeneas' sense of a divine mission together with a father's pride far outweighed his love for Dido. He had his men make ready the ships and tried to think of some way of telling the queen that he must go. But almost at once Dido heard the rumour of his plans. To her reproaches he replied bluntly:

> ' "Fair queen, you never can enough repeat
> Your boundless favours, or I own my debt:
> . . .   .
> This only let me speak in my defence—
> I never hoped a secret flight from hence,
> Much less pretended to a lawful claim
> Of sacred nuptials, or a husband's name." '

Wounded in heart and pride Dido answered him: ' " Go! seek thy promised kingdom through the main." ' Yet when she saw the ships made ready her heart was wrung once more with a vain hope. She sent Anna to ask, not for marriage, or for Aeneas to remain, but simply for a little time—'A pause for grief, an interval from woe.'

But Anna's pleas were vain: against Dido was arrayed the whole force of the Roman *pietas*, the individual's responsibility to the gods and to the state.

Left alone, Dido heard her dead husband's voice calling from the tomb and seemed

> 'To wander in her sleep, through ways unknown,
> Guideless and dark; or, in a desert plain,
> To seek her subjects, and to seek in vain.'

She bade Anna have a pyre built in an inner court, on which she could burn the clothes and sword Aeneas had left behind, to rid herself of his memory. When it was ready she laid upon it an image of her faithless lover.

All night her heart was torn between the desire to beg Aeneas to let her go with him and the thought that she might summon her fleet and stop his sailing. But when morning came she saw that there was no choice: the ships were disappearing over the far horizon.

173. DIDO AND HER SISTER WATCH AENEAS MAKE READY TO LEAVE CARTHAGE. Limoges enamel, 1525–1530, based on a woodcut in the Grüninger Vergil of 1502. New York, Metropolitan Museum of Art. Rogers Fund, 1925.

Looking towards the vanishing ships Dido thought for a moment of pursuit. Then, realizing her helplessness, she called down upon the Trojan and his descendants to the last generation the curse of enmity with her own land. Thus, to the Romans of his own day, Vergil interpreted the rivalry and wars between Rome and Carthage that, after more than a century of struggle, had ended in the complete destruction of the North African city in 146 B.C.

All hope now gone, Dido mounted the pyre and unsheathed the sword. Looking upon the robes Aeneas had worn she spoke her last:

‘ “Dear pledges of my love, while heaven so pleased,
Receive a soul, of mortal anguish eased.
My fatal course is finished; and I go,
A glorious name, among the ghosts below”
. . . .
She said, and struck; deep entered in her side
The piercing steel, with reeking purple dyed.’

And so, released at last by pitying Juno,

‘The struggling soul was loosed, and life dissolved in air.’

174. THE DEATH OF DIDO. Illustration in the *Aeneid*, IV, 641–666, in the Vatican Vergil, fifth century A.D. Rome, Vatican Library, cod.vat.lat.3225, fol.141r.

175. THE DEATH OF DIDO. Illustration from a thirteenth-century manuscript of Heinrich von Veldecke's twelfth-century German romance, *Eneide*. Berlin, State Library, cod.germ.fol.282, XVII.

After leaving Carthage the Trojans stopped on the coast of Sicily, where their women, stirred up by Juno, tried to prevent further wanderings by burning the ships. But the fire was quenched with the loss of only a few vessels, and Aeneas built a city where the weary might remain under the protection of the friendly king, Acestes, a Trojan by descent.

Another misfortune was still to come: Neptune required one life as a sacrifice in return for the Trojans' safe arrival in Italy. He sent the god of sleep to overcome Palinurus, the pilot of Aeneas' ship, so that he fell overboard and drowned. But Neptune himself guided the vessel and at last all reached the mainland at Cumae, near Naples.

Here Aeneas and his companion Achates made their way, as directed by Anchises in a dream, to see the famed Sibyl of Cumae, who dwelt in a cave by Apollo's temple. Following Anchises' counsel Aeneas asked her to lead him to the Underworld, where his father had promised to tell him more concerning the future.

The Sibyl told Aeneas that he must first secure as a gift for Proserpine, queen of the Underworld, a magic golden bough that grew on a tree hidden deep in the forest. This he did and, returning, sacrificed to the gods of heaven and hell at the lake of Avernus, which lay, black and gloomy, in the volcanic country near Vesuvius. At the first hint of dawn the earth groaned and the dogs howled. The

176. AENEAS AND ACHATES COME TO THE TEMPLE OF APOLLO AT CUMAE TO CONSULT THE SIBYL. Illustration from the *Aeneid*, VI, 45–50, in the Vatican Vergil, fifth century A.D. Rome, Vatican Library, cod.vat.lat.3225, fol.45v.

The manuscript illustration does not represent the actual entrance to the Underworld, but the temple of Apollo, from whom the Sibyl received her inspiration and near which lay her cave.

Sibyl, leaving Achates behind, then led Aeneas into the black cavern by the lake which was the entrance to the Underworld.

This journey, which fills the sixth book of the *Aeneid*, was modelled after Odysseus' visit to Hades in the *Odyssey*, but with differences due to changing traditions and beliefs. Fundamentally, the location is different. Some ancient Greek myths, including several passages in the *Iliad*, speak of the realm of the dead as underground, but the Hades which Odysseus visited was not beneath the earth's surface; it simply lay in a realm of darkness beyond the limits of the known world. Vergil's abode of the dead, however, is a true Underworld, approached through a deep cave.

At the entrance to the Underworld dwelt terrible shapes, Grief and Care, Sickness and gloomy Age, Fear, Hunger, and Poverty, Death and Death's kinsman Sleep. On the leaves of a great elm hung false dreams, while nearby lurked monstrous creatures, Gorgons and Harpies and the Chimaera breathing fire. Aeneas drew his sword, and, had not the Sibyl restrained him, would have struck out at these immaterial phantoms.

Soon the two reached the River Styx, which the spirits of the dead must cross to reach whatever fate awaited them. In the division of the dead according to their deeds in life lies another difference between the *Aeneid* and the *Odyssey*. The spirits with whom Odysseus spoke wandered like ghosts in a dim world where there was little difference, except in the case of a few great sinners, between the fates of good and of evil men. The *Aeneid* divides the dead roughly according to past conduct, although this division, like the topography of the Underworld, is not strictly logical —perhaps because there was no 'accepted' tradition in classical antiquity. Vergil's epic, therefore, lacks the clear plan of Dante's medieval Hell and Purgatory and Paradise, but its mystery is none the less effective for its uncertainties.

Charon the ferryman would take across the Styx no spirit of one who lay unburied, until it had wandered for a hundred years. He refused at first to accept Aeneas and the Sibyl, but relented when she showed him the golden bough. As they embarked, the ghost of Palinurus begged to accompany them, but Charon refused. The Sibyl comforted the Trojan however, by saying that burial awaited his body on the coast where it had been washed. The river's opposite shore was guarded by the watchdog Cerberus, three-headed, his neck entwined with serpents, but him the Sibyl quieted with a drugged cake. As the two entered the dim land beyond the river they heard the wailing of young children who had died on the threshold of life, and saw those who had been unjustly condemned to death. Then came the spirits of those who had taken their own lives, and next, in the Wailing Fields, those who had died for love. Here Aeneas saw Dido, 'her bosom bathed in blood'. He told her that he had left her unwillingly and begged her to speak, but she, who had so lately longed for him, now regarded him no more

> 'Than the deaf rocks, when the loud billows roar.'

After this limbo where dwelt those neither outstandingly good nor evil, Aeneas and the Sibyl came to a parting of the ways. One road led to the abode of those destined for punishment, encircled by the fiery flood of the River Phlegethon. Along the other road they made their way to the Elysian Fields, where dwelt the heroes—those who had died for their country, those who had lived pure and generous lives, and poets worthy of Apollo's gift. There they found Anchises meditating happily upon the past and future of his race, while close by ran Lethe, river of forgetfulness, thronged by spirits who were to return to earth for another life, but must first drink this water of oblivion.

Anchises led them to a hill, from which he showed them the great men and events that were to come in Italy. They saw the founders of great cities, statesmen, warriors, and generals marching in triumph up the Capitol Hill in Rome, for at last Aeneas learned that the crown of all his toils would be the founding of Rome by his descendant, Romulus. Among the great of later times they saw Julius Caesar, who traced his line from Aeneas; Caesar's successor, Augustus, in whose honour Vergil wrote; and the young Marcellus, destined to be Caesar's heir, but cut off by death with his bright promise unfulfilled.

177. AENEAS AND THE SIBYL IN THE UNDERWORLD. Painting, perhaps 1619, by Jan Brueghel the Elder (Flemish). Formerly in the Budapest Museum of Fine Arts.

The Romans had to do considerable juggling to connect Aeneas, survivor of the Trojan war in the late twelfth century B.C., with the founding of Rome in the eighth; they achieved it by calling its founder, Romulus, a remote descendant of Aeneas. Anchises, in the Underworld, did not tell his son the story of Romulus and Remus his twin; he merely referred to Romulus as the father of an imperial race. Later in the *Aeneid* Vergil affords Aeneas a glimpse of Rome's site; in describing the shield given to his hero by Venus he alludes more specifically to the legend of the twins.

178. THE FINDING OF ROMULUS AND REMUS BESIDE THE TIBER.
Relief on a Roman altar dedicated in A.D. 124. Rome, Terme Museum.

At the lower left a she-wolf suckles the twins Romulus and Remus, who had been left to die; an imperial eagle hovers over them; at the right the Tiber, personified as a river god, establishes the place. Above are shepherds, one of whom will rescue them.

Most ancient sources agree in saying that long after Aeneas' time Numitor, king of Alba Longa which Ascanius had founded, was deposed by his younger brother, who forced Numitor's only child, a daughter, to become a Vestal Virgin. This daughter, generally called Rhea Silvia, was ravished by Mars the god of war and became the mother of twin boys. The usurper imprisoned her and ordered the children drowned in the Tiber. 'It happened by singular good fortune,' says Livy, 'that the Tiber having spread beyond its banks into stagnant pools afforded nowhere any access to the regular channel of the river.' The men commissioned to drown the infants left them in a basket in one of these pools, and when the water receded the basket remained on dry land. 'A she-wolf, coming down out of the surrounding hills to slake her thirst, turned her steps towards the cry of the infants,' and suckled them so gently that the keeper of the royal flock found her licking them with her tongue as though they were her own cubs. Tradition assigns to this man the name of Faustulus, and adds that he carried the twins to his hut and gave them to his wife Laurentia to rear.

Romulus and Remus grew bold and strong and became leaders among the young men of the countryside. Remus quarrelled with the shepherds of the deposed Numitor, who lived nearby, and was brought before him for punishment. Romulus and Faustulus hastened to his rescue, and the origin of the brothers was discovered. Together they overthrew the usurper, re-established their grandfather on his throne, and then set out to found their own city on the Tiber, where they had been so miraculously preserved.

Almost at once they disagreed about the site. Romulus wished it to be on the Palatine Hill; Remus favoured the Aventine; and each wished the city to be named for him. They agreed that divine omens should decide: soon Remus saw six vultures, but a moment later Romulus saw twelve. They could not agree as to what was indicated by this, and Romulus continued to build the wall he had begun

179. THE FINDING OF ROMULUS AND REMUS. Illustration from a manuscript of the *Aeneid*, VI, 777–850, by Apollonio di Giovanni (Italian), about 1460. Florence, Biblioteca Riccardiana, No.492, fol.66r.

180. THE FINDING OF ROMULUS AND REMUS. Painting, early seventeenth century, by Peter Paul Rubens (Flemish). Rome, Capitoline Museum.

about the Palatine. Remus was either struck down in a quarrel or, as Livy says was more commonly agreed, 'leaped over the new walls in mockery of his brother, whereupon Romulus in great anger slew him, and in menacing wise added these words withal, "So perish whoever else shall leap over my walls!" Thus Romulus acquired sole power, and the city thus founded, was called by its founder's name.' Archaeology agrees with legend in considering the Palatine the oldest walled part of Rome.

The she-wolf, symbol of the city's legendary beginnings, holds an honoured place in the small but significant group of statues that has remained unburied and comparatively unharmed through the disasters of the centuries. Although the present twins are believed to be renaissance additions, such infants were a part of the original: Cicero says that a wolf with twins was struck with lightning on the Capitol in 65 B.C. In the twelfth century, however, when the English traveller, Master Gregory, described the present statue, he made no mention of twins. He lists it among the sights of Rome:

'In the porch of the winter palace of our lord the pope is the bronze statue of that wolf which is said to have suckled Remus and Romulus. But this is a fable. For Wolf was a certain woman of remarkable beauty in Rome in ancient times. She found Remus and Romulus when they had been plunged into the Tiber, and she nursed them as her own. She was called Wolf because men were ravished by her beauty and her enticements.—This bronze wolf is set before the palace on a bronze ram, which pours from its mouth water for the washing of hands. The wolf once poured out water also from each teat, but now its feet have been broken off, and it has been torn from its place.'

By 1509, when Albertini described the group, the twins had been added, and soon it was placed above a door of the outer wall of the old Conservators' Palace on the Capitol, where the Museo dei Conservatori now stands: the Flemish artist, Marten van Heemskerck, sketched it there while he was in Rome between 1532 and 1535. Later it was taken into the palace itself.

When Anchises had shown Aeneas and the Sibyl the glories that were to come he said farewell, and they left the Underworld. Making their way up the coast of Italy

181. THE BRONZE SHE-WOLF OF THE ROMAN CAPITOL. Probably Etruscan, late sixth or early fifth century B.C. Rome, Museo dei Conservatori.

the Trojans came at last to the Tiber, where they landed at Latium, ruled by the old king Latinus. This king's only child and heiress, Lavinia, was sought in marriage by many suitors, the most favoured of whom was Turnus, king of the Rutulians and nephew of Lavinia's mother. Signs from heaven, however, had delayed their marriage, and now Latinus had dreamed that his daughter should wed a man from another land, 'Whose martial fame from pole to pole extends.'

As Aeneas and his men sat upon the shore and ate their meagre meal they were glad to consume the dry wheaten cakes which they used as plates. ' "See, we devour the plates on which we fed," ' cried Ascanius jestingly. Aeneas realized at once that the Harpies' prophecy was fulfilled and hailed their destined home.

> ' "This was that famine, this the fatal place,
> Which ends the wandering of our exiled race.
> Then, on to-morrow's dawn, your care employ,
> To search the land, and where the cities lie,
> And what the men; but give this day to joy.
> Now pour to Jove; and, after Jove is blest,
> Call great Anchises to the genial feast:
> Crown high the goblets with a cheerful draught;
> Enjoy the present hour; adjourn the future thought."
> ... ...
> When next the rosy morn disclosed the day,
> The scouts to several parts divide their way,
> To learn the natives' names, their towns explore,
> The coasts and trendings of the crooked shore.'

Latinus, king of the Latins, received the Trojans favourably, but Juno poisoned the mind of Lavinia's mother against the strangers, told Turnus that he had a dangerous rival, and war soon broke out.

The Tiber god, however, reassured Aeneas that this was his promised land and advised him to seek alliance with the Arcadians, a nearby people ruled by Evander. The Arcadians' city, set high upon a hill, and called Pallanteum, was the very spot to be known centuries later as Rome's Palatine Hill, whose walls Romulus would build. As a sign that this was a true dream the god told Aeneas that he would see upon awakening a white sow with a litter of thirty pigs as white as she. These would signify that in thirty years Ascanius would build here a town and call it Alba, the White.

In the morning the Trojans saw the sow and her litter, and Aeneas, sailing up the river, found Evander sacrificing in a grove outside the city. The Arcadian accepted gladly the offer of alliance and then showed his guests the city, calling prophetic attention to places revered by the Romans of Vergil's time. He pointed out first the Asylum on the Capitol, which Romulus was to make a refuge for outlaws who wished to join his band:

> 'Thence, to the steep Tarpeian rock he leads—
> Now roofed with gold, then thatched with homely reeds.
> A reverent fear (such superstition reigns
> Among the rude) even then possessed the swains.

182. THE ROME THAT WAS TO BE.
Detail from a cassone panel, about 1460, by Apollonio di Giovanni (Italian).
New Haven, Yale University Art Gallery, Jarves Collection.

> Some god, they knew—what god they could not tell—
> Did there amidst the sacred horror dwell.
> The Arcadians thought him Jove; and said they saw
> The mighty Thunderer with majestic awe,
> Who shook his shield, and dealt his bolts around,
> And scattered tempests on the teeming ground.'

And from the Capitol Hill they looked down over what was to be the Roman Forum, filled then with lowing herds.

'The Rome that was to be', shown in Plate 182, is not the city of Vergil, but the artist's Rome, suggested by buildings outstanding in his time as now. The ancient Tomb of Hadrian, or Castle of Sant' Angelo, is in the centre foreground. To the right is the Pantheon. Behind Hadrian's Tomb is the Capitol Hill, where then as now the church of Santa Maria in Aracoeli rose above its long stair on the site of Juno's temple, and the medieval Senator's Palace stands on the lower storey of the Roman Record Office. In the background is the Colosseum. Surrounding the city are the walls built by Aurelian in the third century A.D., most of them standing today.

While Trojans and Arcadians considered together how best to meet war with the Rutulians, they heard three peals of thunder and

> 'Thrice forky lightning flashed along the sky.
> ... ...
> Then, gazing up, repeated peals they hear;
> And in a heaven serene, refulgent arms appear:
> Reddening the skies, and glittering all around.'

Aeneas knew the portent: Venus had promised him if war should threaten, to bring him armour made by Vulcan. The goddess herself called her son apart and laid the arms beneath an oak.

183. VENUS, MOTHER OF AENEAS, PRESENTING HIM WITH ARMS FORGED BY VULCAN. Painting by Nicolas Poussin, about 1635 (French). Toronto, Art Gallery of Toronto. Gift of Reuben Wells Leonard Estate, 1948.

In this episode, as in many others, Vergil followed Homer's pattern. Here he echoed the *Iliad's* description of the armour made for Achilles at the request of Thetis. In both passages the emphasis is laid upon the shield, but there is a notable difference in the decoration of the two. Peaceful pursuits had figured largely on the shield of Achilles; on that of Aeneas, besides an allusion to Romulus and Remus as founders of the city, the celestial smith had stressed the martial history of Rome:

'The wars in order, and the race divine
Of warriors issuing from the Julian line.'

In the shield's centre this history was brought down to 31 B.C., with the defeat of Antony and Cleopatra at Actium. Here again Aeneas saw a vision of the future:

'These figures, on the shield divinely wrought,
By Vulcan laboured, and by Venus brought,
With joy and wonder fill the hero's thought.
Unknown the names, he yet admires the grace,
And bears aloft the fame and fortune of his race.'

Next, advised by Evander, Aeneas made an alliance with the Etruscans, who were also at war with the people of Latium. After this Aeneas returned to his camp to find that Turnus too had gathered allies and was attacking. As the tide of battle surged back and forth Turnus killed Evander's son, Pallas. Out of respect for the young man's bravery Turnus sent the body back to his father but kept the shining sword belt, inlaid with gold. For even this slight pilfering from the dead he was to pay dearly.

Both sides then agreed to a truce for burial of their dead, and the Latins, discouraged, began to urge peace upon their king. He himself felt more and more inclined to believe that Aeneas was his future son-in-law, but Turnus held out fiercely.

Turnus grew even more determined to meet Aeneas face to face and decide in combat the questions of Latium's rule and Lavinia's hand. Lavinia's mother begged him to avoid this conflict as, in the *Iliad*, Hecuba had vainly besought Hector not

184. LAVINIA WRITES A LETTER TO AENEAS AND GIVES IT TO AN ARCHER TO SHOOT FROM A TOWER. Illustration from a thirteenth-century German manuscript of Heinrich von Veldecke's twelfth-century German romance, *Eneide.* Berlin, State Library, cod.germ.fol.282, LXIX.

to fight Achilles. Lavinia, listening, showed her one sign of emotion throughout the *Aeneid*: otherwise she seems to have regarded her marriage realistically as a political convenience. But now

> 'A crimson blush her beauteous face o'erspread,
> Varying her cheeks by turns with white and red.'

The Aeneas romances leave no doubt as to her feelings. From the time she sees Aeneas from her tower she is in love and she manages, as the manuscript illustration shows, to convey her feelings to the Trojan, in whom a similar passion awakes. In his treatment of Lavinia Heinrich von Veldecke emphasizes, however, that her love, though ardent, is a gentle, wholesome affection, unlike that of Dido, which he regarded as ungoverned and ill-omened.

Finally Aeneas and Turnus meet and, after a long and fierce contest, the Trojan pins his adversary to the ground. In his final words to his conqueror, Turnus is at his best:

> ' "I know my death deserved, nor hope to live" '

he says, and, if he is to die, asks only that his body be given to his friends. Moved by this appeal Aeneas would have spared his enemy's life had his eyes not fallen on the sword belt of Pallas which Turnus wore. Crying

> ' "Tis Pallas, Pallas gives this deadly blow."
> He raised his arm aloft, and, at the word,
> Deep in his bosom drove the shining sword.
> The streaming blood distained his arms around,
> And the disdainful soul came rushing through the wound.'

And so, with Lavinia still unwed and Italy's cities still unfounded, the *Aeneid* ends.

Though the *Aeneid* closes with the death of Turnus, the legends of the Trojans in Italy carry the action much further. Vergil gave promise of this when he described a treaty concluded between Aeneas and Latinus before the contest with Turnus, in which the Trojan promises that if he is the victor he will name his city after Lavinia and Trojans shall live with Latins 'joined in their laws, their lands, and their abodes.' Dionysius of Halicarnassus says that after the battle and the marriage of Aeneas and Lavinia both parties combined their customs, laws, and religious ceremonies, 'all calling themselves by the common name of Latins.'

The marriage of Aeneas and Lavinia seals the pact between Trojans and Latins, which was to be the foundation for the coming empire. In the detail from a fifteenth-century cassone shown overleaf in Plate 185 this marriage is given the costume and setting of the Italian Renaissance.

Aeneas did not long enjoy his new realm. Dionysius says that he died in battle and, when his body 'was nowhere to be seen, some concluded that it had been translated to the gods.' Ovid, less sober-minded, says that when Ascanius was ready for the responsibility of rule Aeneas was 'ripe for heaven', and Venus persuaded Jupiter to receive him among the gods. And so, as in his life he had linked Troy with Rome, in his death he set the pattern for Rome's deified emperors.

185. THE MARRIAGE OF AENEAS AND LAVINIA. Detail of a cassone panel by the Master of The Tournament of Santa Croce (Italian), fifteenth century. Paris, Musée de Cluny, No. 1710.

APPENDICES

A PARTIAL LIST OF WORKS OF LITERATURE AND MUSIC

AND

A SELECTION OF WORKS OF ART

Etruscan bronze mirror, c. 300–250 B.C.,
engraved with the names, in Etruscan form, of Menelaus, Helen, Thetis and Achilles.
New York, Metropolitan Museum of Art, 21.88.28. Rogers Fund 1921.

APPENDIX A

A PARTIAL LIST OF WORKS OF LITERATURE AND MUSIC DEALING WITH THE TROJAN WAR

9th–8th Century B.C.

HOMER (900–700 B.C.). *The Iliad.* Greek epic beginning in the war's tenth year with the quarrel between Achilles and Agamemnon concerning Briseis and ending a few months later with the funeral of the Trojan leader Hector.

The Odyssey. Greek epic relating the adventures of the Greek leader Odysseus during the ten years between the end of the war and his return home to Ithaca.

HESIOD (800–700 B.C.). *Theogony.* Greek didactic poem noting briefly the births of Achilles, Aeneas, Circe, and Calypso, and the love of the last two for Odysseus.

Works and Days. Greek didactic poem referring briefly to the sailing of the Greeks for Troy.

Catalogue of Women. Fragments from a Greek didactic poem, Hesiodic type, perhaps seventh century, including an account of the wooing of Helen and the birth of her daughter Hesione, and of the education of Achilles by Cheiron.

8th–6th Century B.C.

THE EPIC CYCLE. Greek epic poems ascribed to various authors relating events in the war before or after those told in the Homeric poems. These are now lost, but a summary made by Proclus in the second century A.D. was preserved by the Byzantine scholar Photius in the ninth century A.D. In generally accepted order of composition, these poems are:

The Aethiopis. Ascribed to Arctinus (8th century) and named from the Ethiopian allies of the Trojans. It included the story of the Amazon queen Penthesilea, whom Achilles killed, the death of the Ethiopian king Memnon, and of Achilles himself, and the dispute of Ajax and Odysseus over Achilles' arms. According to an old commentator it also told of the suicide of Ajax.

The Sack of Ilium. Ascribed to Arctinus. It included the bringing of the Wooden Horse into Troy, the theft of the Palladium, the story of Laocoön, the fall of Troy, the meeting of Menelaus and Helen, the dragging of Cassandra from Athena's altar by Ajax son of Oïleus, the sacrifice of Polyxena on Achilles' tomb, the death of Priam, of Hector's son Astyanax, and the captivity of Andromache, Hector's widow.

The Cypria. Ascribed to Stasinus (8th century?). It contained the material leading up to the *Iliad*, beginning with the decision of Zeus to bring about a war; the quarrel between the three goddesses at the wedding feast of Peleus and Thetis; the judgment of Paris; the abduction of Helen; the gathering of the Greeks at Aulis; the sacrifice of Iphigenia and substitution of a hind in her place; and the war, up to the opening of the *Iliad.*

The Returns (*Nostoi*). Ascribed to Hegias (8th century?). It related the adventures of the Greek leaders returning from the war, except those of Odysseus, already told in the *Odyssey.*

The Little Iliad. Ascribed to Lesches (7th century?), covering much the same material as the *Aethiopis* and the *Sack of Ilium.* It began with the contest between Ajax and Odysseus over Achilles' arms, followed by the madness and suicide of the former, and included the bringing of Philoctetes to Troy, the death of Paris, Helen's marriage to Deiphobus, the building of the Wooden Horse, the theft of the Palladium, the bringing of the horse into Troy, the meeting of Menelaus and Helen, the death of Priam, the death of Astyanax, and the captivity of Andromache.

The Telegonia. Late cyclic epic ascribed to Eugammon (6th century), told of the later adventures of Odysseus not described in the *Odyssey* and of his death at the hands of Telegonus, his son by Circe.

7th–6th Century B.C.

STESICHORUS. Greek choral poet. Lost poems dealing with the war included: *The Destruction of Ilium; Helen; The Palinode,* which denied that Helen went to Troy; *The Returns*; and *The Oresteia.*

SAPPHO. Greek lyric poetess (late 7th century). Various fragments mention Trojan themes, one using Helen's passion for Paris to show the power of love.

ALCAEUS (b. c.620). Greek lyric poet. One fragment of his work contrasts the happiness brought by Thetis to Peleus with the woe Helen brought to Troy.

IBYCUS. Greek lyric poet (6th century). Fragments indicate that he wrote of the sack of Troy; he is also said to have told of the marriage of Achilles and Medea in the Elysian Fields.

6th–5th Century B.C.

SIMONIDES (c.556–468). Greek lyric poet said also to have treated of Achilles and Medea in the Elysian Fields.

EPICHARMUS (c.530–c.440). Greek comic dramatist, whose Trojan farces included *The Cyclops*, *Odysseus on His Own*, *Odysseus Shipwrecked*, *The Sirens*, and *The Trojans*.

AESCHYLUS (525/24–456). Greek tragic dramatist. Of 70 to 90 plays credited to him, only seven remain. *The Oresteia*, a group of three plays dealing with Trojan subjects, is the only remaining example of the Greek trilogy on a related theme. These are: *Agamemnon*, which ends with that hero's death at his wife's hand; *The Choephori* (Libation Bearers), which tells of the vengeance of Orestes; and *The Eumenides* (Furies), which relates the trial and acquittal of Orestes for matricide at the court of the Aeropagus at Athens.
His lost Trojan plays included another trilogy, *The Myrmidons*, *The Nereids*, and *Hector's Ransom*: others were *Palamedes* and *Philoctetes*. *The Weighing of Souls* described Zeus' balancing of the fates of Achilles and Memnon. *The Mysians* and *Telephus* probably dealt with such related Trojan themes as the relationship of Telephus, son of Hercules, with Troy and his marriage with a Trojan princess.

5th Century B.C.

BACCHYLIDES. Greek lyric poet. His *Sons of Antenor* or *The Demanding Back of Helen* is an early account of the Greeks' demand for Helen's return; in his *Ode* on Pytheas of Aegina, victor at the Pancratium about 481, there is a long account of the Trojan attack on the Greek ships.

HERODOTUS. Greek historian. His *History* repudiates the Homeric authorship of the *Cypria* (II.117) and denies that Helen was the cause of the Trojan war (II.120).

HELLANICUS. Greek chronicler. Fragments of his *Pharonis* mention Hercules' capture of Troy; those from his *Troica* deal with events of the war, the final fall of the city, the escape of Aeneas and his followers, and their founding of a city in Italy.

SOPHOCLES (c.496–406). Greek tragic dramatist. Only seven of the over 100 plays credited to him remain: of these, three deal with Trojan themes. These are: *Ajax*, which tells of that hero's madness and suicide; *Philoctetes*, which relates the story of the wounded Greek's return to the war with the arrows of Hercules; and *Electra*, which treats, with completely different emphasis, the material of Aeschylus' *Libation Bearers*.
About one third of Sophocles' plays were said to have dealt with Trojan themes. Among them were: *Alexander* (Paris); *The Madness of Odysseus*, based on the Greek's ruse for evading the war; *Lovers of Achilles*; *The Scyrian Women*; *Laocoön*, a fragment of which tells of the escape of Aeneas and his followers; *Antenor's Sons*; *Palamedes*; *Iphigenia*; *Protesilaos*; and *Polyxena*. *Nausicaä*, *The Phaeacians*, and *The Feasters* were evidently inspired by the *Odyssey*. Other plays dealt with such subjects as the captive maidens, Chryseis and Briseis, the Aethiopian allies of Troy, and the return of various heroes when the war was over.

EURIPIDES (c.485–c.406). Greek tragic dramatist. Ninety or more plays are credited to Euripides, twenty of which are said to have dealt with Trojan subjects. Of the nineteen which remain, eight tragedies and a satyr play belong to this group. These are: *Helen*, which dramatizes Stesichorus' story that Menelaus' wife did not go to Troy and is more a melodrama than a tragedy; *Iphigenia in Aulis*; *Iphigenia in Tauris*; *Hecuba*; *The Trojan Women*; *Andromache*; *Electra*; *Orestes*; and *The Cyclops*, the only surviving example of a satyr play, or comic treatment of a mythological theme with a satyr chorus. Among lost Trojan dramas are *Alexander* (Paris), *Palamedes*, *Philoctetes*, *The Scyrians*, and *Telephus*.

THUCYDIDES (c.460–400). Greek historian. His *History of the Peloponnesian War* discusses the Trojan War as part of a gradual eastern expansion of the Greek mainland, long in duration only because of lack of money and supplies (II.9).

5th–4th Century B.C.

PHILOXENUS. Greek poet. His *Cyclops* tells the story of Polyphemus' love for Galatea; he is said to have represented himself as Odysseus.

MENECRATES. Greek author quoted by Dionysius of Halicarnassus as saying that Aeneas betrayed Troy because of jealousy of Paris.

XENOPHON (c.430–c.354). Greek historian and writer on various subjects, whose lighter works, such as the *Memorabilia* and the *Treatise on Hunting*, contain many references to well-defined traditions associated with the heroes of the war.

4th–3rd Century B.C.

LYCOPHRON. Greek poet. His *Alexandra* represents Cassandra as prophesying the fall of Troy and says that Sinon opened the Wooden Horse and gave the signal for the Greeks to return.

TIMAEUS (c.356–260). Greek historian. His *History of Sicily* may have introduced the story of Dido into classical literature.

LIVIUS ANDRONICUS (c.284–c.204). Latin poet, by birth a Greek of South Italy, regarded as the founder of Latin epic and dramatic poetry. He adapted Greek Trojan plays to Latin, under such titles as *Achilles*, *Ajax*, and *The Trojan Horse*, and translated or paraphrased the *Odyssey* into Latin verse for use as a textbook.

NAEVIUS (c.270–c.201). Latin poet. Among his adaptations of Greek Trojan legends are dramas entitled *Andromache*, *Hector*, *Hesione*, *Iphigenia*, and *The Trojan Women*; the early part of his epic *History of the Punic War* includes the legendary background of Aeneas, and probably strongly influenced the *Aeneid*.

3rd–2nd Century B.C.

APOLLONIUS RHODIUS. Greek scholar and poet. His *Argonautica* related in epic form the story of the Argonauts; his *Medea* may have influenced Vergil's conception of Dido. Later versions of his account of the Argonauts, by Diodorus of Sicily and Valerius Flaccus (*see* below), connected them with the first destruction of Troy, a pattern followed by Dares and medieval romancers.

ENNIUS (239–169). Latin poet. His Trojan dramas, extant only in quotations, included *Achilles*, *Ajax*, *Alexander*, *Andromache*, *Eumenides*, and *Iphigenia*; his *Annals*, an epic chronicle of the adventures of Aeneas, was one of the *Aeneid's* sources.

PACUVIUS (c.220–c.130). Latin dramatist. The titles of his works show a number of Trojan plays, such as an *Award of the Arms*, *Hermione*, *Iliona*, *Protesilaus*, and *The Washing*, which dealt with Odysseus' death.

2nd–1st Century B.C.

ACCIUS (170–c.85). Latin dramatist. Titles and fragments of his work indicate an *Achilles*, *Aegisthus*, *Agamemnon's Children*, *Antenor's Sons*, *Clytemnestra*, *Hecuba*, *Neoptolemus*, *Astyanax*, and *Trojan Women*.

BION (fl.100). Greek lyric poet, whose second *Idyll* tells of the love of Achilles and Deïdamia.

VARRO, MARCUS TERENTIUS (116–27). Latin scholar. His *De Familiis Trojanis*, now lost, traced the lineage of many noble Roman families to heroes of Troy.

1st Century B.C.

CICERO (106–43 B.C.). Latin author, orator and statesman.

CATULLUS (c.84–c.54). Latin lyric poet. Among many allusions to the Trojan story the most extensive is the wedding chant, *On the Marriage of Peleus and Thetis*.

PROPERTIUS (born c.50 B.C.). Latin elegiac poet, throughout whose elegies are scattered many exquisitely phrased Trojan allusions.

DIODORUS OF SICILY. Greek compiler of history (d. 21 B.C. or later). His fragmentary *Historical Library* devotes several books to the Trojan War and links Hercules' capture of Troy with the Argonauts.

DIONYSIUS OF HALICARNASSUS. Greek prose writer (d. after 7 B.C.). His *Roman Antiquities* emphasizes the adventures of Aeneas and the Romans' descent from the Trojans.

VERGIL (70–19 B.C.). Most famous of Latin epic poets, whose *Aeneid*, modelled on the *Odyssey*, established Aeneas as Rome's national hero and made enduring the story of her foundation by the Trojans.

HORACE (65–8 B.C.). Latin poet, whose *Satires* and *Odes* contain many allusions to Trojan incidents, the most famous being the passage 'many heroes lived before Agamemnon, but all are overwhelmed . . . because they lacked a sacred bard'.

1st Century B.C.–*1st Century* A.D.

STRABO (64/63 B.C.–A.D. 21). Greek geographer, whose *Geography* gives traditional Trojan locations, such as the Sirens' island.

LIVY (TITUS LIVIUS) (59 B.C.–A.D. 17). Latin historian, whose *Roman History* gives a well-known version of the founding of Rome by the Trojans.

OVID (43 B.C.–C. A.D. 17/19). Latin poet. Books 11 to 15 of his *Metamorphoses* contain a wealth of Trojan narrative; his *Heroides*, a series of imaginary love letters from famous women, includes correspondence between Paris and Helen, letters from Dido to Aeneas, Hermione to Orestes, and Laodamia to Protesilaus.

SENECA, LUCIUS ANNAEUS (The Philosopher) (c.5 B.C.–A.D. 65). Latin author. His dramas, adapted from the Greek, include *Agamemnon*, *Thyestes*, and *The Trojan Women*; Trojan material abounds in his *Essays* and *Epistles*.

VALERIUS FLACCUS. Latin epic poet (d. before A.D. 90). His *Argonautica* is a Latin paraphrase of Apollonius Rhodius. It links Hercules with Troy, but less fully than Diodorus.

1st Century A.D.

UNKNOWN AUTHOR. *Ilias Latina*. First known Latin translation (or condensation) of the *Iliad*, credited variously to Silius Italicus and Baebius Italicus.

LUCAN (39–65). Latin poet, whose *Civil War* (*Pharsalia*) comments on Caesar's fondness for Troy and his claim to Trojan descent.

PLINY THE ELDER (c.23–79). Latin naturalist and author. His *Natural History*, arranged according to materials employed, describes many outstanding works of painting and sculpture then existing, including many from the Trojan cycle.

STATIUS (c.45–96). Latin poet. His unfinished *Achilleid* tells in detail the early life of Achilles, to his departure from Scyros for Troy.

1st–2nd Century A.D.

DIO CHRYSOSTOM (c.40–after 112). Greek philosopher and orator. His *Trojan Discourses* contain much Trojan material: *On Retirement* propounds the idea that the judgment of Paris was a dream.

PLUTARCH (c.46–after 120). Greek prose writer. Many of his *Parallel Lives*, biographies of Greeks and Latins in pairs, contain Trojan material; the *Life of Romulus* relates the founding of Rome; the *Life of Camillus*, the veneration of Troy's Palladium in Rome.

SUETONIUS (c.69–c.140). Latin scholar and historian. His *Life of Julius Caesar* tells of Caesar's interest in Troy and his idea of making it the capital of the Roman Empire.

2nd Century A.D.

LUCIAN OF SAMOSATA (c.120–c.180). Greek philosopher and satirist. His *Dialogues of the Dead*, *Dialogues of the Gods*, and *Dialogues of the Sea Gods* contain much witty and sparkling handling of the Trojan legend.

APULEIUS. Latin writer. His *Golden Ass* gives a detailed description of a Roman danced mime of the judgment of Paris.

PAUSANIAS. Greek traveller and writer. His *Description of Greece* is invaluable as a record of lost paintings, sculpture, and other antiquities. Though he covers a less wide range than Pliny, his descriptions are more detailed.

APOLLODORUS. The *Library*, a Greek mythological compilation, of immense value for its naming of sources, probably dates from the second century A.D. although it has been attributed to the grammarian Apollodorus of the second century B.C.

HYGINUS. Latin grammarian and author. The *Fabulae*, whose attribution to him is sometimes questioned, has been of great importance in the history of mythology. Among his lost works was one concerning the genealogy of families of Trojan descent.

PROCLUS. Greek grammarian. Compiler of the *Chrestomathia*, or collection of useful information containing the summaries of the epic cycle, which have been preserved in the *Biblioteca* of the ninth-century scholar, Photius.

2nd–3rd Century A.D.

DICTYS in Greek. A papyrus fragment of a Greek version of the *Ephemeris Belli Troiani* (*Diary of the Trojan War*) is dated about A.D. 206. In its Latin form, perhaps two centuries later, this work was one of the great sources of medieval Trojan romance. (See below under *4th Century*, DICTYS in Latin.)

PHILOSTRATUS, FLAVIUS (c.170–c.244). Greek writer. His *Heroicus* is a series of Trojan histories, and much Trojan material is included in his *Life of Apollonius of Tyana*. Writing about the same time as, or slightly later than, Dictys, he uses some of the same versions of the stories.

DARES in Greek. A Greek version of the *De Excidio Troiae Historia* (*History of the Destruction of Troy*) was probably compiled about this time. With Dictys' *Ephemeris*, the Latin version of Dares, dating perhaps from the sixth century, was one of the most important sources of medieval Trojan romance; it was more generally followed than Dictys in Western Europe. (See below under *6th Century*, DICTYS in Latin.)

PHILOSTRATUS, LEMNIUS. Greek writer (b. c.191). His *Imagines* (*Pictures*) describes a series of paintings supposed to have been in a Neapolitan portico, and includes such Trojan themes as the Death of Agamemnon and Cassandra and the Education of Achilles. His grandson of the same name continued the series, with additional Trojan subjects.

AELIAN. Roman philosopher and author writing in Greek. His *Varia Historia* (*Historical Miscellanies*) mentions a Dares who wrote about the Trojan War and gives other information on Trojan matters, such as the anecdote (IV.12) that Zeuxis charged an admission fee to see his painting of 'Helen the Courtesan'.

4th Century

QUINTUS OF SMYRNA. Greek epic poet, author of *The Fall of Troy*, which he embellished with romantic and picturesque details.

SERVIUS. Latin grammarian, composer of a *Commentary on Vergil* designed for use in schools, invaluable for its presentation of comparative versions of mythological subjects and its quotations from various authors.

DICTYS in Latin. The Latin *Ephemeris Belli Troiani* (*Diary of the Trojan War*) may have been composed in this century, although existing manuscripts are much later. This literary forgery, purporting to be an eyewitness account by a man who fought on the Greek side, has a preface stating that it was discovered in the first century A.D. when an earthquake shattered a Cretan tomb, and that it was translated into Greek from strange characters in which it was written. Dictys begins his account of the war with the abduction of Helen and ends with the adventures of Telegonus, Odysseus' son, who unwittingly kills his father. For events before he arrived at Troy, Dictys gives Odysseus as his authority; those after the war's end, he learned from Achilles' son, Neoptolemus, or from the oracle at Delphi. His work is closer to ancient tradition than that of Dares, although he also eliminates battles of the gods and stresses romantic love. Of Hector's death he says that the hero was about to meet Penthesilea when he was ambushed by Achilles. He tells of the Trojan Horse but not of Laocoön.

4th–5th Century

AUGUSTINE, SAINT. Christian bishop and Church Father, of African birth. His *De Civitate Dei* (*City of God*) refutes the charge that Rome's neglect of pagan gods led to the city's sack by the Visigoths in A.D. 410, pointing out that the worship of these same gods had not prevented the sack of Troy.

PAULUS OROSIUS. Spanish presbyter of the Latin Church whose *Historia contra Paganos* (*History Against the Pagans*) draws the same moral as Augustine's *City of God*, and gives valuable additional details concerning knowledge of the story of Troy at that time.

MACROBIUS (c.400). Latin writer, perhaps of African birth, whose *Commentary on the Aeneid* may mark the beginning of medieval tradition concerning Vergil's omniscience, from which it was but a step to endowing the poet with prophetic powers and then with those of a magician. Macrobius' *Saturnalia* also contained Trojan material used by later mythographers.

5th Century

MARTIANUS CAPELLA. His *Marriage of Mercury and Philology* contains much allegorized Trojan mythology used by later Latin writers.

UNKNOWN AUTHOR. *Excidium Troiae.* Latin compendium of the story of the war combined from old sources and evidently meant for a school text, as it is largely in question-and-answer form. It includes the wedding of Peleus and Thetis; the story of Discord and the apple; the early life of Paris; his judgment of the goddesses; a passing reference to the theft of Hesione by the Greeks; the abduction of Helen; the early life of Achilles; a brief mention of his anger with Agamemnon because of Briseis; the death of Patroclus; the death of Hector at Achilles' hand; the ransoming of Hector's body; the death of Achilles through betrayal by Polyxena, who is represented as his wife and is killed after the city's fall; an account of the capture of Troy, largely based on Vergil and including the stories of the Wooden Horse and Laocoön; further incidents in the history of Rome not within the scope of the *Aeneid*; and a brief summary of the blinding of Polyphemus by Ulysses. This account is in general far nearer to classical sources than are Dictys and Dares; it may have been used by the romancers as a reference, but was seldom followed if it disagreed with those two authors.

COLLUTHUS. Greek epic poet, author of *The Rape of Helen*, which mentions that Discord picked the golden apple in the Garden of the Hesperides. Said to have been known in southern Italy early in the Middle Ages.

TRYPHODORUS. Greek epic poet, whose *Taking of Ilion* abounds in elaborate descriptions.

FULGENTIUS. His Latin *Mythology* and *Commentary on the Aeneid* contain much allegorical and mythological material on Troy used by later authors.

6th Century

CASSIODORUS (c.487–583). Latin statesman and minister to Theodoric, whose *History of the Goths*, preserved in abridged form by Jordanes, traces a Trojan pedigree for Theodoric from the son of Hercules and a Trojan princess.

JORDANES. Gothic historian who preserved the abridgement of Cassiodorus' *History*, with the Trojan pedigree of Theodoric.

DARES in Latin. The Latin version of the *Historia* ascribed to Dares the Phrygian may date from this century, although existing manuscripts are considerably later. The book is prefaced by a letter saying that it had been discovered in a Greek manuscript at Athens in the first century B.C. and translated into Latin. Its author stated that he had fought on the Trojan side; hence in Western Europe, with its tradition of Trojan descent, his account was more influential than that of Dictys. Though shorter than Dictys' *Diary*, the *Historia* includes earlier action which Dictys omits; it begins with the expedition of the Argonauts, describing Hercules' capture of Troy, the taking of Hesione, the rebuilding of the city by Priam, and the unsuccessful request for Hesione's return. Paris tells of his judgment of the goddesses as a dream. Like the *Iliad* it says—but briefly—that Achilles killed Hector in flight about the walls of Troy. It omits the theft of the Palladium and the stratagem of the Wooden Horse (consequently, the story of Laocoön), and includes Aeneas in a plot to betray Troy, as Dictys does not. The *Historia* closes with the city's fall, the sacrifice of Polyxena at Achilles' tomb, and the departure of the Greeks for home. No mention is made of Aeneas' founding of an Italian city. Like Dictys, this work eliminates much of the supernatural and stresses love interest.

7th–10th Centuries

FREDEGARIUS (7th century). Frankish chronicler. The *Chronicle of Fredegarius*, traditionally attributed to him, contains what is believed to be the first reference to the French as descended from a Trojan prince, Francus.

NENNIUS. Welsh chronicler. His Latin chronicle (c.826), the *Historia Britonum* (*History of Britain*) includes the story of Britain's settlement by and naming for Brutus, a son of Ascanius.

PHOTIUS (9th century). Byzantine scholar, whose *Biblioteca* has preserved Proclus' summaries of the epic cycle.

LIUDPRAND OF CREMONA (920–972). Italian diplomat and man of letters, whose *Antapodosis* dwells upon the wonders he saw at the Byzantine court, indicating a source for the Eastern marvels which found their way into the romances: for instance, the 'Golden Tree' of Troy.

12th Century

GEOFFREY OF MONMOUTH. Welsh chronicler, whose Latin *History of the Kings of Britain* enlarges and embellishes Nennius' account of the Trojan settlement of Britain. He represents Caesar as saying, 'We Romans and these Britains be of one ancestry, for we also do come of Trojan stock.'

ALBRICUS. His *Images of the Gods*, a Latin handbook of mythology, was much used by later authors.

BENOIT DE SAINTE-MORE. French composer of the verse romance of Troy, the *Roman de Troie*, c.1160, which set the pattern for later works. Benoit drew from Dares and somewhat from Dictys to fill gaps in the story; he also took details from Servius' *Commentary on Vergil*, Hyginus' *Fables*, Ovid, and other sources, as well as filling in from his own imagination. His romance contains the first known version of the love of Troilus and Cressida; stresses courtly love and medieval customs; and is filled with references to Eastern marvels and luxuries. It was translated into many languages, among them the Latin prose of Guido delle Colonne, through which it became most widely known.

UNKNOWN AUTHOR. *Roman d'Enéas*. Anonymous French romance, sometimes ascribed to Benoit, drawn chiefly from Vergil with details from Ovid, from commentaries, and from a book on the seven wonders of the world. Courtly love is stressed, especially in the character of Lavinia, destined wife of Aeneas.

HEINRICH VON VELDECKE. German poet. His *Eneide*, an adaptation of the French *Enéas*, written between 1174 and 1184, was the first influential courtly romance in German.

12th–13th Century

CONRAD OF QUERFURT. Bishop of Hildesheim. Letters written from Italy and Sicily contain some of the earliest references to Vergil as a magician.

HERBORT VON FRITZLAR. German poet, whose *Liet von Troye* (*Song of Troy*), an abbreviated version of Benoit's romance, composed early in the thirteenth century, was the earliest Troy romance (as distinct from an Aeneas romance) in German.

13th Century

UNKNOWN AUTHOR. *Histoire Universelle* (1223–1230), in French, the earliest compilation in the vernacular of a type of historical writing which was very popular in the Middle Ages. It attempts to correlate the chronology of the Old Testament with that of secular antiquity. Latin chronicles of this kind are, of course, much older, having roots at least as far back as the works of Saint Augustine and Paulus Orosius. The *Histoire* drew its Greek sections chiefly from the Troy romances; its Latin ones from the *Aeneid*. Its earliest manuscripts belong to the later thirteenth century, but most come from the fourteenth and fifteenth (*see* Plate 26).

KONRAD OF WÜRZBURG. German poet (d. 1287). His *Trojanerkrieg* (*Trojan War*), though drawn largely from Benoit, incorporates incidents from some less well-known version, perhaps the *Excidium Troiae* or its sources, such as stories of the early life of Paris and the adventures of Aeneas.

GUIDO DELLE COLONNE. Sicilian author whose *Historia Destructionis Trojae*, composed in Latin prose between 1272 and 1287, is an abridgement, without credit, of Benoit's romance. As Latin was the international language of the time this was the most influential single work of the Middle Ages dealing with Troy, being more widely translated and adapted than Benoit's romance, which it superseded as an authority.

SEGHER DIEREGOTGAF. His *Trojaensche Oorlag* (*Trojan War*), a Dutch version of Benoit, is unfinished.

JACOB VAN MAERLANT. Author of the *Istory van Troyen*, a Dutch version of Benoit incorporating much of the *Trojaensche Oorlag*.

13th–14th Century

DANTE ALIGHERI (1265–1321). Italian poet and prose writer. His use of Vergil as his guide in the first part of the *Divine Comedy* reflects the medieval respect for that poet, while his placing of the great characters of Trojan legend indicates the medieval conception of their characters.

JACQUES DE LONGUYON. French poet. His *Vows of the Peacock*, composed about 1310, contains the first known mention of the Nine Heroes or Worthies, including Hector of Troy.

UNKNOWN AUTHOR. *Gesta Romanorum* (*Deeds of the Romans*), a Latin compilation of tales from Oriental, classical, and unknown sources, contains a moralized version of the discovery of Achilles in Scyros (CLVI), taken from Ovid's *Metamorphoses*. Published in English translation by Wynkyn de Worde, c.1510–1515.

14th Century

UNKNOWN AUTHOR. *Moralized Ovid* (early 14th century), in French rhymed couplets, with allegorical and moralized comments, based on the Bible, Ovid, Statius, Hyginus, Fulgentius, and others. Such Ovids were widely used in place of the classical Latin text in the Middle Ages.

PIERRE BESUIRE (d. 1362). French author of a well-known *Moralized Ovid*.

FILIPPO CEFFI translated Guido's Latin Troy romance into Italian prose (1324).

BINDUCCIO DELLE SCELTO translated Benoit's romance into Italian (1332).

UNKNOWN AUTHOR. *Cronica Troyana* (1350), Spanish version of Benoit made for Alfonso XI, Escorial Library, MS H.j.6.

PETRARCH (Francesco Petrarca) (1304–1374). Italian scholar and author, whose interest in Greek was largely responsible for Leo Pilatus' rough translations of the *Iliad* and the *Odyssey* into Latin, the first since ancient times.

GIOVANNI BOCCACCIO (1313–1375). Italian scholar and author, who supervised Pilatus' translations. Boccaccio's own work, outstanding for its Trojan material, includes three Latin treatises and an Italian poem. The Latin works are: *De Casibus Virorum Illustrium* (*Concerning the Fate of Famous People*), *De Claris Mulieribus* (*Concerning Famous Women*), both of which include Trojan characters, and *De Genealogia Deorum* (*The Genealogy of the Gods*), the first important mythological handbook of the Renaissance. It drew copiously from the Latin classics, though often at second or third hand, and mentioned Greek authors. It also gave different versions of legends, sometimes stating sources. It became an important reference work for both artists and authors, referred to, for instance, in Lydgate's early fifteenth-century *Troy Book* and Raoul Lefèvre's Troy romance of 1464. Boccaccio's Italian poem, *Il Filostrato* (*The One Prostrated by Love*) elaborated Benoit's story of Troilus and Cressida.

UNKNOWN AUTHOR. *The Siege and Battle of Troy.* Anonymous English poem in the form of a minstrel's romance, known in several widely differing manuscripts derived from some common source. Unlike most romances it includes a summary of the early life of Paris and of that of Achilles.

GEOFFREY CHAUCER (1340?–1400). English poet. In addition to innumerable Trojan references, his *Troilus and Criseyde* gives an English version of this theme, while his *Legend of Good Women* retells at length the story of Dido, largely from the *Aeneid.*

ANONYMOUS SCENARIST. Pantomime of the capture of Troy (1389) presented at the French court on occasion of the entry of Isabelle of Bavaria, described in Froissart's *Chronicles.*

JACQUES DE GUISE composed the Latin *Chronicle of Hainault* (1390) referring to the Trojan descent of the Burgundian princes.

UNKNOWN AUTHOR. *Gest Historical of the Destruction of Troy* (1390?). English metrical romance based on Guido.

14th–15th Century

CHRISTINE DE PISAN (1363/4–1430). French authoress whose *Epistle of Othéa, Goddess of Prudence, to Hector, Chief of the Trojans,* composed in 1400, contains moralized summaries of Trojan incidents and makes much use of moralized Ovids.

UNKNOWN AUTHOR. *Jeu du Siège de Troie* (*Play of the Siege of Troy*) (1400) produced at Avignon.

UNKNOWN AUTHOR. *Laud Troy Book* (1400?). English metrical romance based on Guido.

JOHN LYDGATE (c.1370–c.1451). English poet; composed his *Troy Book,* based on Guido (1412–1420). One of the most beautiful of English versions.

PEDRO DE CHENCILLA. Spanish poet; composed (1443) his *Conquista de Troye,* a Castilian version derived from Guido.

JEAN WAUQUELIN translated into French (c.1445) part of the *Chronicle of Hainault* (1390) for Philip the Good, Duke of Burgundy, whose library is said to have had 17 volumes devoted to his family's descent from the Trojans.

JACQUES MILET. French dramatist, composed (1450–1452) his play, *The Destruction of Troy the Great,* based on Guido and intended as a four-day presentation.

RAOUL LEFÈVRE. French author, composed (1464) his *Recueil des Histoires de Troie* (*Collection of Trojan Histories*) at the suggestion of Philip the Good, Duke of Burgundy. Based on Guido, it makes one major narrative change, that of having Hercules destroy the city twice.

15th Century

WILLIAM CAXTON (c.1422–1491). English printer and translator. Translated Lefèvre's *Recueil* into English (between 1468 and 1471) at the Burgundian court at the command of the English princess, Margaret of York, wife of Charles the Bold, Duke of Burgundy.
Caxton published (c.1474) his translation of Lefèvre as *The Recuyeil of the Historyes of Troye,* at Bruges, the first book printed in English. In 1490 he translated and published the *Eneydos,* from a French paraphrase of the *Aeneid.*

MATTEO MARIA BOIARDO (c.1434–1494). Italian poet, whose romantic epic, *Orlando Innamorato* (*Roland in Love*), left unfinished at his death, blended the romance cycles of Charlemagne, Arthur, and Troy.

15th–16th Century

ROBERT HENRYSON (c.1430–c.1506). Scottish poet. His *Testament of Cressid* forms a sequel to the story as told by Boccaccio and Chaucer. Cressida, abandoned by Diomedes, becomes a leper; Troilus, learning that she has died in poverty, arranges honourable burial.

JEAN LEMAIRE DE BELGE (c.1473–1525). French poet. His *Illustrations de Gaulle et Singularitéz de Troye* (*Glories of Gaul and Excellencies of Troy*), 1502–1512, is a renaissance version of the medieval Trojan pedigrees. He uses the war as a background for the glorification of the French royal line, stressing the part played by the gods.

LODOVICO ARIOSTO (1474–1533). Italian poet. His romantic epic, *Orlando Furioso* (*Madness of Roland*), continues Boiardo's unfinished *Orlando Innamorato,* incorporating a wealth of Trojan details. His enchantress Alcina is modelled on Circe.

LILIO GREGORIO GIRALDI (1479–1552). *Historia de deis gentium* (*History of the Pagan Gods*), 1548, most important mythological handbook since Boccaccio. Like Boccaccio he treats Trojan incidents in connection with the deities involved.

16th Century

HANS SACHS (1494–1576). German poet and dramatist. Among his works are several Trojan plays: *The Goddess Circe,* 1550; *The Destruction of*

Troy, 1554; *Queen Clytemnestra*, 1555; and *The Wanderings of Ulysses*, 1555.

GIORGIO VASARI (1511–1574). Italian painter and author. His *Lives of the Most Eminent Painters* notes Raphael's use of Trojan subjects. (*See* APPENDIX B under RAPHAEL.)

VINCENZO CARTARI (c.1520–c.1570). Italian scholar. His *Imagini con la spositione de dei degli antichi* (*Images of the Gods of Antiquity, with Explanations*), 1556, carried on the renaissance tradition of mythological handbooks, using Trojan material as subsidiary to discussions of the gods. Detailed descriptions made it especially useful to artists.

NATALE CONTI (c.1520–1582). Italian scholar. His *Mythologiae sive explicationis fabularum* (*Mythology with Explanations*), early 1560's, followed the usual arrangement but made more use of Greek dramatists as sources.

EDMUND SPENSER (c.1552–1599). English poet. Following the example of Boiardo and Ariosto, his *Faerie Queene* blends the various cycles of romance. As a glorification of Elizabeth of England it includes the legend of Trojan settlement, and abounds in allusions to Troy. Books I–III were printed in 1590, but the poem was unfinished at the poet's death.

LODOVICO DOLCE (1508–1568/9). Italian dramatist and translator. His *Trojans*, sung with music by Claudio Merulo in 1566, was an opera in all but action.

PIERRE DE RONSARD (1524–1585). French epic poet. His *Franciade*, 1572, though giving as its sources Homer and Vergil, draws heavily from Jean Lemaire de Belges and continues the tradition of French descent from the Trojans.

TORQUATO TASSO (1544–1595). Italian poet. His *Gerusalemme Liberata* (*Jerusalem Delivered*) includes Armida, an enchantress modelled upon Circe via Ariosto's Alcina.

16th–17th Century

RICHARD BARNFIELD (1547–1627). English poet. His *Cynthia*, 1595, treats a theme popular in Elizabethan literature, in which the golden apple is awarded to Queen Elizabeth instead of Venus. The same volume also contains a *Legend of Cassandra*.

GEORGE PEELE (c.1558–c.1597). English dramatist. His *Arraignment of Paris*, midway between masque and drama, is an outstanding early example of the connection between Elizabeth of England and the judgment of Paris. Presented before the Queen by the Children of the Queen's Chapel in the 1580's, it was printed in 1584.

CHRISTOPHER MARLOWE (1564–1593). English dramatist. *Dr. Faustus*, 1588, presents Helen as the ideal beauty and contains the famous lines echoed from Lucian '. . . the face that launched a thousand ships'. His *Dido, Queen of Carthage*, 1593, may have been the play referred to in *Hamlet*, 'What's Hecuba to him or he to Hecuba.'

WILLIAM SHAKESPEARE (1564–1616). English dramatist and poet. His one Trojan play, *Troilus and Cressida*, 1601–1602, presents the heroine as a faithless wanton. Trojan allusions in other plays include the passage in *The Merchant of Venice*, 'On such a night stood Dido with a willow in her hand.' Act V of *Love's Labour Lost* presents a pageant parodying Nine Worthies, including Hector, 'sweet knight of Troy'.

ALEXANDRE HARDY (c.1569–1631). French dramatist, father of the renaissance theatre in France. Two at least of his plays have Trojan subjects: *Dido* and *The Death of Achilles*.

FRANCIS SABIE (fl.1595). English poetaster. In his *Pan's Pipe* the apple is awarded to Elizabeth.

THOMAS HEYWOOD (died c.1650). English dramatic poet. *The Four Ages*, a group of dramatic spectacles, dealt with various Greek myths: the last, *The Iron Age*, 1632, is devoted to the Trojan War, beginning with the abduction of Helen and continuing through the history of Clytemnestra, Aegisthus, Orestes, etc. He also wrote, in 1609, a long heroic poem, *Troie Brittanica, or Great Britain's Troy*.

17th Century

JOHN MILTON (1608–1674). English poet. Aside from the usual Trojan allusions, his *Comus* has definite connections with the legend of Odysseus, as Comus the enchanter is Circe's son. Milton planned an epic dealing with the Trojan settlement of Britain, mentioned in 1640 in his Latin poem *On the Death of Damon*; his prose *History of Britain*, 1670, includes a section on this legend, drawn from old chroniclers.

CARLO CAPROLI. Italian composer. Music for *The Wedding of Peleus and Thetis* (1654), first Italian opera heard in Paris. Libretto by Buti and ballet music by Lully. Caproli's own score has disappeared.

JEAN-BAPTISTE LULLY (1632–1687). Franco-Italian composer. Besides the ballet music for

Caproli's *Peleus and Thetis*, he wrote the music for the first act of an *Achilles and Polyxena*, with a libretto by Campistron. Unfinished at Lully's death, the score was completed by Colasse.

JEAN RACINE (1639–1699). French dramatist. In his Trojan plays, *Andromaque*, 1667, and *Iphigénie en Aulide*, 1674, strongly influenced by Euripides, he synthesized classical subject matter with Christian attitude. The supernatural element, for instance, is absent in *Iphigénie*, the plot hinging on a misunderstanding, the maiden showing the resignation of a Christian martyr, and the ending being desirably happy.

PASCAL COLASSE (1649–1709). French composer who completed the score for the *Achilles and Polyxena* begun by Lully.

HENRY PURCELL (c.1659–1695). English composer, whose *Dido and Aeneas*, with libretto by Nahum Tate, produced between 1688 and 1690, was the first English opera on a Trojan theme.

17th–18th Century

FRANÇOIS DE SALIGNAC DE LA MOTHE-FÉNELON (1651–1715). French author. His *Télémaque*, the first part of which appeared in 1699 to be followed at intervals by other volumes, was a didactic prose romance based on the *Odyssey's* story of Telemachus' search for his father, in the course of which Fénelon involves him with one of Calypso's nymphs.

CHAPBOOKS AND BALLADS (17th–18th centuries). These centuries saw the heyday of chapbooks, small, cheap books of a popular nature such as ballads, tracts, and short narratives sometimes derived from romances. A number of these, such as *The History of Hector, Prince of Troy*, dealt with Trojan themes. This particular chapbook may have evolved from Caxton's translation of Lefèvre, as it treats briefly of three destructions of the city (Fig. 4).
The ballad of *The Wandering Prince of Troy* can be traced to the early seventeenth century (*see* T. J. B. Spencer, *Robert Wood and the Problem of Troy in the Eighteenth Century*, in *Journal of the Warburg and Courtauld Institutes*, Vol. XX (1957), pp.83–84). In its refrain, 'Waste lie those walls that were so good. And corn now grows where Troy Town stood,' is an echo from Ovid's *Heroides*, 1,53ff. 'Now are fields of corn where Troy once was, and soil made fertile with Phrygian blood waves with harvest ready for the sickle.'
The eighteenth century saw a dawning interest among educated readers in these popular ballads.

ELKANAH SETTLE (1648–1724). English playwright. His *Virgin Prophetess, or The Siege of Troy*, first produced in 1701, was set to music by several composers and was extremely popular, especially with the wide public reached by ballads and chapbooks. It was performed, for instance, at Bartholomew Fair in London, and is said to be the production shown in rehearsal in Hogarth's engraving of that fair, dated 1735.

18th Century

PIETRO METASTASIO (1698–1782). Italian poet and dramatist, who wrote the libretto for Galuppi's *Dido Abandoned*, produced 1741, and for *Achilles in Scyros*, set to music by several composers.

BALDASSARE GALUPPI (1706–1785). Italian composer of a number of Trojan operas: *Dido Abandoned*, 1741; *Penelope*, 1741; *Wedding of Paris*, 1756; *The Arrival of Aeneas in Latium*, 1765; and *Iphigenia in Tauris*, 1768.

THOMAS PERCY, Bishop of Dromore (1729–1811). Collected and edited *Percy's Reliques of Ancient English Poetry* (1765), which marks the interest in folk literature that attended dawning romanticism.

CHRISTOPH WILLIBALD VON GLUCK (1714–1787). German composer, in whose works Trojan opera blossoms: *Paris and Helen*, libretto by Calzabigi, 1769–70; *Iphigenia in Aulis*, libretto by Du Roullet, 1774; *Iphigenia in Tauris*, libretto by Guillard, 1779, the last two stemming from Euripides.

18th–19th Century

ANDRÉ-ERNEST GRÉTRY (1741–1813). French composer. Operas, *Andromaque*, with libretto based on Racine's play of that name, and *Électra*, with libretto by Thilorier, both produced about 1780.

FRIEDRICH VON SCHILLER (1759–1805). German poet. Among his poems in ballad style are several with Trojan themes. His *Cassandra* describes the ill-fated wedding of Achilles and Polyxena; *The Victory Feast*, the Greeks' celebration after the fall of Troy. In his play, *The Robbers*, 1781, he introduced a ballad fragment, *Hector's Farewell*, later issued in different form as a separate poem.

JOHANN WOLFGANG VON GOETHE (1749–1832). German poet. Goethe's classical drama, *Iphigenia auf Tauris*, was produced in prose form in 1779 and given verse form in 1787. In the second part of *Faust*, published after the poet's death, Helen appears as the ideal of classic beauty; the section dealing with her had appeared as a separate poem entitled *Helen, a Classico-Romantic Phantasmagoria* in 1827. Goethe also left an unfinished epic, *Achilleis*, conceived as a sequel to the *Iliad*.

HEINRICH VON KLEIST (1777–1811). German poet. His tragedy, *Penthesilea*, published in 1808, presents the classical story in reverse. Penthesilea, loving Achilles and feeling that she is scorned, slays him and then falls dead upon his body.

GEORGE GORDON, LORD BYRON (1788–1824). English poet, whose one poem touching the Trojan theme celebrates, not Helen herself, but Canova's bust—'the Helen of the heart'.

19th Century

WILLIAM WORDSWORTH (1780–1850). English poet. His *Laodamia* tells the story of the wife of the first Greek to die at Troy, stressing that the gods approved depth rather than passion in emotion.

WALTER SAVAGE LANDOR (1775–1864). English classicist, poet, and prose writer. Many of his Trojan themes appear in Latin and English poetry and in English prose. The English poems are largely grouped in several volumes of *Hellenics*, issued from the 1820's through the 1850's, often varying from edition to edition; the prose tales appear in the *Imaginary Conversations* and *Imaginary Conversations of the Greeks and Romans*. Among these are: *Menelaus and Helen at Troy*; *The Shades of Iphigenia and Agamemnon*; *Achilles and Helen on Ida*; *The Espousals of Polyxena*; *The Death of Paris and Oenone*; *The Wooden Horse*; and *The Last of Odysseus*.

EDGAR ALLAN POE (1809–1849). American poet. Sonnet, *To Helen*, 1825, and several later versions.

HECTOR BERLIOZ (1803–1869). French composer. Music and words for his opera, *The Trojans*, based largely on Vergil, composed 1853–1859.

ALFRED, LORD TENNYSON (1809–1892). English poet. *Oenone*, 1833, revised 1842; *A Dream of Fair Women*, 1833, revised 1842 and later. It was inspired by Chaucer's *Legend of Good Women* and includes brief accounts of Helen and Iphigenia. *The Lotus Eaters*, 1833, revised 1842. *Ulysses*, 1842, gives a glimpse of the hero's adventurous old age.

CHARLES-MARIE-RENÉ LECONTE DE LISLE (1818–1894). French poet. His *Antique Poems*, 1852, include *The Death of Penthesilea* and *Helen*; his *Erinnyes*, 1872, was performed with incidental music by Massenet in 1873.

JACQUES OFFENBACH (1819–1880). Franco-German composer. His witty operetta, *Fair Helen*, with libretto by Meilhac and Halévy, was first performed in 1864.

DANTE GABRIEL ROSSETTI (1828–1882). English poet and painter. As prime mover of the Pre-Raphaelite group Rossetti often illustrated this school's ideal of the unity of the arts by using the same theme in literature and painting. His sonnet, *Cassandra*, accompanied a drawing of 1859, a study for a painting never executed. The ballad, *Troy Town*, 1869–1870, also inspired a drawing for a painting never undertaken.

WILLIAM MORRIS (1834–1896). English poet, prose writer, artist, and craftsman, an influential member of the Pre-Raphaelite group. Between 1857 and 1865 he planned a group of poems centred about Troy. The series was abandoned, but six completed poems, with fragments of others, have been published as *Scenes from the Fall of Troy*. They are: *Helen Arming Paris*; *The Defiance of the Greeks*; *Hector's Last Battle*; *Hector Brought Dead to Troy*; *Helen's Chamber*; *Achilles' Love Letter*; *The Descent from the Wooden Horse*; and *Helen and Menelaus*. Strongly influenced by medieval Troy romances, these poems are the most complete group of such works produced by the romantic revival in England.

SAMUEL BUTLER (1835–1902). English author. His *Authoress of the Odyssey*, 1897, contending that no man of Homer's time could have written so understandingly of women's interests, and hence, a woman, perhaps Nausicaä herself, was the author, was the forerunner of several fictional works on this theme.

ANDREW LANG (1844–1912). English author and translator. Best known for his fairy tales and his part in translations of the *Iliad* and the *Odyssey*, Lang also treated Trojan themes in extended poems, such as *Helen of Troy*, 1882, and shorter poems collected in 1888 and 1898, including *The Shade of Helen* and a group dealing with Odysseus.

20th Century

CAMILLE SAINT-SAËNS (1835–1921). French composer: words and music of the opera, *Hélène*, 1904.

ERNEST MYERS (1844–1921). English classicist and poet. Author of lines on Achilles quoted (p.57).

ROBERT BRIDGES (1844–1930). English poet: dramatic poems, *Achilles in Scyros* and *The Return of Ulysses*.

GIOVANNI PASCOLI (1855–1912). Italian poet and critic: his *Ultimo Viaggio*, 1904, treats of Ulysses' death.

GERHARDT HAUPTMANN (1862–1946). German dramatist and novelist. Play: *The Bow of Odysseus*, 1914.

GABRIELE D'ANNUNZIO (1862–1946). Italian poet and dramatist: his *Laus Vitae* contains poetic treatments of the Ulysses story.

RICHARD STRAUSS (1864–1949). German composer: music for Trojan and other librettos by von Hofmannsthal.

RICHARD LE GALLIENNE (1866–1947). English poet and essayist: his *Orestes*, a verse tragedy, was written for music composed by Massenet for Leconte de Lisle's *Erinnyes*.

HUGO VON HOFMANNSTHAL (1874–1929). Austrian poet and dramatist. His *Elektra*, 1903, adapted from Sophocles, was set to music by Richard Strauss in 1909; his *Egyptian Helen*, a variant of the legend that Helen never went to Troy, produced with music by Strauss, 1927.

JOHN ERSKINE (1879–1951). American author: satiric novels, *The Private Life of Helen of Troy*, 1925; *Penelope's Man*, 1928; *Helen Retires*, 1934.

JOHN MASEFIELD (1878–). English poet and prose writer. His works on Trojan themes are: *A King's Daughter*, 1923 (a verse tragedy on Helen and Jezebel); *The Taking of Helen*, a short story; and *A Tale of Troy*, 1932 (dramatic stanzas in various metres).

JEAN GIRAUDOUX (1882–1944). French dramatist and author: *Elpenor*, 1919, a prose variant of a theme from the *Odyssey*, was translated into English in 1959; *La Guerre de Troie n'aura pas Lieu*, 'The Trojan War Will Not Take Place', was produced in Paris in 1935 and in New York as *The Tiger at the Gates*, in 1955. It suggests that the Trojan war was not inevitable, as it was precipitated by a mere 'incident' after Hector and Ajax had arrived at a peaceful settlement. His *Electra* was produced in Paris in 1937.

JAMES JOYCE (1882–1941). Irish novelist. His *Ulysses*, 1922, sets the story in contemporary Dublin, changes the relationship of the characters, and the motivation of actions.

SARA TEASDALE (1884–1933). American poet: *Helen of Troy*, 1911.

NIKOS KAZANTZAKIS (1885–1957). Greek poet and novelist: *Odysseus*, published in modern Greek verse in 1938 and in English verse translation in 1958 as *The Odyssey, a Modern Sequel*, begins with the hero's adventures near the end of the *Odyssey* and continues in a series of events very different from the *Telegonia*, including an abduction of Helen, the destruction of Knossos, and death in the icy seas.

HILDA DOOLITTLE ALDINGTON (H.D.). (1886–1961). American poet: *Helen in Egypt*, 1961. A semi-dramatic lyric poem based on the legend that Helen did not go to Troy and including her sojourn with Achilles in the White Island.

EUGENE O'NEILL (1888–1953). American dramatist: his *Mourning Becomes Electra*, 1931, is a trilogy modelled on Aeschylus' *Oresteia*, set in a New England seaside town. *The Homecoming* is the equivalent of *Agamemnon*; *The Hunted*, of *The Libation Bearers*; *The Haunted*, of *The Eumenides*.

THOMAS STEARNS ELIOT (1888–). English poet. His drama, *Family Reunion*, based rather distantly on the vengeance of Orestes, is set in contemporary England.

FRANZ WERFEL (1890–1945). Austrian dramatist. His *Trojan Women* was produced in 1914.

CHRISTOPHER MORLEY (1890–1957). American author: his *Trojan Horse*, 1937, retells in contemporary terms the story of Troilus and Cressida.

ARCHIBALD MACLEISH (1892–). American poet: his *Trojan Horse*, a radio play, was produced by the British Broadcasting Corporation in 1952.

ROBERT GRAVES (1895–). English poet, novelist, and translator. *Homer's Daughter*, a novel, 1955, is based on the premise that the *Odyssey* was composed by Nausicaä; *The Anger of Achilles*, 1959, translates the *Iliad* into modern English prose and poetry.

JEAN GIONO (1895–). French author. In his *Birth of the Odyssey*, 1938, Odysseus invents the account of his adventures to explain the time spent on his homeward journey.

STEPHEN VINCENT BENÉT (1898–1943). American author. His two *Visions of Helen* appeared in 1931; the *First Vision of Helen* deals with one of her early loves; the *Last Vision of Helen*, with her disappearance by merging with the Sphinx.

GEORGE ANTHEIL (1900–). American composer: music for Erskine's *Helen Retires.*

HUGH WYSTON AUDEN (1907–). English poet. His *Shield of Achilles*, 1955, reflects the disillusionment of World War II.

ERNST SCHNABEL (1913–). German author. His novel, *On the Voyage Home*, 1957, translated into English in 1958, suggests that Homer manipulated the closing events of Odysseus' voyage to fit his preconceived pattern for the *Odyssey*.

THE CLASSICS ILLUSTRATED. These 'comic books' represent twentieth-century descendants of the chapbooks of Troy (*see* above), but with emphasis on pictures rather than text: No. 77, *The Iliad* (1950); No. 81, *The Odyssey* (1951).

MOTION PICTURES: *Ulysses* (1955), produced by Paramount; *Helen of Troy* (1956), produced by Warner Brothers; *The Trojan Horse* (1962), produced by Colorama Features, Inc.; *Electra*, based on Euripides' play, produced by Michael Cacoyannis, 1962.

JOHN LATOUCHE (1917–1956). American lyricist. Libretto for musical comedy, *The Golden Apple* (1954), which retells the judgment of Paris and abduction of Helen in terms of life in a small American town on the Pacific Coast, near Mount Olympus, about 1900–1910.

JEROME MOROSS (1911–). American composer. Music for *The Golden Apple* (1954).

MICHAEL TIPPET (1905–). English composer. Words and music for the opera, *King Priam*, Coventry and London (1962). It tells the Trojan legend from the birth of Paris to Troy's fall and the death of Priam.

THE SUICIDE OF AJAX. Carnelian scarab (impression, enlarged). Etruscan, late fifth century B.C. New York, Metropolitan Museum of Art, 41.160.489. Bequest of William Gedney Beatty, 1941.

APPENDIX B

A SELECTION OF WORKS OF ART DEALING WITH TROJAN THEMES

Any practicable list of such examples is necessarily even less complete than one of literary sources. This selection can suggest only a small portion of works extant today, and it omits mention of many lost examples, known through such ancient descriptions as those of Pliny (c. A.D. 23–79), *Natural History*, and Pausanias (second century A.D.), *Description of Greece*. Where the material is very plentiful and the objects comparatively similar, as in the case of Greek vases and classical gems, mention has necessarily been summary.

900–700 B.C.

The first mention of the Trojan legend in art occurs in its first expression in literature. Helen (*Iliad*, III,125–128) sits in the palace at Troy

> '. . . . . . weaving a great web
> a red folding robe, and working into it the numerous struggles
> of Trojans, breakers of horses, and bronze-armoured Achaians.'

7th Century B.C. *or Earlier*

JUDGMENT OF PARIS, on an ivory comb from Sparta, is one of the oldest known representations of a scene from Trojan legend, dating within a few centuries of Homer's time. Athens, National Museum. (Pl. 10e in the *Journal of Hellenic Studies*, Vol. LXVIII (1948).)

7th Century B.C.

PAINTED VASES from the Greek world of this time have preserved the greatest number of Trojan scenes from classical culture. Among these are a krater from Caere showing the blinding of Polyphemus (Rome, Conservatori Museum); a vase with Menelaus and his companions (Berlin, Antiquarium, A42); and a Rhodian plate with the combat of Greeks and Trojans over the body of Euphorbus (London, British Museum, Cat. No. A749).

VASE IN RELIEF, recently found in Mykonos, shows the Wooden Horse and the Fall of Troy.

ORNAMENTAL BRONZES with Trojan themes include a relief, perhaps used as furniture decoration, showing two scenes, interpreted as the return of Agamemnon and Clytemnestra killing Cassandra (Pl. 109), Athens Museum. An engraved bronze channel probably showing Peleus choosing Thetis from among the dancing Nereids, dating from the mid-century, is in the Metropolitan Museum, New York (58.11.6). (*See* Dietrich von Bothmer, *Newly Acquired Bronzes*, *Bulletin of The Metropolitan Museum of Art*, new ser., Vol. XIX (Jan., 1961), pp. 136–137, fig. 6.)

7th Century B.C. *and Later*

ENGRAVED GEMS AND CAMEOS dating from this century throughout Roman times abound in Trojan subjects. An early steatite gem in the Metropolitan Museum (42.11.13) shows the suicide of Ajax; an Etruscan scarab in the same museum shows the Greeks emerging from the Wooden Horse (32.11.7) and Achilles wounded in the heel by an arrow (21.88.41). Also in the Metropolitan Museum is a Roman intaglio gem of Odysseus (41.160.766) (Pl. 114). A fifth-century scarab in the British Museum shows the serpents slaying Laocoön and his sons; the parting of Hector and Andromache appears on gems in the State Museum, Berlin.

6th Century B.C.

VASES WITH TROJAN SUBJECTS remain in considerable numbers from the sixth century; eight examples are illustrated in this volume. Favourite themes are Achilles lying in wait for Troilus, as shown in Plates 2 and 40 and the suicide of Ajax. The blinding of Polyphemus appears on a black-figured kylix in the Bibliothèque Nationale, Paris (Pl. 125), and on a Corinthian alabastron in the Metropolitan Museum, New York (X.22.20).

A FRIEZE FROM THE SIXTH-CENTURY TREASURY OF THE SIPHNIANS AT DELPHI shows Menelaus and other Greeks in combat with Hector and other Trojans over the body of Euphorbus (Delphi Museum).

ORNAMENTAL BRONZES. Among surviving examples of decorative arts of this century are such examples as the relief showing the suicide of Ajax (Athens, National Museum), and a bronze shield band with the slaying of Agamemnon (Pl.107), Olympia Museum. (*See* Note on p.132.)

6th–5th Century B.C.

ETRUSCAN BRONZE SHE-WOLF, nurse of Romulus and Remus (Pl.181). Rome, Conservatori Museum. (H. Stuart Jones, *Catalogue of Ancient Sculptures . . . Palazzo dei Conservatori*, Oxford, 1926, pp.56–58, Pl.17.)

5th Century B.C.

VASES PAINTED WITH TROJAN SCENES become too numerous to mention by the fifth century; 25 examples are illustrated in this volume.

POLYGNOTOS (fl.c.475–447). No works by Polygnotos or any of the other great painters of ancient Greece remain, but descriptions by Pliny, Pausanias, and others mention many Trojan scenes.

Polygnotos painted at least two great pictures of the Iliupersis, or Sack of Troy—one in the Painted Porch at Athens (Paus. I, XV), one in the Club Rooms of the Knidians at Delphi (Paus. X,XXVff.). Here he painted also Odysseus in the Underworld (Paus. X,XXVIIIff.).

In the temple of Athena Areia at Plataea he painted 'Odysseus after he had killed the suitors' (Paus. IX,iv).

A number of paintings attributed to him were in the Picture Collection of the Propylaea at Athens: Achilles in Scyros, Diomedes Stealing the Palladium, Odysseus and the Bow of Philoctetes, the Sacrifice of Polyxena, Odysseus and Nausicaä, and Orestes Slaying Aegisthus (Paus. I,XXII).

ARISTOPHON. Greek painter, Polygnotos' brother, was celebrated, says Pliny (XXXV,40) for a picture showing Priam, Helen, Credulity, Odysseus, Deiphobus, and Guile. He also painted the story of Laomedon, Hercules, Poseidon, and the walls of Troy.

APOLLODORUS. Greek painter, painted 'an Ajax struck by lightning' which was at Pergamon in Pliny's time (Pliny, XXXV,36). This was Ajax son of Oïleus, shipwrecked on his homeward way because of his insult to Cassandra.

TIMANTHES. Greek painter, painted several Trojan scenes. The most famous was the sacrifice of Iphigenia, of which the Roman painting (Pl.33) is believed to be a copy. He also won the prize over the slightly younger Parrhasius for his picture of Ajax and the award of Achilles' arms (Pliny, XXXV,36).

PANAEUS. Greek painter, painted on or near the throne of the statue of Zeus in the temple of Zeus at Olympia pictures of Ajax and Cassandra and of Achilles supporting Penthesilea (Paus. V,XI).

PHIDIAS. Greek sculptor, or his pupil Agoracritus (Paus. I,XXIII) carved Leda with Helen and Nemesis, and Agamemnon, Menelaus, and Pyrrhus. Later opinion inclines to assign these to Agoracritus. No original work by Phidias or any of the named Greek sculptors dealing with the Trojan story is known to remain today.

ONATAS. Greek sculptor, made a group of nine bronze statues showing Nestor and the Greek warriors who drew lots to fight Hector in single combat (*Iliad*, VII,161ff.). When Pausanias saw these at Elis (Paus. V,XXV) the figure of Odysseus had been taken to Rome by Nero.

LYCIUS. Greek sculptor, son of Myron, made a group of warriors which Pausanias saw at Olympia (Paus. V,XXII). They were opposing pairs: Paris with Menelaus; Achilles with Memnon; Odysseus with Helenus; Diomedes with Aeneas; and Ajax Telamon with Deiphobus. They were arranged about a group of Thetis and Aurora imploring the favour of Zeus for their sons, Achilles and Memnon.

STRONGYLION. Greek sculptor, made a Trojan horse which Pausanias saw on the Acropolis at Athens (Paus. I,XXIII). The base with the sculptor's name and that of the man dedicating the group, was found on the Acropolis from 1840 to 1890.

Odysseus Slaying the Suitors and other reliefs of a city at war, possibly Troy, appear on the inner wall of a tomb at Gjölbaschi in Lycia, Asia Minor. (These reliefs are discussed and illustrated by C. E. Korte, *Zu dem Fries von Gjölbaschi* in *Jahrbuch der k.k deutsch. Archäol. Instituts*, Vol.XXXI (1916), pp.257–288.)

THE LOST ORIGINAL OF THE STATUE OF PROTESILAUS, a copy of which is in the Metropolitan Museum (25.116) and a torso and base of another copy in the British Museum, may have belonged to the fifth century.

THE LOST GREEK ORIGINAL OF THE STATUE OF DIOMEDES in the Munich Museum was also a work of this century.

TERRACOTTA RELIEFS, characteristic of the fifth century, include a mourning Penelope and an Eurykleia washing the feet of Odysseus (Rome, Vatican), the return of Odysseus (Pl. 147) and Eurykleia washing the feet of Odysseus (Pl.146), both in the Metropolitan Museum (30.11.9 and 25.78.26), and the weighing of the ransom for Hector's body (Toronto Museum).

ANTIPHANES (c.400). Greek sculptor, said by Pausanias (x,IX) to have made a statue of the Trojan Horse dedicated at Delphi.

5th–4th Century B.C.

PARRHASIUS. Greek painter who was defeated by Timanthes in the contest for a picture of Ajax and the award of Achilles' arms, painted other Trojan scenes, of which Pliny says (xxxv, 36) 'His Aeneas, Castor, and Pollux . . . all in the same picture are also highly praised, and likewise a group of Telephus with Achilles, Agamemnon, and Odysseus.' (Compare with same subject in the small frieze of the Altar of Zeus at Pergamon.)

ZEUXIS. Greek painter, painted a Penelope that 'seemed to portray morality' (Pliny, xxxv, 36). He also painted a Helen, which Pliny saw in the Portico of Philip in Rome (xxxv,36). This was evidently the one described by Cicero in *De Inventione* as a composite of the best features of five maidens of Cortona, whose citizens commissioned it. Aelian says (*Varia Historia*, IV, 12) that Helen was painted nude, evidently an innovation, as the artist collected an admission fee for showing it.

4th Century B.C.

THE ETRUSCAN 'TOMB OF ORCUS' at Tarquinia, discovered in 1868, belongs to this century. In it are painted Odysseus blinding Polyphemus and a scene in Hades in which Agamemnon appears.

AN ETRUSCAN SARCOPHAGUS of carved and polychromed stone shows the sacrifice of Trojan prisoners at Patroclus' tomb, the sacrifice of Polyxena, Odysseus attacking Circe, and Odysseus and Tiresias (Orvieto, Museo del Opera). *Art and Archaeology*, Vol.VI, No.5 (Nov., 1917), pp.229–232.

ANTIPHILUS. Greek painter, painted a 'famous picture of Hesione' (Pliny, xxxv,37).

ANTHENION. Greek painter, did 'an Achilles disguised in female dress' (Pliny, xxxv,40).

PAMPHILUS. Greek painter, did an 'Odysseus on his raft' (Pliny, xxxv,36).

EUPHRANOR. Greek painter and sculptor. His painting of Odysseus feigning madness was in Ephesus in Pliny's time (xxxv,40); his statue of Paris, Pliny says (xxxiv,19), displayed the Trojan as at once 'the judge of the goddesses, the lover of Helen, and yet the slayer of Achilles.' This may have been the original of the Vatican statue (255), in which the apple and other portions are restorations.

SCOPAS. Greek sculptor. He produced, according to Pliny (xxxvi,4), at least two Trojan works: Poseidon with Thetis and Achilles, in a temple of the Circus of Domitian in Rome, and an Achilles and Cheiron, also in Rome.

SILANION. Greek sculptor, 'made a famous Achilles' in bronze, says Pliny (xxxiv,19).

4th–3rd Century B.C.

ETRUSCAN BRONZE MIRRORS, largely from these centuries, are engraved on their backs with many scenes and characters of the war. Favourite scenes are the judgment of Paris and the persuasion of Helen. Among examples in the Metropolitan Museum are: the persuasion of Helen, c.400–350 (97.22.16); Achilles slaying Memnon, early fourth century (22.139.84); Odysseus attacking Circe, mid-fourth century (09.221.17); Alexander, Helen, Chryseis (probably an error for Briseis), with Achilles, 300–250 (21.88.27); Menelaus, Helen, Thetis, and Achilles, 300–250 (21.88.28).

ARTEMON. Greek painter, painted 'the story of Laomedon and his bargain with Hercules and Neptune' (Pliny, xxxv,40). This was the story leading up to the first capture of Troy. The tentative date is deduced from the mention of Artemon's painting a portrait of a Queen Stratonice.

THEORUS. Greek painter, made an 'Orestes killing his mother and Aegisthus, and the Trojan war in a series of pictures now in Philippus' Portico in Rome, and a Cassandra in the shrine of Concord' (Pliny, xxxv,40).

3rd Century B.C.

A MARBLE GROUP OF ARTEMIS RESCUING IPHIGENIA, Copenhagen, Ny Carlsberg Glyptothek. (Margarete Bieber, *The Sculpture of the Hellenistic Age*, 1955, pp.77–78, figs.268–271.)

ACHILLES SLAYING TROJAN CAPTIVES AT THE FUNERAL OF PATROCLUS, an early third-century painting, was found at Vulci in 1857 in an Etruscan tomb, called from its discoverer the 'François Tomb' (Pl.73). It and a much damaged Ajax and Cassandra are in the Torlonia Collection, Villa Albani, Rome.

MENELAUS WITH THE BODY OF PATROCLUS, the original sculptured group, copies of which are in the Loggia dei Lanzi and in the Pitti Palace, Florence, and in various other collections, probably dates from this century. One of the copies is the famous battered stump in Rome known as Pasquino.

3rd–2nd Century B.C.

ETRUSCAN BURIAL URNS WITH TROJAN SCENES IN RELIEF belong largely to these centuries, although a number of them are either earlier or later. Examples of favourite subjects are: Paris recognized as the son of Priam (Volterra, Guarnacci Museum); the abduction of Helen (Volterra and British Museum); the sacrifice of Iphigenia (Volterra); Philoctetes in Lemnos (Volterra); the death of Troilus (Volterra); the sacrifice of Trojan prisoners at the funeral of Patroclus (Orvieto, Museo dell' Opera); the sacrifice of Polyxena (Orvieto); the Amazons come to aid the Trojans (Volterra); Odysseus and the Sirens (Volterra; British Museum); Polyphemus hurling rocks at the ship of Odysseus (Leyden Museum); Orestes killing his mother (Rome, Vatican).
(Opinion is considerably divided on the dating of these reliefs. *See* G. M. A. Hanfmann, *Etruscan Reliefs of the Hellenistic Period*, in *Journal of Hellenic Studies*, Vol.LXV (1945), pp.45–57.)

'MEGARIAN' BOWLS OF STAMPED TERRACOTTA frequently display scenes from the Troy legend seemingly based on the epics and on the plays of Euripides. Among such are: a bowl in the Metropolitan Museum (31.11.2), with scenes based on *Iphigenia in Aulis*; a similar bowl in Berlin continuing the action of the play; five bowls in Berlin with scenes illustrating the epics (the exploits of Achilles, Priam begging Hector's body, the arrival of Penthesilea, the murder of Agamemnon, and scenes from the *Odyssey*); a bowl in Athens with the abduction of Helen by Theseus.
(The bowls are published in Kurt Weitzmann's *Ancient Book Illumination*, Harvard University Press, 1959, *passim*, together with other valuable material on Trojan representations.)

2nd Century B.C.

LAOCOÖN AND HIS SONS. The original group, by the sculptors Agesandros, Polydoros, and Athenodorus (Pliny, XXXVI,4), probably belonged to the second century. The copy of it, now in the Vatican, was discovered near Nero's Golden House in Rome in 1506 (Pl.91).

THE SMALL FRIEZE OF THE ALTAR OF ZEUS AT PERGAMON touches upon the Trojan legend, representing incidents from the life of Telephus, son of Hercules and Auge, who became king of Mysia and the local hero from whom inhabitants of the country claimed descent.
Among the incidents shown are: Telephus suckled by a doe while Hercules looks on; Teuthras welcoming Auge; a battle scene; the Greeks about to flee by ship; Telephus at Argos, with Agamemnon and Odysseus (cf. painting by Parrhasius); and Telephus threatening to kill the infant Orestes. Berlin, State Museum. (Described and illustrated by Gerda Bruns, *Der Grosse Altar von Pergamon*, Berlin, 1949.)

1st Century B.C.

TIMOMACHUS. Greek painter. According to Pliny (XXXV,40), he painted an Ajax, an Iphigenia in Tauris, and an Orestes. Some place the artist earlier.

EXISTING WALL PAINTINGS BY UNKNOWN ARTISTS INCLUDE:

The *Odyssey* landscapes, Vatican Library, Rome, discovered on the Esquiline Hill, 1848 (Pls.131,132,135).

Frescoes illustrating the *Iliad* and cyclic epics (House of the Cryptoporticus), Pompeii.
Achilles in Scyros (House of the Centaur), Pompeii.

SCULPTURE

The Aeneas relief on the Altar of Peace in Rome (13–9 B.C.) a purposeful link between Troy and Rome (Pl.157).

1st Century B.C.–*1st Century* A.D.

SCULPTURE

Pictorial reliefs, such as the persuasion of Helen, Naples, National Museum (Pl.21).

METALWORK

Among examples of Trojan scenes in Roman silver of this period are: two cups in the National Museum, Copenhagen, one showing the Greek camp asleep and Priam ransoming Hector's body; the other, scenes from the story of Philoctetes. (*See* K. Friis Johansen, *Hoby-Fundet, Nordiske Fortidsminder*, Vol.II, Pt.3 (1923), with résumé in French by E. Philpot.)
Two silver jugs in the Bibliothèque Nationale, Paris, show scenes from the life of Achilles. On one are the death of Patroclus and the ransom-

ing of Hector's body; on the other, the dragging of Hector's body and Achilles' death. (*See* Ernest Babelon, *Le Trésor d'Argenterie de Berthouville*, Paris, 1916, pp.81–87, Pls.v–viii, and Karl Lehmann-Hartleben, *Two Roman Silver Jugs* in *American Journal of Archaeology*, Vol.xlii (1938), pp.82–105 and Pls.xiii–xv).

The 'Corsini cup', discovered at Anzio, now in the Palazzo Corsini, Rome (1961), shows the judgment of Orestes at the Areopagus. (*See* G. M. A. Richter, *Ancient Italy*, University of Michigan, 1955, pp.59, 94, and fig.269.)

A recently acquired cup in the British Museum (1960.2.11) shows the adventures of Orestes and Iphigenia. (*See* P. E. Corbett and D. E. Strong, *Three Roman Silver Cups, British Museum Quarterly*, new series, Vol.xxiii (April 1961), pp.68–83.)

1st Century A.D.

PAINTING.

PAINTINGS IN SITU IN POMPEII INCLUDE:

Ulysses and Penelope (Macellum). Pl.150.

Iphigenia, Orestes, and Pylades in Tauris (House of Pinarius Cerialis). Pl.112.

Frescoes illustrating the *Iliad* (House of M. Lorei Tiburtini or Octavianus Quartianus).

Agamemnon and the hind of Diana (House of the Vettii).

Orestes and Pylades in Tauris (House of the Vettii).

Building of the walls of Troy; Thetis watching the forging of Achilles' arms (House of Siriacus).

Achilles in Scyros; judgment of Paris; Iphigenia, Orestes, and Pylades in Tauris (House of Holconius Rufus).

Priam begging the body of Hector; Iphigenia, Orestes, and Pylades in Tauris (House of the Centaur).

Wooden Horse brought into Troy; death of Laocoön; meeting of Menelaus and Helen, with Cassandra embracing the image of Artemis (House of Menander).

Aeneas rescuing Anchises and Ascanius (Shop in the Via dell'Abbondanza).

Scenes from the *Iliad* in stucco relief (House of the Lararium or Sacello Iliaca).

(The dating of these paintings is taken from Karl Schefold's *Die Wände Pompeiis*, Berlin, 1957. The *Iliad* series in the House of the Cryptoporticus and the House of Octavianus Quartianus are fully discussed and illustrated in Vittorio Spinazzola, *Pompeii alla luce degli scavi nuovi di Via dell'Abbondanza* (Anni 1910–1923), Rome, 1953, Vol.ii, pp.867 ff. G. E. Rizzo's *La Pittura Ellenistico-Romana*, Milan, 1929, is also invaluable both for illustrations and for descriptions.)

PAINTINGS IN SITU IN ROME INCLUDE:

An almost obliterated disembarkation of Paris and Helen in the 'Hall of Isis' beneath the basilica of the Flavian Palace on the Palatine, probably painted in Caligula's time (37–41). This room was almost destroyed by the foundation walls of Nero's *Domus Transitoria*.

A farewell of Hector and Andromache and a Paris and Helen, on the ceiling of Room 80, Nero's Golden House, A.D. 64–68?

OUTSTANDING PAINTINGS OF TROJAN SCENES IN MUSEUMS INCLUDE:

The judgment of Paris, Naples, National Museum (Pl.9).

Cheiron and Achilles, Naples, National Museum (Pl.29).

Achilles on Scyros, Naples, National Museum (Pl.31).

The sacrifice of Iphigenia, Naples, National Museum (Pl.33).

Athena restraining the anger of Achilles (incomplete), Naples, National Museum.

The surrender of Briseis, Naples, National Museum (Pl.44).

Caricature of Aeneas rescuing Anchises and Ascanius, Naples, National Museum (Pl.165).

The Wooden Horse brought into Troy, Naples, National Museum (Pl.93).

Polyphemus hurling a rock at Odysseus, detail of a painting from Boscotrecase (20.192.17), New York, Metropolitan Museum (Pl.129).

MOSAICS.

Athena restraining the anger of Achilles, Naples, National Museum, probably of this century, shows entire composition corresponding to incomplete painting listed above (Pl.42).

SCULPTURE.

The well-known *Tabulae Iliacae* are usually assigned to this century because of their inscriptions and their emphasis on Aeneas. These *tabulae* are tablets carved in low relief, originally painted, showing scenes from the Trojan war with inscriptions explaining the action. They have been thought to have been used in the teaching of the legend of the Romans' Trojan origin. The largest of these fragments (Fig. 1), together with several smaller pieces, is in the Capitoline Museum, Rome, while others are scattered through various collections; one fragment is in the Metropolitan Museum (24.97.11).

The Vatican Library possesses a fragment with scenes from the *Odyssey*.

Closely related to the *tabulae* is a fragment representing the Shield of Achilles (Pl.63) in the Capitoline Museum, Rome.

For the *tabulae* in general *see* Otto Jahn, *Griechische Bilderchroniken*, Bonn, 1873. The pieces in the Capitoline Museum are published in H. Stuart Jones' *Catalogue of Ancient Sculptures . . . Museo Capitolino*, Oxford, 1912, pp.165–176, Pl. 41; that in the Metropolitan Museum, in G. M. A. Richter's *Catalogue of Greek Sculptures in the Metropolitan Museum*, Cambridge (Mass.), 1954, pp.116–117, Pls.CLXI and CLXII, and by Kazimiere Bulas, *New Illustrations to the Iliad* in *American Journal of Archaeology*, Vol.LIV (1950), pp.112–118, Pls.XVIII–XX A–B. The fragment from the *Odyssey* is published by Kurt Weitzmann, *A Tabula Odysseaca*, in *American Journal of Archaeology*, Vol.XLV (1941), pp.166–181, figs. 1–4.

1st–2nd Century A.D.

MOSAICS.

Among mosaics of this century, one found in Tunisia in the 1890's shows the farewell of Dido and Aeneas (Tunis, Musée Aloui).

A mosaic found at Ampurias shows the sacrifice of Iphigenia. Barcelona, Archaeological Museum. (*Ars Hispania*, Vol.II, 1947, p.154, Pl.1.)

2nd Century A.D.

MOSAICS.

Achilles dragging Hector's body, Rome, Vatican.

Many fine Graeco-Roman mosaics with Trojan subjects have been discovered at Antioch. These are described and illustrated in Doro Levi's *Antioch Mosaic Pavements*, Princeton, 1947.

SCULPTURE.

ROMAN PICTORIAL RELIEFS of Trojan subjects are ascribed to this century. Among them are examples illustrating Paris and Eros, Paris and Oenone, and the theft of the Palladium, Rome, Villa Spada (*see* A. J. B. Wace, *The Reliefs of the Villa Spada*, in *Papers of the British School in Rome*, Vol.V (1910, pp.65–200); the forging of the armour of Achilles, Rome, Conservatori Museum (*see* H. Stuart Jones, *Catalogue of Ancient Sculptures . . . Palazzo Conservatori*, Oxford, 1926, p.281, Pl.112).

THE ALTAR dedicated in A.D. 124, which shows the wolf suckling Romulus and Remus, Rome, Terme Museum (Pl.178).

2nd–3rd Century A.D.

SCULPTURE.

NUMEROUS ROMAN SARCOPHAGI of this period show reliefs of Trojan scenes. Typical examples are: the gods assembling for the marriage feast of Peleus (Rome, Villa Albani, Pl.3); the judgment of Paris (Rome, Villa Medici); the story of Protesilaus and Laodamia, Achilles supporting Penthesilea, and the history of Orestes (Rome, Vatican); the history of Orestes (Rome, Lateran); the history of Orestes (Madrid); Achilles in Scyros (Rome, Capitoline Museum); Odysseus recognized by his dog Argos (Naples, San Martino, Pl.145). (*See* Carl Robert, *Die antiken Sarkophagreliefs*, Berlin, 1890, Vol.II, *Mythologische Cyklen*.)

ROMAN RELIEF OF THE JUDGMENT OF PARIS in a niche of the stage in the theatre at Sabratha, Leptis Magna (Pl.10).

3rd Century A.D.

MOSIACS AND METALWORK.

MOSAIC OF ODYSSEUS ESCAPING FROM THE CAVE OF POLYPHEMUS (early in century), Rome, Terme Museum.

MOSAIC OF ULYSSES AND THE SIRENS, found in Ameixial, Portugal. Belem, Archaeological Museum.

TWO WOODEN SHIELDS WITH TROJAN SCENES are among those discovered at Dura Europos in Mesopotamia in the 1930's. One shows Greeks and Amazons in combat, with Achilles about to slay Penthesilea; the other, the Wooden Horse and the sack of Troy. New Haven, Yale University Museum. (*See Yale University Excavations at Dura Europos, 7th and 8th Seasons*, 1933–34; 34–35, ed. by M. I. Rostovtzeff, F. E. Brown, and C. B. Welles, New Haven, 1939, pp.332–49; 350–53, Pls.XLII, XLV.)

BRONZE RELIEF OF SCENES FROM THE LIFE OF ACHILLES on a Roman triumphal chariot. Rome, Conservatori Museum. (*See* H. Stuart Jones, *Catalogue . . . of the Palazzo Conservatori*, Oxford, 1926, pp.179–187, Pls.68–73.)

4th Century

MOSAICS.

A MOSAIC WITH SCENES FROM THE STORY OF AENEAS AND DIDO, discovered in the bath of a Roman house at Low Ham, Somerset, England, 1945, County Museum, Somerset (Pl.169).

MOSAIC OF ULYSSES AND POLYPHEMUS, Piazza Armerina, Sicily.

SCULPTURE.

A band of marble relief showing scenes from the life of Achilles, beginning with the hero's birth and ending with the dragging of Hector's body. In the Middle Ages this was enclosed in a marble panel and used in the Church of S. Maria in Aracoeli, Rome. Rome, Capitol Collections. (*See* H. Stuart Jones, *Catalogue of Ancient Sculptures . . . Museo Capitolino*, Oxford, 1912, pp.45–47, Pl.9.)

METALWORK.

A silver dish with the story of Achilles' youth, in relief, discovered in 1962 in Switzerland, is assigned to this century. Roman Museum, Augst, near Basel.

5th Century

MANUSCRIPTS.

The only known classical examples of illustrated manuscripts of the *Iliad* and the *Aeneid* are believed to date from this century. These are: the Ambrosiana *Iliad*, Milan, Ambrosian Library, cod.F.205; the Vatican Vergil, Rome, Vatican Library, cod.vat.lat.3225 (Pls. 90,174,176); and the Codex Romanus, Rome, Vatican Library, cod.vat.lat.3867 (Pls.158,170), its *Aeneid* illustrations less classic in style than the preceding.

9th Century

TEXTILE.

A hanging embroidered with the fall of Troy is said, on the doubtful authority of Ingulf's *History of the Abbey of Croylands*, to have been given to this abbey in the ninth century by Witlaf, king of Mercia. This history, however, is probably later than Ingulf (d.1109). (*See* Francisque Michel, *Recherches sur le commerce, la fabrication et l'usage des étoffes de soie, d'or, et d'argent*, Paris, 1852, Vol.I, p.182.)

10th Century

MANUSCRIPT.

One of two illustrated manuscripts of the *Aeneid* done between the fifth and fifteenth centuries dates from this period. Naples, National Library, cod. olim Vienna 58. (*See* Erwin Panofsky, *Meaning in the Visual Arts*, New York, 1955, p.47, n.20 and fig.7.)

12th Century

LITERARY ALLUSIONS.

From this century come such literary allusions to the Trojan story in art as the famous references to wall paintings in *De Claustro Anime* and a passage in Chréstien de Troyes' *Erec et Enide* describing a saddle with the story of Dido and Aeneas carved on its ivory bows.

12th–13th Century

MANUSCRIPT of French *Éneas* romance. Florence, Bibioteca Laurenziana, Plut.XLI, cod.44.

13th Century

MANUSCRIPTS.

Illustrated manuscripts of Troy romances become numerous about 1250. Among outstanding examples are:

MS of Heinrich von Veldecke's *Eneide*, German. Berlin, National Library, cod.germ.fol.282; (Pls. 171,175,184).

MS of von Veldecke's *Eneide*. Munich, State Library, cod.germ.57.

Earliest known illustrated MS of Benoit de Sainte-More's *Roman de Troie*, French (1264). Paris, Bibliothèque Nationale, MS fr. 1610, and four missing pages now in private collection, Holland (Pl.70). (*See* Fritz Saxl, *The Troy Romances* in his *Lectures*, London, Warburg Institute ,1957: von Veldecke, pp.128–129, Pls.72b–73b; Benoit, pp.129–130, Pls.74–75 a–b.)

A MS of the *Histoire Universelle* (c.1285), probably made in Acre. London, British Museum, Add. MS 15268. (*See* Hugo Buchthal, *Miniature Painting in the Latin Kingdom of Jerusalem*, London, Warburg Institute, 1957, pp.79–83, Pls.111, 113c,114c,116c.)

14th Century

PAINTING AND SCULPTURE.

The fourteenth century saw a blossoming in art of scenes from the Trojan legend and of the Nine Heroes or Worthies (including Hector of Troy), who are first met in Jacques de Longuyon's *Vows of the Peacock*, 1310.

Badly damaged frescoes of a Trojan battle scene

(c.1313) still exist in the Loggia dei Cavalieri at Treviso, unidentifiable except for names inscribed. (*See* Note on p.7.)

Frescoes, now lost, in the Visconti Palace at Milan (after 1339), showing ancient and later heroes, including Hector, Aeneas, and Hercules. Not the traditional group.

The Nine Heroes appear as polychromed statues in niches of the Hansa Saal of the Council House at Cologne. (Roger Loomis and Laura Hibbard Loomis, *Arthurian Legends in Medieval Art,* New York, 1938, p.38, date the statues c.1325. Robert L. Wyss, *Die Neun Helden* in *Zeitschrift für schweizerische Archäologie und Kunstgeschichte*, Band 17, Heft II, Basel, 1957, p.86 and Pl.19, dates them later.)

The painted ceiling (1377–1380) of the Palazzo Chiaramonte, 'Lo Steri', at Palermo, presents more scenes from Troy romance than any other known medieval decorative painting (Pl.4). The series begins with the Argonauts: Jason sets out in search of the Golden Fleece; the Argo sails; Laomedon forbids Jason and Hercules to land at Troy; several scenes show Jason and Medea. The Trojan sequence proper continues with Jason and Hercules setting out to attack Troy and the city's capture. Hesione is given to Telamon, Priam rebuilds Troy, and Discord throws the apple. Then follow the judgment of Paris, the proposal to steal a Greek woman as hostage for Hesione, and the abduction of Helen. Paris then conveys Helen to Troy and they are married. Next the Greeks appear. Achilles consults the Delphic oracle and Calchas demands the sacrifice of Iphigenia. Here the sequence ends abruptly, followed by three scenes from the story of Dido and Aeneas: Dido watching the departure of Aeneas, Dido kneeling between two winged figures, and Dido's death. (*See* Note on p.7.)

Statues of the Nine Heroes (c.1385) adorned the keep of Maubergeon, Poitiers. (*See* Loomis, as above, p.38 and Note 76.)

Statues of the Nine Heroes (before 1387) decorated the great hall of the château of Coucy. (*See* Loomis, as above, p.38 and Note 77.)

The Nine Heroes appear (1385–1396) in the decoration of the much-restored Schöne Brunne, Nuremberg.

TAPESTRIES.

The fourteenth century saw the beginning of the great sets of tapestries picturing the Nine Heroes and scenes from the Trojan war. No complete set of either is known to remain today, but a number of scenes remain and many sets and separate pieces are recorded in inventories.

1364. An inventory of the possessions of Louis of Anjou lists a tapestry of the Nine Heroes. (*Bibliothèque de l'École des Chartes*, Vol.L, 1889, p.171.)

1376. Nicolas Bataille of Paris received payment from Louis of Anjou for a tapestry of the history of Hector. (*See* Jules Guiffrey, *Histoire de la tapisserie*, Tours, 1886, p.28.)

1380. Two tapestries of the Nine Heroes are listed in the inventory made at the death of Charles V of France in this year. (*See* Jules Labarte, *Inventaire du Mobilier de Charles V*, Paris, 1879, p.378.)

c.1385. The most nearly complete set of Heroes tapestries known to survive is that in the Metropolitan Museum, The Cloisters: two pagans, two Hebrews, and one Christian. One of the pagans (47.101.2) bears on his shield a lion enthroned, which is used both for Hector and for Alexander. (*See* Note on p.63.)

1396. The Duke of Orléans purchased from Bataille of Paris a History of Penthesilea. (*See* W. G. Thomson, *A History of Tapestry*, London, 1930, p.62.)

1398. An inventory of the English crown tapestries made in the 22nd year of Richard II (1377–1399) lists five pieces of the History of the Greeks and Trojans. (*See* Thomson as above, pp.84–85.)

MANUSCRIPTS.

Illustrated manuscripts dealing with Trojan themes become more plentiful in the fourteenth century. Notable examples include:

The second of the two medieval MSS of the *Aeneid* in the Vatican Library, cod.vat.lat.2761. (*See* Erwin Panofsky and Fritz Saxl, *Classical Mythology in Mediaeval Art*, Metropolitan Museum Studies, Vol.IV, Pt.2 (1933), p.253 and fig.38.)

c.1340. MS of Benoit's *Roman*, Italian. Leningrad, Hermitage, MS F. V. XIV,3. (*See* Fritz Saxl, *The Troy Romances*, in his *Lectures*, London, Warburg Institute, 1957, pp.137–138, Pls.80–81; also Panofsky and Saxl in *Metropolitan Museum Studies* as above, p.262 and fig.49.)

c.1350. MS of the *Cronica Troyana*. A Castilian version of Benoit. Madrid, Escorial, MS h.I.6 (Pl.37). (*See* E. Julian Zarco Cuevas, *Catalogo de los Manuscritos Castellanos de la Real Biblioteca de el Escorial*, Madrid, 1924, Vol.I, p.181 ff.)

c.1350–1360. MS of *Livre des estoires dou commencement dou monde*, Neapolitan. British Museum, Royal MS 20,D.1. More than 150 of its illustrations deal with the Trojan war or related themes. (*See* Fritz Saxl and Hans Meier, ed. by Harry Bober, *Catalogue of Astrological and Mythological Manuscripts of the Latin Middle Ages*, III, *Manuscripts in English Libraries*. London, Warburg Institute, 1953, pp.223–243, Pls.XXIX, XXX, 80–81, XXXVIII, 77.) (Pl.99.)

After 1350. MS of Benoit's *Roman*, Italian. Venice, Marciana, Fr.17 (Pls.82,105).

MS of Benoit's *Roman*, Italian. Rome, Vatican Library, cod.reg.lat.1505.

MS of Benoit's *Roman*, Viennese. Vienna, National Library, MS 2571.

MS of Benoit's *Roman*, Viennese. Paris, Bibliothèque Nationale, Fr.782.

1370–1380. MS of Guido's *Historia*, Italian. Milan, Ambrosiana, cod. H.86 sup.

1375–1400. MS of Guido's *Historia*. London, British Museum, Add. MS 15477 (Pl.54).

ENAMELS.

Trojan themes appear in an inventory (1364–1365) of Louis, Duke of Anjou, which lists a *hanap* or drinking vessel and a *thiphenie* or shallow dish used at the feast of the Epiphany, both enamelled with the Nine Heroes. (*See* E. S. J. Marquis de Laborde, *Notices des émaux du Musée du Louvre*, Paris, 1853, Vol.II, pp.71 and 100.)

14th to 15th Century

IVORIES AND PAINTINGS.

Ivory carvings of the early life of Paris, including the judgment scene, were made in great numbers by the Embriacchi family in Venice. Caskets carved with these scenes are in many collections, including the Museo Civico, Bologna; Musée de Cluny, Paris; the Museo Civico, Venice; the Museo Civico, Catania; and the Walters Collection, Baltimore. (The most complete list of these ivories is that by Julius von Schlosser, *Die Werkstatt der Embriacchi in Venedig*, in *Jahrbuch der Kunstsammlungen des allerhöchsten Kaiserhauses*, Vienna, Vol.XX (1899), pp.220–280.)

Hector as one of the Nine Worthies is painted on the balcony of the Summer House, Castle Runkelstein (Roncolo) near Bolzano, Tyrol. (*See* Loomis, *Arthurian Legends*, as above, pp. 48–49, and Wyss, *Die Neun Helden*, as above, pp.85–86.)

15th Century

ENAMELS, STAINED-GLASS, PAINTINGS.

1416. Among objects listed in the inventory of possessions after the death of Jean, Duke of Berry, in 1416, were a *nef*, or table ornament in the form of a ship, and a basin for washing hands at the table, both enamelled with the Nine Heroes. (*See* Jules Guiffrey, *Inventaires de Jean duc de Berri*, Paris, 1894–96, Vol.II, p.209.)

c.1420. The Nine Heroes appear in a stained-glass window of the Council House at Lüneburg. (*See* Loomis, as above, p.39, and Wyss, as above, p.87.)

1420–1430. The Nine Heroes and Penthesilea, from a group of the Nine Heroes, considerably repainted, still adorn the great hall of Castle Manta near Saluzzo in North Italy (Pl.48). (*See* Loomis, as above, p.39, and Wyss, as above, p.79.)

c.1450 or later. The Nine Heroes, badly damaged, decorate the walls of the Castle of Valeria at Sion, Switzerland. (*See* Loomis, as above, p. 39, and Wyss, as above, pp.91–92 and Pl.23.)

About 1457 Peter Kaltenhaff (or Kaltenofer) d. c.1490, painted the Nine Heroes among the princes of Germany in the Amtstube of the Weberhaus in Augsburg. These paintings have been removed to the Bavarian National Museum, Munich. (*See* Wyss, as above, pp.88–89 and Pl.24.)

c.1465–1470. A group of large panel paintings attributed to the workshop of Antonio Vivarini (Italian, fl.1450–1499) show scenes from the story of Paris and Helen: the embarkation of Helen for Cythera; the abduction of Helen and her companions (Pl.25); and the reception of Helen at Troy. These paintings, almost 19 feet in length, were probably used as decorations above a supporting cornice. Baltimore, Walters Art Gallery.

CASSONI.

The largest number of Trojan paintings in the fifteenth century are to be found on Italian chests (*cassoni*) and wooden salvers for bearing gifts. Examples of favourite subjects include:

The marriage of Peleus and Thetis. Paris, Louvre.

The judgment of Paris. Cambridge (Mass.), Fogg Museum of Art.

The judgment of Paris, salver. Florence, Museo Nazionale (Pl.12).

The abduction of Helen. Le Havre, Musée-bibliothèque.

The abduction of Helen, attributed to Benozzo Gozzoli (1420–1498). London, National Gallery.

The story of Paris, Florentine. New York, Metropolitan Museum, 32.75.1a (Pl.24).

The story of Paris. Prague, Rudolphinum.

Achilles in Scyros. Verona, Museo Civico.

Achilles and Briseis. Paris, Musée de Cluny.

Siege of Troy and story of the Wooden Horse. Cambridge, Fitzwilliam Museum; Paris, Musée de Cluny; Paris, Musée des arts décoratifs.

History of Aeneas and Dido. New Haven, Yale University Museum (Jarves Coll.), attributed to Apollonio di Giovanni (Pls.159,160); Paris, Musée de Cluny (Pl.185); Hanover, Kestner Museum.

Adventures of Ulysses. Liverpool, Walker Art Gallery; Paris, Musée de Cluny.

(*See* Paul Schubring, *Cassoni*, Leipzig, 1905, and Supplement, 1923.)

TAPESTRIES.

The fifteenth century saw the greatest production of tapestries dealing with the Trojan war:

1393–1407. The workshop of Dourdain made for Queen Isabelle of France a tapestry of the destruction of Troy. (*See* Guiffrey, *Histoire de la tapisserie*, Tours, 1886, p.38.)

1404. An inventory of the possessions of Philip the Bold, Duke of Burgundy, after his death in this year, records a tapestry of Hector of Troy. (*See* Alexandre Pinchart, *Histoire de tapisserie dans les Flandres*, Paris, 1878–85, p.15.)

1416. In an inventory of the possessions of the Duke de Berri is listed a tapestry of the Nine Heroes. (*See* Guiffrey, *Inventaires de Jean duc de Berri*, Paris, 1894–96, Vol.II, p.209.)

1420. An inventory of the possessions of the dukes of Burgundy made the year after the accession of Philip the Good (1419) includes a tapestry of the Nine Knights and the Nine Amazons, enriched with gold, and another, also with gold, of the Nine Knights alone. (Part of this inventory is published in W. G. Thomson's *History of Tapestry*, London, 1930, pp.91 ff.)

c.1472. A set of 11 tapestries of the Trojan war was ordered from Pasquier Grenier, leading merchant-weaver of Tournai, by the magistrate of Bruges and the castelan of the Castle of le Franc de Bruges as a gift for Charles the Bold, Duke of Burgundy. Payments were made in 1472 and 1474 and it is believed that the hangings were delivered in the latter year.

No complete set of Troy tapestries is known today. The best idea of a full series is probably given by drawings in the Louvre, perhaps preliminary sketches, perhaps drawings from a completed set. Known tapestries corresponding to these drawings date from the last quarter of the fifteenth century. Several important scenes in existing hangings do not appear in the drawings, but some of these have been mutilated and others may have been lost. (For these drawings *see* Paul Schumann, *Der Trojanische Krieg*, Dresden, 1898.)

The first in order of the Louvre drawings shows Priam sending Antenor to Greece to demand the return of Hesione, the Greeks' refusal, and the judgment of Paris as a dream. A tapestry belonging to the cathedral of Zamora shows the first two incidents, and, instead of the judgment scene, the abduction of Helen.

The second drawing has lost its centre. What remains shows the arrival of the Greeks before Troy and the first battle. No known tapestry exactly corresponds to this.

The third drawing represents another battle and Helen and Hecuba welcoming Aeneas and other heroes to the Chamber of Beauty, an apartment in the Trojan Palace set apart for women. Again, no known tapestry corresponds to the drawing.

The fourth drawing consists of two fragments. One shows the arming of Hector, with Andromache and Priam begging him not to fight. A tapestry corresponding to this is in the Metropolitan Museum (39.74; Pl.66). The other fragment shows Paris killing Palamedes and the Greeks urging Achilles to return to battle. A strip of tapestry in the Higgins Collection, Worcester, corresponds closely to this second fragment, although the characters in the foreground emphasize Calchas rather than the ambassadors sent by the Greeks to Achilles. The centre of this drawing, now lost, probably showed a battle in which a centaur-archer or *sagittary* fights the Greeks and is killed by Diomedes, and also a scene in which Hector and Achilles meet to discuss combat. A tapestry in the Metropolitan Museum (52.69; Pl.64) shows these two scenes together; another, somewhat earlier, fragment in the Metropolitan Museum shows only the heads of the heroes in conference (55.39). The Higgins Collection has a *sagittary* alone. A tapestry in Zamora corresponds more closely than any other to what may have been in the complete drawing. It lacks Paris killing Palamedes and the fighting *sagittary*, but shows the conference of Hector and Achilles, a battle scene, and the arming of Hector.

The fifth drawing represents the death of Achilles at the hand of Paris (Pl.81) and the death of Paris. These appear in a tapestry at Zamora.

The sixth drawing, which shows the arrival of Penthesilea and the arming of Achilles' son is paralleled by a tapestry in the Victoria and Albert Museum. (Pl.84 shows the arming.)

The seventh drawing shows the death of Penthesilea, the false peace conference at Troy arranged by Antenor, the theft of the Palladium, and an eagle snatching the Trojan sacrifice. All these appear in a tapestry in the collection of the Duke of Alba. (The right side is illustrated in Pl.87.) A piece in the Montreal Museum of Fine Arts shows the conference.

The eighth and last drawing represents the fall of Troy, with the fatal horse; Helen, Hecuba, and other women; the death of Priam; and the sacrifice of Polyxena. A tapestry in Zamora corresponds to this drawing (Pls.94,103).

Important scenes not shown in the drawings but represented in existing tapestries include: the embassy of Ulysses and Diomedes to demand the return of Helen, in tapestries in the Burrell Collection, Glasgow (Pl.39) and with Duveen Brothers; the funeral of Hector (Pl. 76), Glasgow; and the Sagittary already mentioned.

A tapestry (c.1475) of the history of Brutus, Flemish, shows Brutus about to land in Britain. Saragossa, Cathedral.

Three scenes, less Gothic than the preceding, are in the possession of Duveen Brothers. These are: the embassy of Ulysses and Diomedes to Priam to demand Helen's return, the arrival of Paris and Helen at Troy, and their marriage (Pl.27). Neither in style nor composition do these resemble the Louvre drawings. A fourth tapestry sometimes called the reconciliation of Menelaus and Helen, also with Duveen's, is slightly later than the others and the subject is less certain.

A tapestry of the fall of Tenedos was in a private collection in 1929.

Tapestries showing the capture of Troy by Hercules may have formed a separate set. Priam forbidding Jason and Hercules to land (Pl.18) appears in an example in the Joslyn Art Museum, Omaha; the same scene, without the inscription, and a defeat of Laomedon by Hercules are in the possession of French and Company.

Two tapestries in the Boston Museum (Pls.116, 117) show Ulysses and Penelope. They may have belonged to a set of famous women.

The fate of some of the great lost sets of tapestries remains an enigma, though from time to time pieces which may have belonged to one or another come to light.

One of these sets was that woven (1472–1474) for Charles the Bold. They were believed to have been captured when Charles was defeated at Nancy in 1477. According to tradition some Trojan tapestries in the château at Aulhac before the French Revolution came from this plunder. Later these were taken to the court house at Issoire and at some time were cut into sections. In 1838, while they were at Issoire, Achille Jubinal published them in water-colour drawings, which do not necessarily show the complete group, as some may already have been removed. Some time after this publication the hangings disappeared from Issoire, but several pieces corresponding to the illustrations have reappeared in recent years.

Another important lost group of the late fifteenth century consisted of five hangings which were in the Painted Chamber at Westminster in the reign of Charles II. These were sold in 1800, resold in 1880, and have since disappeared. Fortunately they had been sketched, though very roughly, at the end of the eighteenth century.

PUBLICATIONS OF THE TAPESTRIES LISTED ABOVE:

The Zamora Trojan tapestries are published by Manuel Gomez-Moreno, *La gran tapiceria de la guerra de Troya*, in *Arte Español*, Vol.IV, No.6 (1919), and in Armando Gomez Martinez' *Los tapices de la catedral de Zamora*, Zamora, 1925.

The Metropolitan Museum's arming of Hector (39.74) is published by James J. Rorimer in the *Bulletin of The Metropolitan Museum of Art*, Vol. XXXIV (1939), pp.224–227; the *sagittary* and the conference of Hector and Achilles and the fragment with the heroes' heads are published by William H. Forsyth in the Museum's *Bulletin*, new series, Vol.XIV (1955–1956), pp.76–84, which also mentions the Higgins' pieces.

The Victoria and Albert's tapestry of the arrival of Penthesilea and the arming of Pyrrhus is discussed by A. F. Kendrick in the *Catalogue of Tapestries in the Victoria and Albert Museum*, London, 1914, pp.29–31.

For the Duke of Alba's tapestry showing the conference in Troy and theft of the Palladium *see* G. L. Hunter, *Practical Book of Tapestries*, Philadelphia, 1925, p.80.

The Montreal tapestry showing the conference in Troy is published in *2000 Years of Tapestry Weaving*, 1952, a catalogue of an exhibition held at the Wadsworth Atheneum, Hartford, and the Baltimore Museum of Art, p.35, No.74, Pl.IX.

For the Zamora tapestry of the fall of Troy and Horse of Brass, *see*, besides Gomez-Moreno and Gomez Martinez as above, *Los Joyas de la Exposicion historico-europea*, Madrid, 1893, an invaluable *de luxe* catalogue of an international exhibition held at Madrid the previous year.

The embassy of the Greeks to demand the return of Helen (Pl.39), Glasgow, is discussed by Betty Kurth in the *Connoisseur*, Vol.117 (March, 1947), p.7; the funeral of Hector (Pl. 76) in the same collection is published by Betty Kurth in the *Glasgow Art Review* (Scottish Art Review), Vol.I (1946–1947), pp.4–6.

For the Brutus tapestry *see* Heinrich Göbel, *Tapestries of the Lowlands*, New York, 1924, p.59, Pl.225.

The Duveen Paris and Helen tapestries are published in G. L. Hunter's *Practical Book of Tapestries*, Philadelphia, 1925, pp.80–81.

The fall of the Port of Tenedos, and the tapestries in the hands of French and Company (1929), including the defeat of Laomedon and the uninscribed Laomedon and Hercules are published by A. M. Frankfurter in *International Studio*, Vol.92 (1929).

The Joslyn Museum's Laomedon refusing Hercules and Jason, then in the hands of French and Company, is published in Hunter as above, p.81.

The Ulysses and Penelope tapestries are published by Gertrude Townsend in the *Bulletin of the Museum of Fine Arts*, Boston, Vol.XXVII (1929), pp.2–10, and by Walter H. Siple, *Cardinal Ferry de Clugny's Tapestries, International Studio*, Vol. 92 (1929), pp.39–43.

For the history of the Trojan tapestries of Charles the Bold, *see* James J. Rorimer, *Bulletin of The Metropolitan Museum of Art*, Vol.XXXIV (1939), pp.224–227.

The lost tapestries of the Painted Chamber are published by H. C. Marillier in the *Burlington Magazine*, Vol.XLVI (1925), pp.35–42.

MANUSCRIPTS.

A few outstanding examples suggest the richness of fifteenth-century illustrated manuscripts dealing with the Troy story:

c.1400. MS of *Les livres des histoires du commencement du monde*, North French. London, British Museum, Stowe MS 54. Fifteen of its illustrations deal with the Trojan story. (*See* Saxl and Meier, *Catalogue* . . . III, as above, pp.268–272, Pls.XXX–XXXII.)

Early 15th century. MS of Statius' *Achilleid* and *Thebaid*, French. London, British Museum, Burney MS 257. The *Achilleid* fragment has seven illustrations. (*See* Saxl and Meier, as above, p.114, Pl.XXII.)

MS of Boccaccio's *De Claris Mulieribus*, French. London, British Museum, Royal MS 16 G.V. (Saxl and Meier, as above, pp.204–207, Pl.XLI.)

MS of Christine de Pisan's *Épître d'Othéa*, French. Paris, Bibliothèque Nationale, MS fr. 606.

1409–1419. MS of *Des cas des nobles hommes et femmes*, French translation of Boccaccio's *De casibus virorum illustrium*. Paris, Bibliothèque d'Arsenal, MS 5193. (*See* Henry Martin, *Le Boccace de Jean sans Peur*, Brussels, 1911.)

1414. MS of Boccaccio's *Il Filostrato*, Neapolitan. New York, Pierpont Morgan Library, M 371.

First half of century. MS of Guido's *Historia*, in French translation, French. London, British Museum, Royal MS 16 F.IX.

Mid-century. MS of Paulus Orosius' *Histoire ancien jusq'a César*, French. New York, Pierpont Morgan Library, M 212.

MS of Vergil's *Opera*, Italian. London, British Museum, Add. MS.14815.

c.1459. MS of *Des cas du nobles hommes et femmes*, French translation from Boccaccio, believed to be illustrated by Jean Foucquet. Munich, State Library, cod.gall.369. (*See* Paul Durrieu, *Le Boccace de Munich*, Munich, 1909.)

1450–1460. MS of the *Aeneid*, illustrated by Apollonio di Giovanni (Master of the Vergil Codex), Italian, Florentine. Florence, Biblioteca Riccardiana, N.492 (Pls.101,161,162,179). (*See* E. H. Gombrich, *Apollonio di Giovanni* in *Journal of the Warburg and Courtauld Institutes*, Vol.XVIII, No.1 (1955), pp.16–34.)

c.1460. MS of Christine de Pisan's *Épître*, Flemish, School of Vreelandt. Erlangen University Library, MS.2361.

1461. MS of Jacques Milet's play, *The Destruction of Troy the Great*, French. Oxford, Bodleian Library, Douce MS.356.

1461. MS of Christine de Pisan's *Épître*, Flemish, illustrated by Jean Miélot. Brussels, Bibliothèque Royale, MS fr.9392 (Pls.5,79,126,136).

c.1470. MS of Boccaccio's *De Casibus* in French translation, by Laurent Premierfait, French. London, British Museum, Add. MS.35321.

c.1470. MS of the *Chronique Universelle dite de la Bouquechardière* of Jehan de Courcy, Flemish. New York, Pierpont Morgan Library, M 214 (Pl.26).

3rd quarter. MS of French translation of Boccaccio's *Il Filostrato*, French. Oxford, Bodleian Library, Douce MS.331. (*See* Saxl and Meier, *Catalogue* . . . III . . ., as above, pp.359–360, Pl.XXIV.)

MS of Lydgate's *Troy Book*, English. Manchester, John Rylands Library, Ryl. Eng. No. 1. (*See* Lydgate's *Troy Book*, ed. by Henry Bergen, Early English Text Society, Extra Series, CXXVI, Part IV, London, 1935, pp.29–36.) (Fig.2.)

MS of Lydgate's *Troy Book*. London, British Museum, Royal MS D.II. The first 12 illustrations are English, fifteenth century, the others Flemish, sixteenth century. (*See* Bergen, Early English Text Society, as above, pp.15–19, and Saxl and Meier, as above, pp.215–216.)

MS of Christine de Pisan's *Épître*, French, last third of century. Oxford, Bodleian Library, MS.421.

c.1475. MS of Raoul Lefèvre's *Recueil*, Flemish. London, British Museum, Royal MS.17 E.II, entitled *Le Livre nommé Hercules*.

MS of German version of Guido's *Historia*, Rhenish. Munich, National Library, cod.lat.61 (Pls.108,111).

Late 15th century. MS of Lefèvre's *Recueil*, French. Paris, Bibliothèque Nationale, Fr.59.

MS of Lefèvre's *Recueil*, French. Paris, Bibliothèque Nationale, Fr.22552 (Pls.11,19,28,34,95).

MS of Vergil's *Opera*, Italian. London, British Museum, King's MS.24.

MS of Jacques Milet's play, *The Destruction of Troy the Great*, French. Paris, Bibliothèque Nationale, Fr.12601.

1500. MS of Guido's *Historia*, French, illustrated by Jean Colombe. Paris, Bibliothèque Nationale, *nouv. acq.* Fr.24920, formerly in St. Petersburg, Imperial Library.

PAINTING.

LUCA SIGNORELLI (c.1441–1523). Italian painter: Scenes from the *Iliad* and *Aeneid* accompanying his medallions of Homer and Vergil in Orvieto Cathedral, c.1499–1502.

LIBERALE DA VERONA (c.1445–c.1526–29). Italian painter: *Death of Dido*, London, National Gallery.

PINTORRICCHIO (1454–1513). Italian painter: *Telemachus and Penelope*, London, National Gallery (Pls.143,144).

LUCAS CRANACH the Elder (1472–1553). German painter: *Judgment of Paris*, c.1528, New York, Metropolitan Museum (28.221; Pl. 15); other versions in Graz, Landesgalerie and Frankfurt-on-the-Main, private coll. (1930).

GIORGIONE (1478–1510). Italian painter. Scenes from the story of Paris: *Birth of Paris*, fragment, Budapest; *Finding of Paris*, Allington Castle, Kent, England; *Paris Given to Nurse*, Allington Castle; *Paris Exposed*, Princeton, Mather Collection; *Paris and the Three Goddesses*, four versions. Dresden Gallery and collections of the Earl of Malmesbury, E. Albuzio, Venice, S. Larpent, Oslo. (*See* Sir Martin Conway, *Giorgione*, London, 1929.)

DOSSO DOSSI (1479–1542). Italian painter: *Circe and Her Lovers in a Landscape*, Washington, National Gallery (Pl.137); *The Enchantress Circe*, Rome, Borghese Gallery; *Dido*, Rome, Doria-Pamphili Gallery.

16th Century

PAINTING.

RAPHAEL (Raffaele Sanzio) (1483–1520). Italian painter: *Young man rescuing an old*, detail of *Fire in the Borgo*, Rome, Vatican, Stanze dell' Incendio. (Inspired, according to Vasari, by the story of Aeneas and Anchises.) To Raphael are also credited by Vasari the designs, now lost, for a *Judgment of Paris*, engraved by Marcantonio (Pl.13), woven as tapestries, and used as ceramic designs, and also an *Abduction of Helen*, engraved by various artists, and used in ceramics and tapestries.

DOMENICO BECCAFUMI (1486–1551). Italian painter: *Penelope Spinning*, Venice, Seminario Patriarcale.

GIOVANNI BATTISTA ROSSO (1494–1540). Italian painter and stucco worker: Trojan subjects in the Gallery of Francis I at Fontainebleau include *The Education of Achilles* and *The Shipwreck of Ajax*.

MARTEN VAN HEEMSKERCK (1498–1574). Flemish painter: *The Abduction of Helen*, Baltimore, Walters Art Gallery; *Vulcan Gives Thetis the Shield for Achilles*, Vienna, Private Coll. (1911).

GIULIO ROMANO (1499–1546). Italian painter: Trojan frescoes in the Ducal Palace, Mantua, c.1536–39, include *The Judgment of*

Paris; *The Dream of Andromache*; *The Rape of Helen*; *The Fight over the Body of Patroclus* (Pl.59); *Laocoön*; *Thetis with the Weapons of Achilles*; *The Trojan Horse*. Scenes from the *Aeneid* decorate the Hall of the Aeneid.

JOACHIM PATINIR (fl.c.1515–1524). Flemish painter, att. to: *Landscape with Judgement of Paris*, Toledo (Ohio) Museum. The figures are treated as accessories to the landscape.

LUCA PENNI. Italian painter, assisted Primaticcio in his Trojan frescoes at Fountainebleau (c.1556). Some drawings for these lost works are preserved.

FRANCESCO PRIMATICCIO (1504–1570). Italian painter: carried out, series of Trojan scenes in the Royal Chamber at Fontainebleau, c.1533–1535 (work now destroyed). With assistants, especially Niccolo dell'Abbate, painted an *Odyssey* series in the Hall of the Odyssey at Fontainebleau, 1541–1570. Work now destroyed but many drawings remain in Stockholm (Pl.152), the Albertina in Vienna, and Chantilly. Among his other Trojan frescoes at Fontainebleau are decorative scenes including a *Discord at the Feast* (overpainted). Surviving easel paintings include: *Penelope and Ulysses*, Castle Howard, and *Helen Swooning*, Collection of Lord Pembroke, Wilton House. (*See* Dimier, *French Painting in the Sixteenth Century*, London, 1904, pp.146–186 and *passim.*)

NICCOLO DELL' ABBATE (c.1512–1571). Italian painter: frescoes illustrating the *Aeneid* at Castle Scandiano near Modena, now in the Modena Museum; also work on the *Odyssey* frescoes at Fontainebleau.

UNKNOWN ITALIAN PAINTER (first half 16th century), Veronese: *The Rape of Helen*, New York, Metropolitan Museum (12.57).

HANS EWORTH (fl. c.1545–1580). Flemish painter working in England. To him is attributed the *Queen Elizabeth and the Judgment of Paris*, dated 1569, Royal Collection, Hampton Court. (This painting is the artistic counterpart of the treatment of this theme by Peele, Barnfield, and others. Illustrated in E. C. Wilson's *England's Eliza*, Cambridge (Mass.), 1939, Pl. opp. p.238, and in *Queen Elizabeth or Astrea* by Frances A. Yates, in *Journal of the Warburg and Courtauld Institutes*, Vol.x (1947), Pl.19a.)

TAPESTRIES.

A tapestry (c.1500) showing Penthesilea with drawn sword, Angers Museum of Tapestries, may have come from a set of Nine Famous Women or Amazons, companions to the Nine Heroes. (*See Handbook to the Loan Exhibition of French Tapestries*, New York, Metropolitan Museum, 1947, p.15.)

Two Brussels tapestries (early 16th century) of the Trojan war, Trojans and Greeks fighting over the body of Sarpedon, and a contest of Paris and Menelaus. Collection of the Duke of Berwick and Alba, sold in 1877. (*See* illustrated sales catalogue, *Collection . . . de duc de Berwick et Alba . . .*, Paris, Hôtel Drouot, Vol.35, April 20, 1877, pp.56–57, nos.17–18 and Pl. opp. p.57.)

In 1522 Cardinal Wolsey purchased a tapestry of the Nine Heroes; it is believed that he usually collected contemporary hangings.

A Flemish tapestry (c.1515–1525) in the Royal Ontario Museum presents a series of Trojan incidents suggestive of a mythological handbook as a source. The incidents are: Ulysses feigning madness (not a romance subject); Ulysses discovering Achilles at Scyros; Priam receiving Ulysses and Diomedes who ask Helen's return; and the theft of the Palladium.

Six Flemish tapestries (c.1525) after designs by Bernard van Orley in the Spanish Royal Collections show scenes from the story of Romulus and Remus, including Romulus and Remus cast into the Tiber, Remus presented to Amulius, and Romulus and Remus tracing the walls of Rome. (*See Los Tapices de la Casa del Rey N.S.*, Elías Tormo Monzó and Francisco J. Sánchez Cantón, Madrid, 1919, pp.47–50; a French translation follows the Spanish text.)

An inventory of Crown tapestries (1547) made after the death of Henry VIII of England includes various pieces of Troy and of the Nine Heroes. The '6 pieces of Tapestries of the IX Worthies having borders with the late Cardinal's arms' was probably that noted above, and confiscated from Wolsey. The inventory also lists '3 pieces of Hector', '4 pieces of tapestry of Troy', '9 pieces of tapestry of the history of Troy', and '11 pieces . . . of the siege of Troie'. Most of these are believed to have been comparatively new at the time; a few notations such as '8 pieces of old tapestry of Hector' are thought to refer to fifteenth-century hangings. (*See* W. G. Thomson, *History of Tapestry*, London, 1930, pp.248, 250, 252, 258.)

ROCK CRYSTALS.

An entertaining use of Trojan themes in minor arts appears in engraved rock crystals of Italian workmanship of the sixteenth century in the Austrian National Collections, Vienna: the

Trojan Horse, Aeneas and Anchises, and the Abduction of Helen, after Marcantonio's engravings.

METALWORK.

Silver-gilt ewer and basin with the Nine Worthies by Christoph Jamnitzer (1563–1618). German. Vienna, Austrian National Collections.

An embossed shield (c.1585), probably made in Brescia, decorated with the Trojan Horse and the burning of Troy, New York, Metropolitan Museum (25.163.2).

MAIOLICA.

Italian maiolica was often decorated with Trojan themes, chiefly taken from engravings. Among pieces in the Metropolitan Museum are: the rape of Helen, from engraving ascribed to Marcantonio (41.49.4) (Fig.3); the death of Achilles, plate, from an illustration in the Ovid published by Marcantonio Giunta in 1497 (84.3.2); the judgment of Paris, plate after Raphael's design (18.129.1); Aeneas carrying Anchises from Troy (27.97.27), influenced by Raphael's painting of the Fire in the Borgo.

ENAMELS.

Painted enamels made at Limoges in this century often represent scenes from the *Aeneid.* A large group of these in the Metropolitan Museum, dated c.1525–1530, was directly inspired by the woodcuts of the Grüninger *Aeneid*, Strassburg, 1502. (Metropolitan Museum, 88.3.85; 25.39.1–5; 25.40.1–2; 25.41; 45.60.3–6; 45.60.29–30.) (Pls.163,168,173.)

16th–17th Century

PAINTING AND SCULPTURE.

FEDERIGO BAROCCIO (1526?–1612). Italian painter: *Aeneas Carrying Anchises from Burning Troy*, c.1598, Rome, Borghese Gallery.

TIBALDI (Pellegrino de Pellegrini) (1527–1596). Italian painter: ceiling paintings of the *Odyssey* in the palace of Cardinal Poggi, Rome; scenes from the *Odyssey*, Bologna, University.

EL GRECO (Domenico Theotocopuli) (1541–1614). Spanish painter: *Laocoön.* Washington, National Gallery of Art (Pl.92).

CORNELISZ. OF HAARLEM (1562–1638). Dutch painter: *Wedding of Peleus and Thetis*, The Hague, Mauritshuis.

JAN BRUEGHEL the Elder (1568–1625). Flemish painter: *Aeneas and the Sibyl in the Underworld*, formerly in the Museum of Fine Arts, Budapest (Pl.177). *See* note on p.206.

ANNIBALE CARRACCI (1560–1609). Italian painter. Scenes from the *Odyssey* on the ceiling of the small Camerino, Palazzo Farnese, Rome: *Ulysses and Circe*; *Ulysses and the Sirens*; easel painting, *Cheiron and Achilles*, Galleria Doria-Pamphili, Rome. Annibale and Agostino Carracci. Ceiling paintings: *Venus and Anchises*, *Mercury Giving Paris the Apple*, Carracci Gallery of the Farnese Palace, Rome; *Neptune Stilling the Storm*, Bordeaux Museum. Annibale, Agostino, and Lodovico Carracci: scenes from the *Aeneid* (1580–1585) in the Palazzo Fava, Bologna.

ABRAHAM BLOEMAERTS (1564–1651). Dutch painter: *Wedding of Peleus and Thetis*, The Hague, Mauritshuis.

GUIDO RENI (1575–1642). Italian painter: *The Abduction of Helen*, Paris, Louvre; *The Sacrifice of Polyxena*, Paris, Louvre; *Ulysses and Nausicaä*, Naples, National Gallery.

LIONELLO SPADA (1576–1622). Italian painter: *Aeneas and Anchises*, or, *The Burning of Troy.* Paris, Louvre.

ADAM ELSHEIMER (1578–1610). German painter: *The Burning of Troy*, Munich, Alte Pinakothek (Pl.167).

FRANCESCO ALBANI (1578–1660). Italian painter: scenes from the story of Aeneas, Bologna, Palazzo Fava.

PIETER LASTMAN (1583–c.1633). Dutch painter: *Odysseus and Nausicaä*, Braunschweig, Ducal Collection (Pl.124); another version in the Paintings Gallery, Augsburg; *Orestes and Pylades*, Amsterdam, Rijksmuseum.

PETER PAUL RUBENS (1577–1640). Flemish painter: *Judgment of Paris*, versions in London, National Gallery (Pl.16), Prado, Madrid; an early composition in the Picture Gallery, Dresden, believed to be the work of pupils; *Romulus and Remus*, Rome, Capitoline Museum (Pl.180); *Odysseus and Nausicaä*, figures by Rubens, landscape by Lukas van Uden, Florence, Pitti Palace; *Landscape with the Shipwreck of Aeneas*, Boston, Museum of Fine Arts; *Marriage of Peleus and Thetis*, Chicago, Private Collection (1940); *Polyphemus*, Madrid, Prado; *Dido and Aeneas* and *Death of Dido*, location of last two unknown in 1940.

Eight oil sketches by Rubens for tapestry cartoons of the History of Achilles, 1630–1632: *Achilles Dipped in the Styx*, Rotterdam, Boymans

Museum; *The Education of Achilles*, Rotterdam, Boymans Museum (Pl.30); *Achilles in Scyros*, Haarlem, Private Collection (1940); *The Anger of Achilles*, Rotterdam, Boymans Museum; *Thetis Receiving the Armour of Achilles from Vulcan*, Rotterdam, Boymans Museum (replica at Pau Museum); *The Death of Hector*, Rotterdam, Boymans Museum (replica at Pau Museum); *Briseis Returned to Achilles*, Detroit Institute of Arts; *The Death of Achilles*, Rotterdam, Boymans Museum.
(These oil sketches are fully discussed and illustrated in Leo van Puyvelde's *Les Esquisses de Rubens*, Bâle, 1940.)

FRANCESCO ALLEGRINI (1587–1663). Italian painter: the following ceiling paintings of the story of Dido in a room of the Palazzo Doria-Pamphili, Piazza Navona, Rome, are sometimes attributed to Allegrini: *Juno and Venus Confer*; *Aeneas Relating the Fall of Troy*; *The Death of Dido*; *Aeneas Seeing Dido's Shade in the Underworld.*

GIOVANNI FRANCESCO BARBIERI (Guercino) (1591–1666). Italian painter: *Death of Dido*, Rome, Spada Gallery.

NICOLAS POUSSIN (1594–1665). French painter: *Achilles on Scyros*, Richmond, Virginia Museum of Fine Arts (Pl.32); *Ulysses Discovering Achilles in Scyros*, Boston, Museum of Fine Arts; *Ulysses Discovering Achilles in Scyros*, Paris, Louvre; *Landscape with Dido and Aeneas*, London, National Gallery; *Venus Giving Aeneas the Arms Made by Hephaestus*, Toronto Art Gallery (Pl.183); *Venus Giving Aeneas the Arms Made by Hephaestus*, Rouen Museum; *Polyphemus* (location unknown, the story of Ulysses is merely incidental to that of Polyphemus and Galatea); *Alexander Adorning the Tomb of Achilles*, Leningrad, Hermitage. (This is the incident related by Arrian, 1,12,1, and others, that Alexander laid a wreath upon the so-called tomb of Achilles, accounting him happy that he had had Homer to keep his memory green.)
Among Poussin's Trojan drawings are a *Judgment of Paris* and *Venus Giving Arms to Aeneas*, both in the École des Beaux-Arts, Paris.

PIETRO DA CORTONA (1596–1669). Italian painter and architect: scenes showing the arrival of Aeneas in Latium in the ceiling decoration of a gallery in the Palazzo Doria-Pamphili, Piazza Navona, Rome; *Venus Appearing to Aeneas as a Huntress*, Paris, Louvre; *Finding of Romulus and Remus*, Paris, Louvre.

GIOVANNI BERNINI (1598–1680). Italian sculptor and architect: group of *Aeneas, Anchises, and Ascanius*, Rome, Borghese Gallery; group of *Neptune and Triton*, London, Victoria and Albert Museum (inspired by the *Aeneid*, I, 132ff.).

17th Century

PAINTING.

ANTHONY VAN DYCK (1597–1691). Flemish painter: *Venus Asks Vulcan for the Weapons for Aeneas*, Paris, Louvre; *Venus Receives from Vulcan the Weapons for Aeneas*, Vienna, Kunsthistorisches Museum; a number of oil sketches in various collections, probably after designs by Rubens.

CLAUDE LORRAIN (1600–1682). French painter: *Ulysses Returning Chryseis to Her Father*, Paris, Louvre; *Sinon before Priam*, London, National Gallery; *Aeneas at Delos*, London, National Gallery; *Judgment of Paris*, Collection of the Duke of Buccleuch (1937); *Ascanius Shooting Sylvia's Stag*, Oxford, Ashmolean Museum; *The Trojan Women Setting Fire to the Greek Ships*, New York, Metropolitan Museum, 55. 119. (This shows an incident related by Strabo, *Geography*, VI,I.12, according to which certain Greek ships, separated from their companions during the return from Troy, landed near Crotona in Calabria. While the men were reconnoitring, the captive Trojan women, weary of their journeying, burned the ships and all were forced to remain, thus planting one of the many Greek colonies of Southern Italy.)
Claude's Trojan drawings are innumerable. Among those in the British Museum are: *The Departure of Paris for Troy*, *Paris and Oenone*, *Paris as a Child on Mount Ida*, *Paris Giving the Apple to Venus*, *The Flight of Helen*, *The Death of Priam.* (In spite of their titles Claude's works are actually landscapes with subsidiary figures to give narrative content.)

MATHIEU LE NAIN (1607–1677). French painter: *Venus at the Forge of Vulcan*, Rheims, Museum.

GIOVANNI FRANCESCO ROMANELLI (1610–1662). Italian painter and tapestry designer: *Venus Healing the Wounds of Aeneas*, Paris, Louvre; *Sacrifice of Iphigenia*, New York, Metropolitan Museum (54.166). *See also Aeneid* tapestries after his designs.

JAN VAN RYN OR REYN (1610–1678). Dutch painter: *The Wedding of Peleus and Thetis*, Madrid, Prado.

PIERRE LEMAIRE (1612–1688). French painter: *Achilles among the Daughters of Lycomedes*, Los Angeles County Museum.

SÉBASTIEN BOURDON (1616–1671). French painter: *Death of Dido*, Leningrad, Hermitage.

SALVATOR ROSA (1615–1673). Italian painter: *Odysseus and Nausicaä*, versions in Leningrad, Hermitage, and Los Angeles County Museum.

PAOLO DE MATTEIS (1622–1728). Italian painter: *Achilles at the Court of Lycomedes*, Leningrad, Hermitage.

JAN STEEN (c.1626–1679). Dutch painter: *Sacrifice of Iphigenia*, Amsterdam, Rijksmuseum.

LUCA GIORDANO (1632–1705). Italian painter: *The Rape of Helen*, Hartford, Wadsworth Atheneum; *The Judgment of Paris*, versions in Berlin, State Museum, and Leningrad, Hermitage.

GÉRARD DE LAIRESSE (1641–1711). Dutch painter: *Achilles Recognized by Ulysses*, The Hague, Mauritshuis; *Circe*, Cambridge, Fitzwilliam Museum; *Landing of Aeneas*, Aix-la-Chapelle.

MARCANTONIO FRANCESCHINI (1648–1729). Italian painter: *Judgment of Paris*, Leningrad, Hermitage.

SEBASTIANO RICCI (1659–1734). Italian painter: *The Abduction of Helen*, Parma, University.

TAPESTRIES AND EMBROIDERIES.

Ten tapestries of the History of Achilles (before 1643), woven after Rubens' designs, were noted in an inventory of Rubens' father-in-law made in this year. Six subjects based on these sketches are known today. In the Royal Museum, Brussels, are: *Achilles Dipped in the Styx*; *The Education of Achilles*; *The Death of Hector*; *The Return of Briseis*; and *The Death of Achilles*. The sixth, *The Anger of Achilles*, is in the Museum of Fine Arts, Boston. (These tapestries are discussed by Marthe Crick-Kuntzinger in the *Bulletin des Musées Royaux d'Art et d'Histoire*, Brussels, Series 3 (1934–35), pp.2–12.)

To this period belongs a group of Sino-Portuguese embroideries in the Metropolitan Museum, probably made at Macao, combining Chinese and Portuguese influences. *Calchas Sacrificing* (50.97.2) shows the portent of the serpent and the birds indicating the duration of the war. *The Sacrifice of Polyxena* (51.152) has also been called the 'Sacrifice of Iphigenia'.

c.1635. Several sets of French tapestries of the History of Ulysses after designs by Simon Vouet are in various collections. One complete set in the château de Gheverny, Loir-et-Cher (1903) includes: *Ulysses Saying Farewell to Aeolus*; *Ulysses at Circe's Isle*; *The Greeks in Circe's Palace*; *Ulysses Victorious over Circe*; *The Funeral of Elpenor*; *Ulysses and the Sirens*; *Ulysses Landing at Ithaca*; *Ulysses Recognized by Argos*.

The Museum of Besançon has four pieces: *The Greeks at Circe's Palace*; *Ulysses and the Sirens*; *Ulysses Landing at Ithaca*; *Ulysses Recognized by Argos*. Pieces from other sets have been sold separately or in groups from time to time. (The Ulysses tapestries are discussed in Fenaille's *État Général des Tapisseries de la Manufacture des Gobelins*, Paris, 1903, Vol.I, pp.329–334.)

Tapestries illustrating the *Aeneid* were woven (1635–1645) by Flemings after designs by Giovanni Romanelli. The subjects include: *The Meeting of Venus and Aeneas*; *Cupid in the Guise of Ascanius Presenting Dido with Gifts*; *Dido Sacrificing to Juno*; *Dido Showing Aeneas the Plans of Carthage*; *Dido and Aeneas Seeking Shelter from the Storm* (Pl.172); *Mercury Bidding Aeneas Leave Dido*; *The Parting of Dido and Aeneas*; *The Death of Dido*.

A complete set of these is in the Austrian National Collections; practically identical sets, except that spiral columns replace the Atlantes, are in the Swedish State Collections and in the Cleveland Museum. The latter set was made for the Barberini family. (The Dido and Aeneas tapestries are discussed by Dorothy M. Schullian in *Vergilius*, Feb., 1940, pp.23–30.)

Two pieces of a set of tapestries of the History of Achilles, Brussels, of the second half of the seventeenth century, show *The Return of Briseis* and *The Death of Achilles*, the designs influenced by Rubens. Musées Royaux du Cinquantenaire, Brussels.

1686–1704. Between these years several sets of French tapestries were woven at the Gobelins manufactory after Raphael's Trojan designs for *The Judgment of Paris* and *The Abduction of Helen*. The first set, dated 1686–90, and the second, 1690–1703, are in the French National Collections; the third, 1693–1704, in the Austrian National Collections. (*See* Maurice Fenaille, *État Général*, as above, Vol.II, pp.267–272. The tapestry of the *Judgment of Paris*, the reverse of Marcantonio's engraving (Pl.13), is illustrated.)

17th–18th Century

PAINTING.

LORENZO DE' FERRARI (1680–1744). Italian painter: decorations of the story of Aeneas and Dido in the Palazzo Cataldi, Genoa.

ADRIAN VAN DER WERFF (1659–1772). Dutch painter: *Dido Sorrowing*, Braunschweig,

Ducal Collection; *Judgment of Paris*, versions in Dresden Picture Gallery and Dulwich College Museum, London; *Paris and Oenone*, Turin, Picture Gallery.

JACOPO AMIGONI (1675–1752). Italian painter: *The Embarkation of Helen for Troy*, Private Collection.

18th Century

PAINTING.

JEAN-ANTOINE WATTEAU (1684–1721). French painter: *Judgment of Paris*, Paris, Louvre.

GIOVANNI BATTISTA PITTONI (1687–1767). Italian painter: *Sacrifice of Polyxena*, Paris, Louvre (also attributed to Ricci); other versions in the Brera, Milan, and Museo Civico, Vicenza; *Achilles Among the Daughters of Lycomedes*, Berlin, State Museum.

JOHANN HEINRICH KELLER (1692–1765). Swiss painter: *Aeneas Rescuing Anchises*, Amsterdam, Rijksmuseum.

GIOVANNI BATTISTA TIEPOLO (1696–1770). Italian painter: Trojan frescoes of scenes from the *Iliad* and *Aeneid* at Villa Valmarana near Vicenza, c.1757 (Pls.35,36,43); *Sacrifice of Iphigenia*, Washington, National Gallery; *Building of the Trojan Horse*, versions in London, National Gallery, and Hartford, Wadsworth Atheneum (Pl.89); *Procession of the Trojan Horse*, London, National Gallery; *Sacrifice of Polyxena*, Brussels, Royal Museum; *Abduction of Helen*, Milan, Private Collection; *Ulysses Discovering Achilles at Scyros*, Vicenza, Private Collection; *Aeneas Received into the Temple of Immortality*, Boston, Museum of Fine Arts; *Telemachus and Mentor*, Amsterdam, Rijksmuseum.
(The Villa Valmarana frescoes and change in dating from 1737 to c.1757 are discussed by Michael Levey, *Tiepolo's Treatment of Classical Story at Villa Valmarana*, in *Journal of the Warburg and Courtauld Institutes*, Vol.xx (1957), pp.298–317.)

CHARLES JOSEPH NATOIRE (1700–1777). French painter: *Venus and Vulcan*, *Venus and Aeneas*, Bordeaux, Museum; *Telemachus and Calypso*, *Calypso's Nymphs Burning the Ships of Telemachus*, Leningrad, Hermitage.

FRANÇOIS BOUCHER (1703–1770). French painter: *Judgment of Paris*, London, Wallace Collection; *Venus at the Forge of Vulcan with the Armour for Aeneas*, Paris, Louvre.

POMPEO BATONI (1708–1787). Italian painter: *Thetis Entrusts Achilles to Cheiron*, Parma, Picture Gallery; *The Education of Achilles* and *Achilles at Scyros*, Florence, Uffizi; *Venus Showing Aeneas the Arms Made by Vulcan*, Vienna, Liechtenstein Gallery; *Thetis Rising from the Sea to Console Achilles for the Loss of Briseis* and *Aeneas Abandoning Dido*, Collection of Brinsley Ford, London.

JOSEPH-MARIE VIEN (1716–1809). French painter: *Anger of Achilles*, Rouen Museum; *Briseis Led from the Tent of Achilles*, Angers Museum (also woven as tapestry); *Return of Priam with Hector's Body*, Angers Museum; *Parting of Hector and Andromache*, Epinal Museum.

DOMENICO CORVI (1721–1803). Italian painter: *Sacrifice of Polyxena*, Viterbo, Museo Civico.

JOHANN HEINRICH TISCHBEIN the Elder (1722–1789). German painter: *Anger of Achilles* and *Surrender of Briseis*, Hamburg, Kunsthalle; *Dido and Aeneas*, *Menelaus and Paris*, *Thetis and Achilles*, and *Death of Dido*, Cassel, Landesmuseum.

GAVIN HAMILTON (1723–1798). British painter: *The Story of Paris*, ceiling decoration in a room of the Villa Borghese, Rome; *Venus Presenting Helen to Paris*, *Rape of Helen*, and *Death of Achilles*, Rome, Museo di Roma, designed as part of the decoration of the same room. (*See* L. Ferrara, *La stanza di Elena e Paride nella Galleria Borghese*, in *Riv. dell'Ist. Naz. di Arch. e Storia dell'Arte*, New series (III), Rome, 1954, pp.242–256.) Also *Andromache Mourning the Dead Hector*, Collection of the Duke of Hamilton; *Achilles Dragging Hector's Body*, Collection of the Duke of Bedford.

SIR JOSHUA REYNOLDS (1723–1792). British painter: *Death of Dido*, Buckingham Palace. (*See* Sir Lionel Cust, *The Royal Collection of Paintings at Buckingham Palace and Windsor Castle*, London, 1903–1906, Vol. 1.)

ANTON RAPHAEL MENGS (1728–1779). German painter: *Judgment of Paris*, Leningrad, Hermitage.

TAPESTRIES.

A series of Flemish tapestries of the story of Troy (c.1700) in the North Carolina Museum of Art, Raleigh, N.C., includes *Helen of Troy; Ladies Guarding the Treasures of Helen*; *Quarrel of Achilles and Agamemnon*; *Thetis Taking Leave of Poseidon*; *Combat of Ajax and Hector*; *Combat of Paris and Menelaus*; *Thetis at the Forge of Vulcan*; *Priam Seeking the Body of Hector*; *Death of Achilles*.

An incomplete set of French tapestries, Gobelins, 1717–1730, after designs by Antoine and Charles Coypel, illustrates scenes from the Trojan story: *The Wrath of Achilles, the Sacrifice of Iphigenia,*

Achilles Seeking Vengeance for Patroclus, *Farewell of Hector and Andromache* (fragment), *Dido and Aeneas*. French National Collections. (*See* Fenaille, *État Général*, as above, Vol.I, pp.292–302.)

Two pieces of a set of Spanish tapestries, 1731–1735, in the Spanish Royal Collections show an incident from Fénelon's *Télémaque*: *Telemachus and Mentor Encountering Calypso*. (*See Los Tapices de la Casa del Rey, N.S.*, as above, pp.131–134 and Pl.XLIV.)

A set of eighteenth-century Flemish tapestries, first half of century, in the Spanish Royal Collections, show further incidents from Fénelon. (*Los Tapices de la Casa del Rey, N.S.*, as above, pp.135–136. Pl.XLV illustrates *Neptune Stilling the Storm which has Shipwrecked Telemachus and Mentor*.) A similar set is in the Austrian National Collections (Pl.155).

Six French tapestries woven at Beauvais c.1766, after designs by Deshayes, are in the Spanish Royal Collections. They show *Cassandra Prophesying that Paris Will Bring Destruction to Troy*; *The Abduction of Helen*; *Hector, Paris, and Helen*; *Calchas Demanding the Sacrifice of Iphigenia*; *Agamemnon Consenting to the Sacrifice*; *Diomedes and Aeneas in Combat before the Walls of Troy*. (*See Los Tapices de la Casa del Rey, N.S.*, as above, pp.147–148, Pl.XLVIII.)

CERAMICS.

JOSIAH WEDGWOOD (1730–1795). English manufacturer of ceramics. Wedgwood ware, with designs in relief, includes such Trojan subjects as the following: Plaques: *Sacrifice of Iphigenia, Priam ransoming the body of Achilles* (Metropolitan Museum 09.29), *Birth of Achilles, Thetis dipping Achilles in the Styx, Achilles and the daughters of Lycomedes, Judgment of Paris, Cheiron and Achilles, Achilles victorious over Hector*. Inkstand: *Thetis dipping Achilles in the Styx* (Metropolitan Museum, 10.85.2).

18th–19th Century

PAINTING AND SCULPTURE.

THOMAS BANKS (1735–1805). British sculptor: *Thetis Dipping Achilles in the Styx*, London, Victoria and Albert Museum; *Thetis and Her Nymphs Consoling Achilles for the Death of Patroclus*, London, Victoria and Albert Museum; *Achilles Arming*, terracotta model, Private Collection; *Achilles Enraged at the Loss of Briseis*, original plaster model, 1784, probably destroyed.

BENJAMIN WEST (1738–1820). American painter: *Helen Brought to Paris*, Milwaukee, Walker Art Center. (This is the picture mentioned by John Galt, *Life, Studies, and Works of Benjamin West, Esq.*, London, 1820, p.223, as 'Helen brought to Paris, in the possession of a family in Kent.' Galt also notes: 'a picture of Pylades and Orestes' (p.222); 'Hector parting with his Wife and Child' (p.225); 'Chryseis returned to her father' (p.225); 'the picture of Chryseis on the Sea-Shore' (p.226); 'Aegisthus viewing the Body of Clytemnestra' (p.227); 'Calypso and Telemachus on the Sea-shore' (p.229); 'the sketch of Priam soliciting of Achilles the Body of Hector' (p.232); and 'the death of Dido' (p.232).

ANGELICA KAUFFMANN (1741–1807). Swiss painter. Most of her pictures were painted in several versions. Among them are: *Telemachus and Mentor Feasted by Calypso and Her Nymphs* (Metropolitan Museum, 25.110.187) and *Telemachus Crowned by the Nymphs of Calypso* (Metropolitan Museum, 25.110.188), both based on Fénelon; *Zeuxis Choosing Models for His Picture of Helen*, Annmary Brown Memorial, Providence; *Achilles Discovered by Ulysses at Scyros*; *Hector Reproving Paris*; *Flight of Paris and Helen*; *Achilles Lamenting the Death of Patroclus*; *Ulysses and Calypso*; *Penelope Weeping over Ulysses' Bow*; *Penelope Awakened by the News of Ulysses' Return*.

HENRY FUSELI (1741–1826). Anglo-Swiss painter and illustrator: drawings for the *Iliad* and the *Odyssey* (Pl.151). Large collections of these in the British Museum, the Kunsthaus, Zürich, and other collections. Paintings include *Odysseus and His Companions Escaping from the Cave of Polyphemus*, Private Collection (Pl.127).

BERNARDINO NOCCHI (1741–1812). Italian painter: *Ulysses Abandoning Calypso*, Lucca, Picture Gallery.

VINCENZO PACETTI (1746–1820). Italian painter: *Achilles and Penthesilea*, Rome, Academy of Saint Luke.

JACQUES-LOUIS DAVID (1748–1825). French painter: *Paris and Helen*, Paris, Louvre (Pl.22); *Hector*, Montpellier Museum; *Andromache Bewailing Hector*, Paris, École des Beaux-Arts.

VINCENZO FERRARI. Italian painter: *Sacrifice of Iphigenia*, 1794, Parma, National Gallery.

19th Century

PAINTING AND SCULPTURE.

JOHN TRUMBULL (1756–1843). American painter: *Priam Receiving the Body of Hector*, Boston, Museum of Fine Arts.

JOHANN HEINRICH WILHELM TISCHBEIN (1751–1829). German painter, nephew of Johann Heinrich the Elder: *Orestes and Iphigenia*, Private Collection (Orestes said to be modelled on the young Goethe, Iphigenia to be a portrait of Lady Hamilton); *Odysseus and Nausicaä*, Cassel, Landesmuseum.

JOHN FLAXMAN (1755–1826). British sculptor and illustrator: illustrations for the *Iliad* and the *Odyssey*, engraved by Piroli and originally published 1793. Many of the drawings are in the British Museum, Victoria and Albert Museum, University College, London; several are in the Diploma Gallery of the Royal Academy, London, and *Achilles and the Shade of Patroclus* in the Metropolitan Museum (18.132.1) (Pl.72). Flaxman's sculptured *Shield of Achilles* was cast in silver-gilt for the King of England, the Duke of York, Lord Lonsdale, and the Duke of Northumberland; there are several bronze versions and plaster casts. Drawings for the shield are in the British Museum. (*See* W. G. Constable, *John Flaxman*, London, 1927, pp. 68–69, 72, 94–95.)

ANTONIO CANOVA (1757–1822). Italian sculptor: among Canova's Trojan sculptures are statues of Hector, Venice, Palazzo Treves; Paris, Munich, Alte Pinakothek. A statue of Pauline Bonaparte as Venus Victrix, with the apple, is in the Borghese Gallery, Rome. The bust of Helen which inspired Byron's line, 'In this beloved marble see', is in a private collection, Venice.

FELICE GIANI (b. 1757–60; d. 1823). Italian painter and illustrator: drawings for the *Iliad*, many of which are in the Cooper Union Museum for the Arts of Decoration, New York (Pl.50).

WILLIAM BLAKE (1757–1827). British painter and poet: *Judgment of Paris*, watercolour, London, British Museum.

BERTEL THORWALDSEN (1768?–1844). Danish sculptor. Replicas of many of Thorwaldsen's Trojan works are in various collections. Among the works in the Thorwaldsen Museum, Copenhagen, which includes many original models as well as marble versions, are reliefs (both original models and marbles): *Cheiron Teaching Achilles to Cast the Spear*; *The Surrender of Briseis* (Pl.45); *Hector Upbraiding Paris for Cowardice*; *Farewell of Hector and Andromache*; *Priam Imploring Achilles for Hector's Body* (Pl.75); *Achilles and Patroclus*; *Achilles and Penthesilea* (Pl.78); *Ulysses Receiving the Armour of Achilles* (model only); *Thetis Dipping Achilles in the Styx* (model only). Sculpture in the round: *Venus with the Apple* (original model and marble).

ETIENNE GARNIER (1759–1849). French painter: *Lamentation over the Death of Hector*, Paris, Luxembourg; *Odysseus and Nausicaä*.

ANNE LOUIS GIRODET DE ROUSSY-TRIOSON (1767–1824). French painter and illustrator: illustrations for the *Aeneid*, lithographs after, published by M. Pannetier, Paris, 1826, 1827.

LUIGI SABATELLI (1772–1850). Italian painter: worked with his son Francesco in 1819 on decorations of the Hall of the Iliad, Florence, Pitti Palace.

FRANÇOIS GÉRARD (1770–1837). French painter: *Judgment of Paris*, *Achilles Mourning Patroclus*, Caen, Musée; illustrations for an edition of Vergil.

PIERRE GUÉRIN (1774–1833). French painter: *Andromache and Pyrrhus*, Paris, Louvre (another version in the Bordeaux Museum); *Clytemnestra about to Stab Agamemnon* and *Aeneas Relating to Dido the Misfortunes of Troy*, both in the Louvre, Paris. Another version of the latter in the Bordeaux Museum.

JOSEPH WILLIAM MALLORD TURNER (1775–1851). British painter: *The Goddess of Discord Choosing an Apple in the Garden of the Hesperides*, *Aeneas Relating to Dido the Story of His Adventures*, *Dido and Aeneas Leaving for the Hunt*, *Mercury Sent to Announce to Aeneas that He must Leave Carthage*, *Departure of Aeneas' Fleet*, *Aeneas and the Sibyl;* all in London, Tate Gallery; *Ulysses Deriding Polyphemus*, London, National Gallery (Pl.130).

JÉRÔME-MARTIN LANGLOIS (1779–1838). French painter: *Priam and Achilles*, Paris, École des Beaux-Arts; *Cassandra Imploring the Vengeance of Minerva*, Paris, Louvre.

WASHINGTON ALLSTON (1779–1843). American painter: *Dido and Anna*, Boston, Museum of Fine Arts.

JEAN-AUGUSTE-DOMINIQUE INGRES (1780–1867). French painter: *Thetis Imploring Jupiter to Honour Achilles*, Aix Museum; *The Ambassadors of Agamemnon at the Tent of Achilles*, Paris, École des Beaux-Arts; *Apotheosis of Homer*, Paris, Louvre.

CHRISTOFFER WILHELM ECKERSBERG (1783–1853). Danish painter: *Hector's Farewell to Andromache*, Copenhagen, Thorwaldsen Museum.

WILLIAM ETTY (1787–1849). British painter: *Ulysses and the Sirens*, Manchester, City Art Gallery.

EUGÈNE DELACROIX (1796–1863). French painter: *Education of Achilles*, ceiling lunette, Chamber of Deputies, Paris; *Education of Achilles*, easel painting, same composition, Private Collection.

GASPARO MARTELLINI (1785–1857). Italian painter: *Return of Ulysses*, ceiling painting, Hall of Ulysses, Florence, Pitti Palace.

FRANCESCO SABATELLI (1803–1829). Italian painter, worked with his father Luigi on decorations in the Hall of the Iliad, Florence, Pitti Palace (Pl.56).

ANTOINE-JOSEPH WIERTZ (1806–1865). Belgian painter and sculptor. Paintings: *Combat over the Body of Patroclus*; *Polyphemus Devouring the Companions of Ulysses*, Brussels, Wiertz Museum. Sculpture: *Laocoön and His Sons*, Brussels, Wiertz Museum.

HONORÉ DAUMIER (1808–1879). French painter, lithographer, sculptor: *Histoire ancienne*, a series of lithographs caricaturing ancient history and mythology, including 17 related to the story of Troy, published in *Charivari*, Paris, 1841–1842 (Pls.153,154.)

PIO FEDI (1816–1892). Italian sculptor: *Polyxena Carried to Sacrifice*, Florence, Loggia dei Lanzi.

GUSTAVE MOREAU (1826–1898). French painter: *Helen on the Walls of Troy*, several versions in the Gustave Moreau Museum, Paris, and at least one other, location unknown; *Circe*, *Polyphemus*, several versions, Gustave Moreau Museum.

JEAN-BAPTISTE CARPEAUX (1827–1875). French sculptor: *Hector Imploring the Gods on Behalf of Astyanax*, Paris, École des Beaux-Arts.

ARNOLD BÖCKLIN (1827–1901). German-Swiss painter: *Odysseus and Calypso*, Basel Museum; *Iphigenia*, or *The Villa by the Sea*, Munich, Schach Gallery; *Polyphemus*; *Odysseus on the Sea Shore*.

ANSELM FEUERBACH (1829–1880). German painter: *Iphigenia in Tauris*, Darmstadt Museum; *Iphigenia in Tauris* (later version), Stuttgart, Picture Gallery; *Judgment of Paris*, Hamburg, Kunsthalle.

FREDERICK LEIGHTON (1830–1896). British painter: *The Captive Andromache* (Pl.106), and *Helen on the Walls of Troy*, both Manchester, City Art Gallery; *Clytemnestra Awaiting the Return of Agamemnon*, London, Leighton House; *Electra at the Tomb of Agamemnon*; *Penelope and Her Women*.

DANTE GABRIEL ROSSETTI (1828–1882). British painter: *Helen of Troy*, oil; *Troy Town*, crayon and wash, design for a picture to illustrate the artist's ballad of that name; *Cassandra*, pen and ink, illustrating two sonnets of that name, London, British Museum; *Penelope*, crayon drawing.

EDWARD BURNE-JONES (1833–1898). British painter: *The Feast of Peleus* (Pl.6), Birmingham, City Museum and Art Gallery; *The Story of Troy*, unfinished triptych, and *Helen Captive in Burning Troy*, watercolour cartoon for right side of triptych, also in the Birmingham Gallery; *Helen of Troy*, watercolour drawing, Cambridge (Mass.), Fogg Art Museum, Winthrop Bequest; *The Wine of Circe* (Pl.138), Collection of the Marquess of Normanby.

HENRI FANTIN-LATOUR (1836–1904). French painter and lithographer: *Judgment of Paris*, painting, Rheims Museum; *Helen*, painting, inspired by Goethe's *Faust*, Paris, École des Beaux-Arts; *The Apparition of Hector to Aeneas before the Fall of Troy*, several versions, inspired by Berlioz' opera, *The Trojans*; *Duet from the Trojans*, lithograph and painting, inspired by Berlioz; *The Trojans at Carthage*, painting, inspired by Berlioz.

19th–20th Century

PAINTING AND SCULPTURE.

AUGUSTE RODIN (1840–1917). French sculptor: *Polyphemus*, several versions in various sizes; *Hecuba*, several versions in various sizes; *Education of Achilles*, several versions in various sizes.

PIERRE-AUGUSTE RENOIR (1841–1919). French painter and sculptor. Paintings: *Judgment of Paris*, several versions, Collections of Charles Laughton, Henry P. McIlhenny, Germantown, Pa. (Pl.17); Barnes Foundation, Merion, Pa. Sculpture: *Judgment of Paris*, bronze relief, several versions, including Collections of Dr. and Mrs. Harry Bakwin, New York, and Cleveland Museum of Art; *Venus Victorious*, standing bronze figure, several versions, including Collection of Dr. and Mrs. Harry Bakwin, New York, and Modern Gallery, Vienna.

HENRI REGNAULT (1843–1871). French painter: *Thetis Bringing Achilles the Armour Made by Vulcan*, Paris, École des Beaux-Arts; *Automedon and the Horses of Achilles*, Boston, Museum of Fine Arts.

HENRI-PAUL MOTTE (1846–1922). French painter: *The Trojan Horse*, Washington, National Gallery of Art.

JOHN WILLIAM WATERHOUSE (1849–1917). British painter: *Odysseus and the Sirens*, Melbourne, National Gallery; *Circe Offering Odysseus the Drugged Cup*.

JOHN SINGER SARGENT (1856–1925). American painter: *Achilles and Cheiron*, relief in the rotunda of the Museum of Fine Arts, Boston.

MAX KLINGER (1857–1920). German painter and sculptor: *Judgment of Paris*, painting; *Cassandra*, sculpture, both in Leipzig Museum.

LOVIS CORINTH (1858–1925). German painter: *The Trojan Horse*, Berlin, State Museum.

HERBERT DRAPER (1864–1920). British painter: *Ulysses and the Sirens*, Hull Museum.

MAX SLEVOGT (1868–1932). German painter and illustrator: *Achilles*, a series of lithographs illustrating the *Iliad* (Pl.68).

BRYSON BURROUGHS (1869–1934). American painter: *Abduction of Helen*, *Toilet of Helen* (Pl.96), *Calypso's Island* (Pl.121), *Nausicaä and Her Maidens*, Baltimore, Mrs. Bryson Burroughs.

CARLO CARRÀ (1881–). Italian painter: *Penelope* (Pl.119), Collection of Carlo Frua de Angeli, Milan.

PABLO PICASSO (1881–). Spanish painter: *Ulysses and the Sirens*, 1946. Antibes, Museum.

PAUL MANSHIP (1885–). American sculptor: *Briseis*, bronze statue and also several bronze statuettes.

GIORGIO DE CHIRICO (1888–). Italian painter: *Hector and Andromache* (1916?), Private Collection; *Hector and Andromache* (1917), Gianni Mattioli Collection, Milan (Pl.51); *Hector and Andromache* (1918), Private Collection, Houston, Texas; *Hector and Andromache* (1924), Collection of Vittorio De Sica, Rome (Pl.52).

KARL ZERBE (1903–). American painter: *The Trojan Horse*, Racine, Wisconsin, Collection of the Friends of Art of Racine.

BASALDELLE MIRKO (1910–). Italian sculptor: *Hector*, abstract bronze figure (1949), Dallas, Texas, Collection of Stanley Seeger, Jr.

Needless to say no list of locations of works of art can long remain accurate: works in private collections change hands, either by sale or inheritance, or by gift to public collections. Some that are noted here may have disappeared or changed location during or after World War II; others entered as 'unknown' may at any time come to light. And works in the great public collections such as London, Paris, and Rome are frequently moved from museum to museum within their cities.

THE GREEKS DESCEND FROM THE WOODEN HORSE.
Cornelian scarab, Etruscan, early fifth century B.C. (enlarged).
New York, Metropolitan Museum of Art, 32.11.7.
Fletcher Fund 1932.

NOTES

INTRODUCTION

The following works are invaluable for any consideration of the scope and persistence of the Troy legend in literature and art:

For the Greek and Roman worlds: *Real-Encyklopädie der klassischen Altertumswissenschaft*, ed. by Pauly, Wissowa, Kroll, and others, Stuttgart, 1894–1957; The *Oxford Classical Dictionary*, Oxford, 1949; Moses Hadas, *Ancilla to Classical Reading*, for general background; Sir James Frazer's notes to the Loeb Classical Library edition of Apollodorus' *Library*, London, 1922, 2 vols., for comparative versions of various themes; Tenney Frank, *Life and Literature in the Roman Republic*, University of California Press, 1930; John Wight Duff, *A Literary History of Rome from the Origins to the Close of the Golden Age*, New York, 1960, and *A Literary History of Rome in the Silver Age*, New York, 1960; J. W. Mackail, *Latin Literature*, New York, 1895, 1923.

A most useful list of heroic subjects on Greek vases is Frank Brommer's *Vasenlisten zur Griechischen Heldensage*, Marburg/Lahn, 1960.

For the classical influence in the Middle Ages and Renaissance: R. R. Bolgar, *The Classical Heritage and Its Beneficiaries*, Cambridge (Eng.), 1954, which carries the theme through the Renaissance and in its Appendices gives invaluable lists of Greek MSS. in Italy during the fifteenth century and of the translations of Greek and Roman classics before 1600; Ernst R. Curtius, *European Literature and the Latin Middle Ages*, trans. by W. R. Trask, New York [1953], Bollingen Series XXXVI; H. O. Taylor, *The Classical Heritage of the Middle Ages*, 3rd ed., New York, 1911; Wilhelm Greif, *Die mittelalterlichen Bearbeitungen der Trojanersage: ein neuer Beitrag zur Dares- und Dictysfrage*, Marburg, 1885.

For surveys of the influence of Greek and Latin literature upon later periods: J. E. Sandys, *A History of Classical Scholarship*, Cambridge (Eng.), 3 vols., 1908–1921, Vol. I, Seventh Century B.C. to the End of the Middle Ages, Vol. II, From the Revival of Learning to the End of the Eighteenth Century (except Germany), Vol. III, The Eighteenth Century in Germany and the Nineteenth Century in Europe and the United States of America; Gilbert Highet, *The Classical Tradition*, New York, 1949, which outlines this tradition almost to the date of publication and, with copious notes, forms the most comprehensive modern survey in the field; *A Bibliography of the Survival of the Classics*, 2 vols., London, 1934, 1938 (German text), which covers a wide range of books and articles on the subject.

For the persistence of classical motives in art: Erwin Panofsky and Fritz Saxl, *Classical Mythology in Medieval Art*, *Metropolitan Museum Studies*, Vol. IV, New York, 1933, pp.228–280; Erwin Panofsky, *Meaning in the Visual Arts*, New York, 1955, chapter on Iconography and Iconology: an Introduction to the Study of Renaissance Art; Jean Seznec, *The Survival of the Pagan Gods*, trans. by Barbara F. Sessions,

New York, 1953, Bollingen Series XXXVIII; Arthur M. Young, *Troy and Her Legend*, University of Pittsburgh, 1948.

Manuscripts are treated in Fritz Saxl's *Lectures*, London, Warburg Institute, 1957, chapter on The Troy Romances in French and Italian Art; Fritz Saxl, *Verzeichnis astrologischer und mythologischer illustrierter Handschriften des lateinischen Mittelalters*, Vol. I, Handschriften in römischen Bibliotheken, Heidelberg, 1915, Vol. II, Handschriften der National-Bibliothek in Wien, Heidelberg, 1927, Vol. III, Fritz Saxl and Hans Meier, ed. by Harry Bober, Manuscripts in English Libraries, London, Warburg Institute, 1953 (German text); and Hugo Buchthal, *Miniature Painting in the Latin Kingdom of Jerusalem*, Oxford, 1957.

For the Trojan story in music *see* Grove's *Dictionary of Music and Musicians*, 5th edition, ed. by Eric Blom, London and New York, 1954, under names of composers or titles and subjects of operas, and Arthur M. Young, *Troy and Her Legend*, section on opera, pp.164–173.

Page IX

The emergence of an actual Troy from a mass of confused legend has been the result of roughly a hundred years of excavation. From the early Middle Ages until well into the nineteenth century the city's very site was in doubt. This doubt had arisen, indeed, in the second century B.C., but for some hundreds of years longer Greek and Roman tradition held to the site approved today. Later, however, various locations were associated with Homeric heroes. On the coast, south of the Cape of Sigeum, the remnants of the Graeco-Roman city of Alexandria Troas, some of its columns emerging picturesquely from the sea, were called those of Priam's city. Standing there, where grain waved among the ruins, travellers, especially those of the seventeenth century, quoted Ovid's lines from the *Heroides*: '*iam seges est, ubi Troia fuit*—Now are fields of corn where Troy once was.'

In the eighteenth and much of the nineteenth century antiquaries favoured two sites farther from the shore: Burnabashi, the Turkish Balli Dağ, lying inland north of Alexandria Troas, and, a little nearer the coast, a hill near the Turkish village of Hisarlik, less than four miles from the sea. As early as 1822 Charles Maclaren had identified Hisarlik as the site of Homeric Troy, but it remained for Heinrich Schliemann, excavating there in a fury of devotion between 1870 and 1890, to demonstrate this identification forcibly.

Mistaken in many details, such as which of the many ruined cities lying one above the other on the hill was Priam's Troy, Schliemann nevertheless established Hisarlik as the only possible site. His successors, notably Wilhelm Dörpfeld, his colleague in the last years of his life, and Carl W. Blegen, who led the excavations of the University of Cincinnati from 1932 to 1938, unearthed the ruins of a city whose buildings and the manner and time of whose destruction coincided remarkably with those credited to Homeric Troy.

The hill of Hisarlik was covered by the débris of nine successive occupations, each consisting of several phases. These have been numbered in order from the bottom, as Troy I through IX. Schliemann, confident that Priam's Troy lay deeply buried, dug down in the centre to (and through) the second of these layers, Troy II, and missed the walls surrounding the cities of the upper layers. At this low level, rich in evidences of a conflagration from which the inhabitants had fled, abandoning many objects of gold, bronze, and copper, he announced that he had found the city captured by Agamemnon. Later excavations have shown that this layer belonged to a culture far older than the period assigned to the Trojan war—certainly in the third millennium B.C.

The seventh city, now generally accepted as Homeric Troy, itself consisted of two layers, known as VIIa and VIIb, that destroyed during the Trojan war being called VIIa. The objects found here, pottery especially, suggest a date of about 1300–1250 B.C., some generations earlier than that given by Eratosthenes for the fall of Troy, 1184 B.C. This layer, too, was destroyed by fire, and the crowding of small houses within its walls, as well as the great number of large storage jars, suggests a time of siege.

The dating here sheds an interesting light on the traditional first destruction of Troy in the time of Priam's father, Laomedon. The citadel (VI) immediately below VIIa was overthrown by earthquake, perhaps about 1300. Traditionally, it was destroyed by Jason and Hercules, but behind their action lay the anger of Poseidon at Laomedon's failure to keep his promises (*see* page 24 and Note)—and Poseidon was the Earthshaker.

Above the ruins of Homeric Troy, where, for a time, some survivors carried on a humbler way of life, rose a later Greek city, and above this, which was sacked by the Roman general Fimbria in 86–85 B.C., a Graeco-Roman city. This, too, although mentioned as late as the fourth century A.D., also decayed and was replaced by the olive groves of the Byzantine Greeks.

Next to Troy itself, Agamemnon's city of 'Mycenae, rich in gold', lying in the plain of Argos on the Greek mainland, commands attention. It has had little recorded history since about the third century B.C., but its site has seldom been questioned. The evidence suggests that Mycenae reached its greatest power about 1400–1200 B.C. It sent a small army to fight against the Persians in the fifth century B.C.; later in the same century it was sacked by jealous fellow-Greeks and little was heard of it thereafter. Some of its outstanding structures have always been visible: its Cyclopaean walls, its famous Lion Gate, and many of its beehive tombs, often named for various Homeric heroes.

Schliemann began to excavate here in 1876 and soon proclaimed that he had found the tomb of Agamemnon as well as golden treasures which fitted Homer's descriptions. Later archaeologists, including Chrestos Tsountas, John Papadimitrious, Ephor of Antiquities for Attica and the Argolid, A. J. B. Wace of the British School at Athens, Spyridon Marinatos, Head of the Antiquities Department of the Greek Ministry of Education, and George Mylonas of Washington University, have carried on the work. They have demonstrated that the tombs antedate Agamemnon's period by perhaps several centuries, although ruins of many buildings suggest those mentioned in Homeric epics. The Lion Gate, though older than the Trojan war, stood, nevertheless, in Agamemnon's time.

Pylos, 'stately citadel of Nestor', Agamemnon's wisest counsellor, has yielded rich results to excavators. Begun in 1939 and renewed in 1952, excavations here have revealed a wealthy city controlling one of the best harbours of Greece, on the western shore of the peninsula of the Peloponnesus. A joint Hellenic-American enterprise has been carried on: Blegen, with the University of Cincinnati, digging in and near a rich and spacious palace such as that in which Telemachus might have visited Nestor (*Odyssey*, Book III); Marinatos excavating elsewhere in the district. As mentioned in the Note on p.33, Pylos, in Dares and the medieval romances, supplanted Crete as the place to which Menelaus sailed from Sparta, leaving Helen alone to be abducted if she so wished.

For Homeric geography, excavations, and all phases of background, *see* A. J. B. Wace and Frank H. Stubbings, *Companion to Homer*, London, 1962, chapters on Troy and Pylos by Carl Blegen, on Mycenae by Wace, on Ithaca by Stubbings.

In addition, *see* for specific sites:

TROY

C. W. Blegen, *Troy and the Trojans*, New York, 1963.

C. W. Blegen, C. G. Boulter, J. L. Caskey, M. Rawson, and J. Sperling, *Troy: Excavations Conducted by the University of Cincinnati, 1932–1938*, 4 vols., Princeton, 1950–1958.

W. Dörpfeld, *Troja und Ilion*, Athens, 1902.

W. Leaf, *Troy: A Study in Homeric Geography*, London, 1912.

D. L. Page, *History and the Homeric Iliad*, University of California Press, 1959.

H. Schliemann, *Ilios, the City and Country of the Trojans*, London, 1880.

H. Schliemann, *Troy and Its Remains*, London, 1875.

MYCENAE

Annual of the British School at Athens, reports by A. J. B. Wace and others on excavations: Vol. 45 (1950), pp.203–228; Vol. 49 (1954), pp.231–296; Vol. 50 (1955), pp.175–230; Vol. 51 (1956), pp.103–131; Vol. 52 (1957), pp.193–223.

Edward Bacon, *Digging for History*, London, 1960, pp.84–89.

George E. Mylonas, *Ancient Mycenae: the Capital City of Agamemnon*, Princeton, 1957.

H. Schliemann, *Mycenae, A Narrative of Researches and Discoveries at Mycenae and Tiryns*, New York, 1880.

A. J. B. Wace, *Mycenae: An Archaeological History and Guide*, Princeton, 1949.

Pylos

American Journal of Archaeology, reports on Pylos, especially the 'Palace of Nestor', by Carl W. Blegen: Vol. 43 (1939), pp.557–576; Vol. 57 (1953), pp.59–64; Vol. 58 (1954), pp.27–32; Vol. 59 (1955), pp.31–37; Vol. 60 (1956), pp.95–101; Vol. 61 (1957), pp.129–135; Vol. 62 (1958), pp.175–191; Vol. 63 (1959), pp.121–137; Vol. 64 (1960), pp.158–164; Vol. 65 (1961), pp.153–163; Vol. 66 (1962), pp.145–152.

Edward Bacon, *Digging for History*, London, 1960, pp.89–94.

The quotation from *De Claustro Anime* is taken from A. Thomas, *De Claustro Anime and the Roman de Troie*, *Romania*, Vol. XLII, pp.83–85.

Page XII

The reference to Varro's Trojan genealogies in *De Familiis* is from Gilbert Highet's *Classical Tradition*, as above, p.665, note 17.

The reference to St. Augustine is to his *City of God*, trans. by John Healey, London [1931], Book III, Ch. VIII, pp.113–114.

The quotation from Paulus Orosius is from his *Seven Books of History Against the Pagans*, trans. by Irving W. Raymond, New York, 1936, pp.65–66.

Pages XII–XIII

For the dating of Dictys and Dares *see* Mary Elizabeth Barnicle, *The Seege or Batyle of Troye*, Early English Text Society, Original Series, No.172, London, 1927, Appendix B, pp.216–231; Wilhelm von Christ, *Geschichte der Griechischen Literatur*, Munich, 1924, Vol. II, Pt. ii, pp.811–812; Wilhelm Greif, *Die mittelalterlichen Bearbeitungen der Trojanersage*, Marburg, 1885; Pauly-Wissowa, *Real-Encyklopädie*, Vol. V, p.590; Karl Voretzsch, *Introduction to the Study of Old French Literature*, New York, 1931, p.251. A clear and succinct treatment in English of the fragment of a Greek Dictys found 1899–1900 is Nathaniel E. Griffin's *The Greek Dictys*, *American Journal of Philology*, Vol. 29 (1908), pp.329–335. For the Latin text of Dictys *see Dictys Cretensis, Ephemeridos Belli Troiani*, ed. by Werner Eisenhut, Leipzig, 1958.

Page XIII

The translation from Benoit's *Prologue*, lines 45ff., was made by Hannah McAllister.

Page XVII

Morris' Trojan fragments are published in *The Collected Works of William Morris*, London, 1915, Vol. 24, Scenes from the Fall of Troy. The Introduction by May Morris, pp.xxvii ff., gives a list of the projected poems. *See also* J. W. Mackail, *The Life of William Morris*, London and New York, 1907, 2 vols., Vol. I, pp.166–178.

Page XVIII

Peele's *Arraignment of Paris* is published in *The Collected Works of George Peele*, London, 1828, Vol. I.

BEFORE THE ILIAD

Page 3

The opening quotations from the *Cypria* are from *Scholiast on Homer, Iliad*, I.5 as given in Hesiod, *The Homeric Hymns and Homerica*, Loeb Classical Library, London and New York, 1914, p.497. All quotations from the summaries of the epic cycle and other material pertaining to them are from this edition.

Page 4

The apple appears on the wrist of Paris in a fourth-century Campanian lekythos in the Metropolitan Museum, acc.no.06.1021.223.

For the ivory carving from Sparta with the debatable apple *see* R. M. Dawkins, *The Sanctuary of Artemis Orthia at Sparta*, *Journal of Hellenic Studies*, *Supplementary Papers*, London, Vol. V (1929), p.223, No.4, and Pl.CXXVII; also C. Clairmont, *Das Paris-Urteil in der antiken Kunst*, Zürich, 1951, pp.14–15.

Pages 5-6

The dialogue of Panope and Galene is from Lucian, *Dialogues of the Sea Gods*, V, trans. by H. W. and F. G. Fowler, Oxford, 1905.

Page 6

Guido tells of the apple in his *Historia Destructionis Troiae*, ed. by Nathaniel E. Griffin, Medieval Academy of America, Cambridge (Mass.), 1936, p.62, the standard edition of Guido's text.

Pages 6-7

The quotation from Lydgate's *Troy Book* is from the edition published by the Early English Text Society, Extra Series 97, 103, 106, 126, 4 vols., London, 1906–1935, Vol. I, Book II. Here, and in similar quotations, the spelling and more archaic phrases have been modernized by the author.

Page 7

The paintings of the Palermo ceiling are described and illustrated in *Lo Steri di Palermo*, by Ettore Gabrici and Ezio Levi, Milan (n.d.).

The Treviso Trojan war frescoes of about 1313 are described and illustrated from drawings by Julius von Schlosser in *Jahrbuch der kunsthistorischen Sammlungen des Allerhöchsten Kaiserhauses*, first series, Vol. XIX (1898), pp.240–246.

Page 8

For moralized Ovids *see* Karl Voretzsch, *Introduction to the Study of Old French Literature*, New York, 1931, pp.244–246; Jean Seznec, *The Survival of the Pagan Gods*,

Bollingen Series, XXXVIII, trans. by Barbara F. Sessions, New York, 1953, pp.174–175; Sanford Brown Meech, *Chaucer and the Ovide Moralisé*, Modern Language Association Publication No.46, New York, 1931, pp.182–204; Gilbert Highet, *The Classical Tradition*, New York, 1949, p.62; L. K. Born, *Ovid and Allegory*, *Speculum*, Vol. IX (1934), pp.362–379; and Fausto Ghisalberti, *Mediaeval Biographies of Ovid*, *Journal of the Warburg and Courtauld Institutes*, London, Vol. IX (1946), pp.10–59.

The quotation from Christine de Pisan is from a fifteenth-century translation (modernized by the author) by Stephen Scrope, *The Epistle of Othéa to Hector; or The Booke of Knyghthode . . .*, ed. from a MS in the library of the Marquis of Bath by George F. Warner, London, Roxburghe Club, 1944. A sixteenth-century translation, probably by Anthony Babyngton, has been edited by James D. Gordon from Harleian MS 838 and published in Philadelphia, 1942.

Page 9

Burne-Jones' *Feast of Peleus* is described in the *Catalogue of the New Gallery Exhibition of the Works of Sir Edward Burne-Jones*, London, 1898–99, p.38, No.29.

Page 11

The quotation from *The Trojan Women* is from the translation by Gilbert Murray, New York, 1912.

Pages 12-13

Apuleius' description of the danced mime is from his *Golden Ass*, Book X.

Page 13

Ovid refers to the three goddesses as nude in *Heroides*, XVIII, 115.

Pages 13-14

Lucian's description of the judgment of Paris is from his *Dialogues of the Gods*, XX.

Page 15

Dio Chrysostom suggests that Paris dreamed in *Discourses*, XX, *Retirement*, 22.

Page 16

Raoul Lefèvre's description of the judgment of Paris as a dream is from *The Recuyell of the Historyes of Troye*, Caxton's translation, ed. by H. Oscar Sommer, London, 2 vols., 1894, Vol. II, pp.521–22. All other quotations from Lefèvre are from this text, with modernizations by the author.

'Four ladies of Elfin land' and 'Maidens in chamber' are from *The Seege or Batyle of Troye*, ed. by Mary Elizabeth Barnicle, Early English Text Society, Original Series, No.172, London, 1927, pp.41–42, with spellings modernized by the author.

Page 18

Raphael's indebtedness to the sarcophagus now in the Villa Medici is discussed by Anton Springer, *Raffael und Michelangelo*, ed. by Robert Dohme in *Kunst und Künstler des Mittelalters und der Neuzeit*, Vol. II, Pt. 2, Leipzig, 1878, pp.310–312.

The sarcophagus is described and discussed by Karl Robert in *Die antiken Sarkophagreliefs*, Vol. II, Berlin, 1890, pp.13–16; and by M. Cagiano de Azevedo, *Le Antichità di Villa Medici*, Rome, 1951, p.68, no.54 and Pl.XXVIII, no.43.

Page 20

Cranach's *Judgment of Paris* is published by Harry B. Wehle in *Metropolitan Museum Studies*, Vol. II (1929–1930), pp.1–12; the legend of the King of Mercia is discussed in Paul Durrieu's *Le Légende du Roi de Mercie*, in *Fondation Eugène Piot, Monuments et Mémoires, Académie des Inscriptions et Belles-Lettres*, Vol. 24 (1920), pp.149–182; and in Emile Moliner, *Les Bronzes de la Renaissance: Les Plaquettes*, Paris, 1886, Vol. II, pp.176–183.

Page 23

Renoir's reliefs of the judgment of Paris are discussed in Paul Haessert's *Renoir Sculptor*, New York, 1947, p.26 and Pls.X–XIII.

Page 24

The tapestry of Laomedon forbidding Jason and Hercules to land is described and its inscription translated by G. L. Hunter, *The Practical Book of Tapestries*, Philadelphia, 1925, p.81.

The *Iliad* refers to Hercules' capture of Troy in Book V, 640–643.

Poseidon's complaint is given in the *Iliad*, Book XXI, 435–460.

Apollodorus gives a typical account of Hercules' capture of Troy in his *Library*, II, V, 9; II, VI, 4.

Corrigendum, line 20: *for* Aristophon *read* Artemon.—Pliny mentions Artemon's painting of the story of Laomedon in his *Natural History*, XXXV, 40.

Diodorus of Sicily links the stories of Hercules' capture of the city with the Argonauts in his *Historical Library*, IV, 32–42, 49.

Ovid mentions this capture in *Metamorphoses*, XI, 198–220. Dares discusses it in his *History*, Ch.2.

Boccaccio's account of the exposure and rescue of Hesione is given in his *Genealogy of the Gods*, Book VI.

Page 28

The other fragments of the krater showing Helen are described by Cedric Boulter in *Shards from a White-ground Krater*, *American Journal of Archaeology*, Vol. 54 (1950), p.120, pl.XXI.

The dialogue concerning Helen is from Lucian's *Dialogues of the Dead*, XVIII.

For an exhaustive treatment of the abductions and return of Helen in ancient literature and art *see* Lilly B. Ghali-Kahil, *Les Enlèvements et le Retour d'Hélène*, Paris, 2 vols., 1955.

Page 30
The relation between David's painting and Gluck's opera is discussed by Edgar Wind in *The Journal of the Warburg and Courtauld Institutes*, Vol. IV, London (1940–1941), pp.135–138; and by Martin Cooper in *Gluck*, New York, 1935, pp.138ff.

Pages 31-32
Hecuba's speech is from the translation of *The Trojan Women* by Gilbert Murray, New York, 1912.

Pages 32-33
The cassone panel with scenes from the story of Helen is described by Edward S. King in *The Legend of Paris and Helen*, *Journal of the Walters Art Gallery*, Vol. II (1939), pp.55–72, together with the panels of the same story in that collection attributed to the studio of Antonio Vivarini. The most complete work on cassone paintings is Paul Schubring's *Cassoni: Truhen und Truhenbilder der italienischen Frührenaissance*, Leipzig, 1915, and Supplement, 1923.

Page 33
Benoit de Sainte-More, following Dares (Ch. IX), changed the place to which Menelaus sailed from Crete to Nestor's city of Pylos, a change followed by other romancers. In the light of recent excavations, Lydgate's description seems especially apt, '. . . Pylos, a famous and strong city.'

Page 34
The Abduction of Helen, School of Antonio Vivarini, is published by Edward S. King in the *Journal of the Walters Art Gallery*, as given in note on pp.32–33.

Page 36
Dictys' account of the relationship of Helen and Hecuba is from I, 9–10.

Page 37
The tapestry of the marriage of Paris and Helen is from a set formerly in the Château de Cany near Yvetot, Normandy. It and two companion pieces showing the arrival of Paris and Helen at Troy and the embassy of Ulysses and Diomedes

to ask for Helen's return, also in the possession of Duveen Brothers, were for a long time unidentified, although their inscriptions were noted in 1886 by Jules Guiffrey in his *Histoire de la Tapisserie*, Paris, 1886, pp.155–156.

Page 39

Odysseus' description of the sacrifice of Calchas is from the *Iliad*, Book II, 299. Ovid tells of it in *Metamorphoses*, XII, 10–24.

Page 40

References to Achilles' vulnerable heel are found in Hyginus' *Fabulae*, 107, and in Quintus of Smyrna, *Fall of Troy*, III, 60.

A delightful description of the education of Achilles is given in Pindar's *Nemaean Odes*, III, 43, as well as in Statius' *Achilleid*, Book I, as quoted.

Page 41

Rubens' oil sketches for the Achilles tapestries are discussed by Leo van Puyvelde in *Les Esquisses de Rubens*, Bâle, 1940. The tapestries are published by Marthe Crick-Kuntziger in the *Bulletin des Musées Royaux d'Art et d'Histoire*, Brussels, Series 3, 1934, pp.2–12.

Page 44

Timanthes' painting of the sacrifice is described in Pliny's *Natural History*, XXXV, 36.

Page 45

Dictys' account of the sacrifice appears in Book I, 20–22.

Page 46

Dares tells of the placating of Diana in Ch. XV. All quotations from Dares and references to his *Historia* are taken from the translation by Margaret Schlauch in *Mediaeval Narratives*, New York, 1934.

Benoit's reference to Agamemnon's offence is given in Book XI, 593ff. All references to this author are to *Le Roman de Troie par Benoit de Sainte-Maure*, ed. by Leopold Constans, Paris, 6 vols., 1904–1912, the standard edition. Numbers indicate lines.

Ovid tells of the substitution of the hind in *Metamorphoses*, XII, 28–36; XIII, 184–194 gives the other version of the story in which the actual sacrifice is not made certain.

Boccaccio tells both forms of the story in Book XII of his *Genealogy of the Gods*.

Page 48

For Tiepolo's frescoes in the Villa Valmarana *see* P. G. Molmenti, *Tiepolo, la Villa Valmarana*, Venice, 1928; and Michael Levey, *Tiepolo's Treatment of Classical Story at Villa Valmarana* in *Journal of the Warburg and Courtauld Institutes*, Vol. XX (1957), pp.298–317.

Page 50
Ovid tells the story of Protesilaus and Laodamia in *Heroides*, XIII.

Page 51
The vase showing Menelaus and Odysseus demanding the return of Helen is published by J. D. Beazley as an excerpt from the *Proceedings of the British Academy*, Vol. XLIII (1958), London, Oxford University Press, pp.236–237. Bacchylides' version of the story is discussed.

The tapestry of the embassy of Diomedes and Ulysses to Priam is discussed by Betty Kurth in *Masterpieces of Gothic Tapestry in the Burrell Collection*, *Connoisseur*, Vol. 117 (March, 1946), p.7 and Pl.5.

Teuthras, whom Achilles slays here, did not play so active a part in the war in Greek legend, where his greatest importance seems to have lain in his relationship to his protégé or adopted heir, Telephus, son of Hercules and Auge. In these legends Achilles wounded but did not kill Telephus, who was eventually won over to the Greek side. Among valuable sources for the story of Telephus, aside from the summary of the *Cypria*, are Apollodorus (*Library*, III, ix) and Hyginus (*Fabulae*, CI). Hyginus says that he married Laodice, daughter of Priam. The legend of Telephus appears on the reliefs of the small frieze of the Altar of Zeus from Pergamon (Appendix B, p.235).

In Dares, Achilles and Telephus together sacked Mysia while Diomedes and Ulysses were demanding Helen's return at Troy. Teuthras was, therefore, the only prominent Mysian enemy with whom Achilles could engage in combat, and Dares says that he was killed by the Greek champion. The romances in general followed Dares, although they sometimes changed the exact time of the engagement.

Cassiodorus used Hyginus' story of Telephus' marriage to a Trojan princess to provide a Trojan ancestry for Theodoric, the East Gothic ruler of Rome. (Jordanes, *De origine actibusque Getorum*.)

The marvellous tree at the court of Constantinople is described in the *Antapodosis*, included in *The Works of Liudprand of Cremona*, trans. by F. A. Wright, London, 1930, p.207.

Page 53
The vase showing Achilles lying in wait for Troilus and seeing Polyxena is published by Gisela M. A. Richter, *Greek Paintings; Four Newly Acquired Vases*, *Bulletin of The Metropolitan Museum of Art*, New Series, Vol. 3 (March, 1945), pp.169–170; and by J. D. Beazley in *Attic Black-Figure Vase-Painters*, Oxford, 1956, p.85, no.2. The scene occurs on a number of black-figured vases, including the François vase,

and in an Etruscan painting of the sixth century B.C. in the Tomb of the Bulls at Corneto (without Polyxena). The painting is described and illustrated in Massimo Pallottino's *Etruscan Painting*, trans. by M. E. Stanley, New York (n.d.), pp.29–32.

THE ILIAD

All quotations from the *Iliad* are from the translation by Richmond Lattimore, University of Chicago Press, 1951.

Page 57
The prophecy concerning Achilles is quoted from Catullus, *Poems*, LXIV.

Pages 58-60
Dares (Ch. XIII) does not hint that Briseis had a story, but gives a description followed by later writers, especially regarding the detail of her 'joined eyebrows'. Dictys (II, 17, 19, 33, 34, 36, 49, 51; III, 12; IV, 15) tells the classical story with many details not in the *Iliad*, but calls her by the old name, Hippodamia. *See* W. H. Roscher, *Ausführliches Lexikon der griechischen und römischen Mythologie*, Leipzig, 1886–1890, under *Hippodamia*.

Page 63
The paintings of the Nine Heroes at La Manta are discussed by Paolo d'Ancona, *Gli Affreschi del Castello di Manta*, in *L'Arte*, Vol. VIII (1905), pp.94–106; 183–198; and by Francesco Novati, *Un Cassone Nuziale Senese e la Raffigurazione delle Donne Illustri nell'Arte Italiana dei Secoli XIV e XV*, *Rassegna d'Arte*, Vol. XI (1911), pp.61–67; and also, with other examples, in *Arthurian Legends in Medieval Art*, New York, 1938, by Roger Sherman Loomis and Laura Hibbard Loomis, pp.39–40; and in *Die Neun Helden* by Robert L. Wyss, *Zeitschrift für Schweizerische Archäologie und Kunstgeschichte*, Band 17, Heft 2, pp.73–106, Basel, 1957. The passage from Jacques de Longuyon concerning Hector was translated by R. S. Loomis from the text printed in J. Barbour's *Buik of Alexander*, ed. by R. L. G. Ritchie, Edinburgh, 1925. Professor Loomis also translated the inscription beneath the Castle Manta painting.

Pages 63-65
The Heroes tapestries at The Cloisters are published by James J. Rorimer and Margaret B. Freeman in the *Bulletin of The Metropolitan Museum of Art*, New Series, Vol. 7 (1948–49), pp.243–260).

Page 67
De Chirico's Hector and Andromache series is discussed by James Thrall Soby in his *Giorgio de Chirico*, New York, Museum of Modern Art (n.d.), pp.129, 143.

Page 69
Dares refers to Hector's order that the fire be removed from the Greek ships in Ch. XIX of his *History*.

Page 73
Dares tells of Patroclus' death in Ch. XIX; Dictys, in III, 3ff.

Pages 73-74
The relationship of Giulio Romano's painting and the Roman sarcophagus is discussed by Erwin Panofsky and Fritz Saxl, *Classical Mythology in Mediaeval Art*, in *Metropolitan Museum Studies*, Vol. IV, Pt.2, New York, 1933, p.263.

Page 78
The relief of the shield of Achilles is published in H. Stuart Jones' *Catalogue of the Ancient Sculptures Preserved in the Municipal Collections of Rome, by Members of the British School in Rome*, Vol. I, *The Sculptures of the Museo Capitolino*, Oxford, 1912, pp.172–175.

Pages 79-80
The tapestry of the centaur-archer with the conference of Hector and Achilles is published by William H. Forsyth in the *Bulletin of The Metropolitan Museum of Art*, New Series, Vol. 14 (1955–56), pp.76–84.

Page 80
The origin of the *sagittarius* as the symbol of the constellation is discussed by Paul V. C. Baur in *Centaurs in Ancient Art: The Archaic Period*, Berlin, 1912, pp.2–3.

The Sagittary appears in Benoit, 6900ff, 12353ff, 12404ff; Hupon the Great (whom Dares calls Hippothous and Benoit, Hupot), is introduced also and his death related, 12044ff, 12648ff; Hector's challenge to Achilles appears in 13121ff.

Pages 82-83
The tapestry of the arming of Hector is published by James J. Rorimer in the *Bulletin of The Metropolitan Museum of Art*, Vol. 34 (1939), pp.224–227.

Page 84
For Milet's play, *The Destruction of Troy the Great, see* Voretzsch, *Introduction to the Study of Old French Literature*, New York, 1931, p.496; Gustave Cohen, *Le Théatre en France au Moyen Age*, Paris, 1931, Vol. II, pp.62–63, pls.XXXV–XXXIX; Louis Petit de Julleville, *Histoire du Théatre en France*, Paris, 1880, Vol. II, pp.569–574; and Grace Frank, *The Medieval French Drama*, Oxford, 1954, pp.206–209.

Pages 86-87

Dares tells of Hector's death in Ch. XXIV of his *History*; Dictys describes it in his *Ephemeris*, III, 15. Benoit de Sainte-More's description of the hero's death is in lines 16231ff.

Page 90

The Etruscan paintings from Vulci are discussed in Franz Messerschmidt's *Nekropolen von Vulci*, *Jahrbuch des deutschen archäologischen Instituts*, Vol. XII, Berlin (1930), pp.153–163; and by J. D. Beazley in *Etruscan Vase-Painting*, Oxford, 1947, pp.89–92.

Page 93

The tapestry of the funeral of Hector is published by Betty Kurth in the *Glasgow Art Review* (Scottish Art Review), Vol. I (1946–47), pp.4–6.

THE FALL OF TROY

Pages 96-97

For late classic accounts of Penthesilea *see* Diodorus Siculus, *Varia Historia* (Historical Library), II, 46,5; Apollodorus, *Epitome*, V, I; Quintus of Smyrna, *Fall of Troy*, Book I, 610–674; and Dictys, IV, 2ff. All these say that she was killed by Achilles.

Page 97

The quotation from Propertius is from the *Elegies*, Book III, XI, 14.

Page 98

In Dares, Ch. XXXVI, however, Penthesilea is killed by the son of Achilles.

Dictys tells of Achilles' meeting with Polyxena in III, 2 and III, 20–27.

Pages 98-99

Philostratus tells of Polyxena's meeting with Achilles in *Heroicus*, written about A.D. 215, a little later than the Greek fragment of Dictys. For this reference *see* Gilbert Highet, *The Classical Tradition*, New York, 1949, pp.574–575, note 9.

Dares tells of Achilles' first sight of Polyxena in Ch. XXVII.

Page 99

The sixth-century vase showing Achilles dead with an arrow through the ankle was formerly in the Pembroke-Hope Coll.: its present location is unknown. It is published in Andreas Rumpf, *Chalkidische Vasen*, Berlin and Leipzig, 1927, pp.9–10 and Pl.XII; and H. B. Walters, *History of Ancient Pottery*, New York, 1905, Vol. I, pp.322–323, where it is incorrectly assigned to the Deepdene Collection.

For the killing of Tenes at Tenedos *see* Apollodorus, *Epitome*, III, 26 and note, in Loeb Classical Library ed., Vol. II, p.194.

Hector's prophecy of Achilles' death is quoted from the *Iliad*, XXII, 355–360.

Hyginus tells of Achilles' wound in the heel in *Fabulae*, 107; Apollodorus, in the *Epitome*, V, 4.

Pausanias tells of Achilles in the White Island in *Description of Greece*, III, xix.

Philostratus' account of Achilles' after-life is given in *Heroicus*. *See* Gilbert Highet, *The Classical Tradition*, as above, pp.574–575, note 9.

Page 102
Apollodorus mentions Medea as Achilles' bride in the *Epitome*, V, 5–6.

The quotation from the *Odyssey* on Achilles in the Otherworld is from Book XXIV, 10ff.

Dictys tells of Achilles' death in IV, 10ff.; Dares in Ch. XXXIV.

The *Excidium Troiae* says that Achilles had married Polyxena, who betrayed the secret of his vulnerable spot. *See Excidium Troiae*, ed. by E. Bagby Atwood and Virgil R. Whitaker, Mediaeval Academy of America, Cambridge (Mass.), 1944, Latin text, pp.12, 20, and note, p.66. This note also lists various versions of Achilles' death; p.xlvi speaks of the wounding in the soles of the feet.

Pages 102-103
For the origin and development of the story of Troilus and Cressida *see* R. K. Gordon, *The Story of Troilus*, London, 1934, which includes pertinent passages from Benoit and Boccaccio in translation and the versions of Chaucer and Henryson. For Dictys' use of the old name Hippodamia for Briseis *see* Note on pp.58–60.

Pages 106-107
For a description of the Palladium *see* Apollodorus, *Library*, III, 12, Loeb Classical Library ed., Vol. 2, p.39 and note on pp.38–41.

The story of Diomedes on Odysseus' shoulders is told in Conon's *Narratives* (first century B.C.–first century A.D.), as preserved in the *Biblioteca* of the ninth century Byzantine scholar, Photius. *See* Loeb Classical Library ed. of Apollodorus, *Library*, Vol. 2, note on p.228.

For Odysseus as a comic figure, *see* the *Oxford Classical Dictionary*, Oxford, 1949, p.323, under Epicharmus; Margarete Bieber, *History of the Greek and Roman Theatre*, Princeton, 1939, pp.73, 79, 92–94, 265–267, 413; and Allardyce Nicoll, *Masks, Mimes, and Miracles*, London, 1931, pp.38–40, 54.

Page 108
The role played by Antenor in Lycophron's *Alexandra* is mentioned in a note on the

Roman Antiquities of Dionysius of Halicarnassus, I, 46, Loeb Classical Library ed., Vol. I, p.146, Note I.

The *Iliad's* reference to the anger of Aeneas is in Book XIII, 460.

Dionysius of Halicarnassus quotes Menecrates on Aeneas' betrayal of Troy in his *Roman Antiquities*, I, 48, 3.

Dictys tells of the peace conference, V, 4–5; Dares in Ch. XXXVII–XL.

Dictys tells of the stealing of the Palladium in V, 5.

Dares mentions Aeneas' treason in Ch. XLI.

The name Theano inscribed above the priest of Minerva in the tapestry reflects a radical change from ancient sources. According to Greek tradition (*Iliad*, VI, 297 ff, and Bacchylides, *Antenor's Sons*, p.51 and Note, and other sources), Theano was the priestess of Athena, guardian of the Palladium, and wife of Antenor. Late classical tradition made her share her husband's treachery: in *Dictys*, V, 8, and Benoit, 25451ff., she helps him to obtain the Palladium. Guido, Ch. XXVIIII, and other romances make Theano a man and Minerva's priest. Guido spells his name Thoans.

Pages 108-109
The Duke of Alba's tapestry showing the conference in Troy and the theft of the Palladium is discussed by G. L. Hunter in *The Practical Book of Tapestries*, Philadelphia, 1925, p.80.

Page 109
Dionysius of Halicarnassus describes Aeneas' rescue of the Palladium in *Roman Antiquities*, I, 69, 2–3.

Plutarch notes that the Palladium was brought to the Temple of Vesta in Rome in his *Life of Camillus*, XX.

Page 110
The vase showing Athena building the horse is described by Nickolaus Yalouris in *Athena als Herrin der Pferde*, *Museum Helveticum*, Vol. VII (1950), p.48 and fig.8.

Page 111
The quotation from the *Odyssey* concerning the horse is from Book VII, 492ff.

Vergil's description is from the *Aeneid*, II, 250–267.

Pausanias speaks of the bronze horse at Delphi in his *Description of Greece*, X, ix–x; of the horse on the Athenian Acropolis in I, xxiii.

Tiepolo's *Building of the Trojan Horse* is published in the *Wadsworth Atheneum Bulletin*, Second Series, No.24 (April, 1951), p.2.

Page 113

Pliny tells of the carving of the Laocoön in his *Natural History*, XXXVI, lv; Rodolfo Lanciani discusses its finding in *Storia degli Scavi*, Vol. I (1902), pp.139ff.

Page 115

The Roman painting of the horse brought into Troy is discussed by Christopher M. Dawson in *Romano-Campanian Mythological Landscape Painting*, Yale Classical Studies, Vol. IX, New Haven, 1944, p.86, no.13.

The wooden horse is mentioned in Dictys, V, 9; the horse's head over the gate in Dares, XL.

Guido describes the horse of bronze in his *History*, Book XXX.

Page 116

For marvels in the Alexander romances *see* A. Wallis Budge, *Life and Exploits of Alexander the Great*, London, 1896, pp.120–121; 368–369; 394–395 and *passim*.

Geoffrey of Monmouth describes the brazen horse and rider in his *History of the Kings of Britain*, VII, 3. This is translated in Everyman's Library, London (n.d.), by Sebastian Evans, p.118.

Page 117

For Conrad of Querfurt's account of the horse of Naples *see* Domenico Comparetti, *Vergil in the Middle Ages*, London, 1895, pp.259, 268.

Page 119

The quotation from *The Trojan Women* is from the translation by Gilbert Murray, New York, 1912.

Page 120

The immortality of Menelaus is mentioned in the *Odyssey*, IV, 560–563.

Page 121

Pausanias tells the story of Helen in Rhodes in his *Description of Greece*, III, xix, 9.

The quotation from Euripides' *Helen* is from the translation by Arthur S. Way, Loeb Classical Library, *Euripides*, Vol. I.

Page 126

Polyxena's speech is from the translation of Euripides' *Hecuba* by Arthur S. Way, Loeb Classical Library, as above.

Ovid describes Polyxena's death in *Metamorphoses*, XIII, 441–482.

Seneca tells of Achilles' request for Polyxena's death in his *Trojan Women*, 170ff.

Philostratus tells of Polyxena's self-immolation in *Life of Apollonius of Tyana*, IV, xvi.

Pausanias describes Polygnotos' Polyxena in his *Description*, I, xxii.

The quotation 'in her eyes . . . ' is from the *Greek Anthology*, XVI, 150.

Euripides' story of Hecuba's transformation is given in his *Hecuba*, 1265–1273.

Ovid tells of Hecuba's madness in *Metamorphoses*, XIII, 561–571.

Quintus of Smyrna describes the fate of Hecuba in his *Fall of Troy*, XIV, 347–351.

Page 127

For the classical account of the death of Ajax son of Oïleus *see Odyssey*, IV, 499–511, and Apollodorus, *Epitome*, VI, 6.

Dictys says (V, 12) that Cassandra took refuge in the temple of Minerva and that Ajax son of Oïleus took her thence; Dares (XLI), that she and Andromache took refuge there, that she was freed by the Greeks (XLII), and went to the Chersonesus (XLIII).

Page 128

Benoit also names the son of Oïleus and says that Andromache was with Cassandra (lines 26211ff.). Guido (XXX) names Ajax Telamon, but says (XXXII) that the other Ajax was shipwrecked. Lefèvre follows Guido. Lydgate confuses the two even more.

Page 130

Vergil's reference to Andromache and Helenus is in the *Aeneid*, III, 294ff.

Dares tells of the freeing of Andromache in Chs. XLII–XLIII; Dictys, of her captivity in V, 13 and VI, 12.

THE ORESTEIA

Page 132

The shield band showing the murder of Agamemnon is published by Ernst Kunze in *Olympische Forschungen, Archaische Schildbänder*, Berlin, 1950, pp.167–168.

Page 134

The relief of Clytemnestra and Cassandra is published by Carl W. Blegen, *Prosymnia: Remains of Post-Mycenaean Date*, in *American Journal of Archaeology*, Vol. XLIII (1939), pp.415–418.

Page 139

The drawing for the setting of Gluck's *Iphigénie* is published by Agne Beijer, *Slottsteatrarna pa Drottningholm och Gripsholm*. Malmö, John Kroon, (1933), Pl.XXV, with a description of the plates in English.

THE ODYSSEY

All quotations from the *Odyssey* are from the translation by George Herbert Palmer, Boston, 1891.

Page 143
The statuette of Ulysses is published in Wolfgang Helbig's *Guide to the Public Collections of Classical Antiquities in Rome,* trans. by James F. and Findlay Muirhead, Leipzig, 1895, Vol. I, pp.70–72, No.124.

Pages 144-145
The Ulysses and Penelope tapestries are published by Gertrude Townsend in the *Bulletin of the Museum of Fine Arts,* Boston, Vol. XXVII (1929), pp.2–10.

Page 146
The statue of Penelope is published in Helbig, as above, pp.124–125, No.191.

Page 147
For the work of Carrà *see* James Thrall Soby and Alfred H. Barr, Jr., *Twentieth-Century Italian Art,* New York, Museum of Modern Art, 1949, pp.21–23, and Guglielmo Pacchioni, *Carlo Carrà,* Milan, 1945. The quotation on the metaphysical school is from James Thrall Soby's *Giorgio de Chirico,* New York, Museum of Modern Art, rev. ed. (n.d.), p.54.

Page 148
The cheek-piece showing Odysseus is discussed by Ludwig von Sybel, *Zwei Bronzen,* in *Jahrbuch des kaiserlichen deutschen archäologischen Instituts,* Berlin, 1887, Vol. II, pp. 15–16.

Pages 150-151
The vase with Odysseus and Nausicaä is published in Edouard Gerhard's *Auserlesene griechische Vasenbilder,* Berlin, 1847, Vol. III, pp.132–134, Pl.CCXVIII.

Page 153
The kylix with the blinding of Polyphemus is published in the *Corpus Vasorum,* France, fasc. 7, Bibl. Nat., 1928, pp.18–19, Pls.22, 1–4; 23, 5.

Page 154
Dictys' account of Polyphemus is found in VI, 5; Benoit tells of him in lines 28629ff.; Guido, in Book XXXIII; Lydgate in his *Troy Book,* V, 1898, 1950, 1995ff.

Ovid tells of Polyphemus in *Metamorphoses,* XIV, 160–200.

For Christine de Pisan's moralized account of Polyphemus see her *Epistle,* XIX.

Pages 156-157
The Roman painting with Polyphemus hurling rocks and its relation to Philoxenus is discussed by Christine Alexander in *Metropolitan Museum Studies,* Vol. I (1928–1929), pp.181–186; and by Christopher M. Dawson in *Romano-Campanian Mythological Landscape Paintings,* Yale Classical Studies, Vol. IX, New Haven, 1944, pp. 100–101, No.42; 145–146.

Pages 158–159
The Graeco-Roman *Odyssey* paintings in the Vatican Library are fully described by Wolfgang Helbig, *Guide to the Public Collections of Classical Antiquities in Rome*, Leipzig, 1896, Vol. II, pp.178–181, and are discussed by Mary Hamilton Swindler, *Ancient Painting*, New Haven, 1929, pp.326, 328, 338, 366, 415.

Page 159
For the transformation of Circe's island into a mainland promontory *see* Pliny, *Natural History*, Book II, 87; and Strabo, *Geography*, v, 3, 6, 'a mountain which has the form of an island'.

Page 162
Christine de Pisan moralizes on Ulysses and Circe in her *Epistle*, XCVIII.

Page 163
The quotation from Ariosto's *Orlando Furioso* is from the translation by William Stewart Rose, London, 1905, Canto VI.

Page 164
Burne-Jones' *Wine of Circe* is discussed and Rossetti's sonnet quoted in full in the *Catalogue of The New Gallery Exhibition of the Works of Sir Edward Burne-Jones*, London, 1898–1899, pp.49–50.

Page 166
For the landscape showing Odysseus in Hades *see* above, Note on p.158–159.

Strabo, *Geography*, I, 2,12 says that some place the Sirens at Cape Peloris (Cape Faro, in Sicily), others on the Sirenussae, a three-pointed rock in the Bay of Naples, but he himself favours 'three uninhabited rocky little islands called the Sirens', which lay the other side of the headland from that bay—i.e. in the Gulf of Salerno where the Galli islands are.

Page 171
The relief of Odysseus and his dog is published in Karl Robert, *Die antiken Sarcophagreliefs*, Berlin, 1890, Vol. II, pp.161–162 and Pl.53, No.150.

Page 172
The relief of Odysseus and Eurykleia is published by Gisela M. A. Richter in the *Bulletin of The Metropolitan Museum of Art*, Vol. 21 (1926), pp.80–82.

Page 173
The relief of Odysseus' return is published by Gisela M. A. Richter in the *Bulletin of The Metropolitan Museum of Art*, Vol. 24 (1930), pp.279ff.

Page 177
For the Odysseus paintings at Fontainebleau *see* L. Dimier, *Fench Painting in the Sixteenth Century*, London, 1904, pp.146–186 and *passim.*

Page 180
The quotation from Fénelon's *Telemachus* is from *The Adventures of Telemachus by Fénelon*, translated by D. Hawkesworth, ed. by O. W. Wright, New York, 1860, pp.154–155.

THE AENEID

All quotations from the *Aeneid* are from the translation by John Dryden.

Page 182
The rule of Aeneas and his descendants is predicted in the *Iliad*, xx, 307–308. For the growth of the Trojan legend before Vergil *see*: Henriette Boas, *Aeneas' Arrival in Latium*, Amsterdam, 1938, especially pp.15–24 dealing with Hellanicus; Lionel Pearson, *Early Ionic Historians*, Oxford, 1939, which gives a translation of Hellanicus; and *P. Vergili Maronis Opera*, London, 4th ed., 1884, Vol. II, *Introduction* by John Conington and *A Story of Aeneas' Wanderings* by Henry Nettleship.

The site of Lavinium is believed to be the modern Pratica de Mare near the shore south of Rome, but Vergil changed it to the Tiber's mouth, practically at Ostia. *See* Bertha Tilly, *Vergil's Latium*, Oxford, 1947, pp.1–30; 54–65. Castel Gandolfo in the Alban Hills is thought to occupy the site of Alba Longa.

For the custom of tracing Trojan ancestry *see* Jean Seznec, *The Survival of the Pagan Gods*, trans. by Barbara F. Sessions, New York, 1953, Bollingen Series, XXXVIII, pp.19–36; and Karl Voretzsch, *Introduction to the Study of Old French Literature*, New York, 1931, pp.15, 63, 65 ff.; for the Trojan pedigree evolved for Theodoric the Great by Cassiodorus and preserved by Jordanes, *see* Thomas Hodgkin, *Italy and Her Invaders*, London, 1885, Vol. III, pp.324–327.

The figure sacrificing on the Altar of Peace is identified by Mrs. Arthur Strong in *Roman Sculpture*, London, 1907, p.46, as perhaps a personification of the Roman Senate, but by later writers as Aeneas. *See* Giuseppe Moretti, *L'Ara Pacis Augustae*, Rome, Libraria dello Stato, 1938, and Dorothy M. Robathan, *Monuments of Ancient Rome*, Rome, 1950, p.150.

Page 185
The cassone panel showing Aeneas' ship tossed by storm is described in Oswald Sirén, *Descriptive Catalogue of the Pictures in the Jarves Collection, Yale University*, New Haven, 1916, pp.87–88; the attribution to Apollonio di Giovanni is discussed by E. H. Gombrich in *Apollonio di Giovanni, Journal of the Warburg and Courtauld Institutes*, Vol. XVIII (1955), pp.16–34.

Page 189
The first of several groups of *Aeneid* enamels in the Metropolitan Museum is published by Joseph Breck in the *Bulletin of The Metropolitan Museum of Art*, Vol. 20 (1925), pp.95–98.

Page 190
For the flight of Aeneas *see* Dionysius of Halicarnassus, *Roman Antiquities*, I, 46–47; Xenophon, treatise *On Hunting*, I, 15–16; Apollodorus, *Epitome*, V, 21.

Pausanias describes Polygnotos' painting of the Sack of Troy at Delphi in his *Description of Greece*, X, XXV–XXVI. His authorities for the name Eurydice are the *Cypria* and *Little Iliad*.

Page 194
For Elsheimer's *Burning of Troy*, *see* Heinrich Weizsäcker, *Adam Elsheimer, der Maler von Frankfurt*, Berlin, 1936, Vol. I, pp.174–177.

Page 196
Dionysius of Halicarnassus, *Roman Antiquities*, I,51,3, says that the Trojans landed at several places along the east shore of Italy, those with Aeneas at 'a place named after Minerva, where Aeneas himself chanced to set foot first in Italy. This place is a promontory that offers harbour in the summer, which from that time has been called the Harbour of Venus.' (*Portus Veneris* below *Castrum Minervae*.)

Page 197
The Aeneas mosaic found at Low Ham was first published in the *Journal of Roman Studies*, Vol. XXXVI (1946), p.142 and Pl.XI, and again in Vol. XLIV (1954), pp. 99–100. It is discussed fully by C. A. R. Radford and H. S. L. Dewar in *The Roman Mosaics from Low Ham*, Somerset County Museum Publications, 2, 1954 and by J. M. C. Toynbee in *Art in Roman Britain*, London 1962 (second ed. 1963), pp.203ff.

Page 198
For Heinrich von Veldecke's *Eneide*, *see* Helmut de Boor and Richard Newald, *Geschichte der deutschen Literatur*, Munich, 1953, Vol. II, pp.41ff.; and Gustav Ehrismann, *Geschichte der deutschen Literatur bis zum Ausgang des Mittelalters, Part II, Mittelhochdeutsche Literatur*, Munich, 1927, pp.79–95.

The refuge under a tree is described in *Heinrich von Veldecke's Eneide, mit Einleitung und Anmerkungen herausgegeben von Otto Behagel*, Heilbronn, 1882, lines 1812–1845. For the MS illustrated here and later *see* Margareta Hudig-Frey, *Die älteste Illustration der Eneide des Heinrich von Veldecke*, Strassburg, 1921. The French romance of *Eneas* is discussed in Karl Voretzsch, *Introduction to the Study of Old French Literature*, New York, 1931, pp.248–251; von Veldecke's *Eneide* is mentioned on p.250.

Pages 204-206
The sources of Vergil's description of the Underworld and its differences from that of the *Odyssey* are discussed in the Introduction and Notes of H. E. Butler's *The Sixth Book of the Aeneid*, Oxford, 1920.

Page 206
Jan Brueghel's painting of Aeneas and the Sibyl, formerly in the Museum of Fine Arts, Budapest, disappeared during World War II. *See* Catalogue (in Hungarian) of the Budapest Museum's paintings, 1954, p.10.

Page 208
Livy tells the story of Romulus and Remus in his *Roman History*, I, iii–viii; Dionysius of Halicarnassus in *Roman Antiquities*, I, *passim*; Plutarch, *Parallel Lives*, *The Life of Romulus*.

Page 209
The quotation from Livy is from the *Roman History*, I, v.

Page 210
Albertini mentions the statue of the wolf in his *Opusculum de Mirabilibus novae et veteris urbis Romae*, Rome, 1510, Book II.

The history of the bronze she-wolf is discussed in H. Stuart Jones' *Catalogue of the Ancient Sculptures Preserved in the Municipal Collections of Rome*, Vol. II: *The Sculptures of the Palazzo dei Conservatori*, Oxford, 1926, pp.56–58.

Master Gregory's description of the wolf is translated in George B. Parks' *The English Traveler in Italy*, Vol. I, *The Middle Ages*, Stanford University Press (n.d.), p.268.

Van Heemskerck's drawing of the Conservators' Palace with the wolf is published in *Die Römischen Skizzenbücher von Marten van Heemskerck*, by Christian Hülsen and Adolf Michaelis, Vienna, Vol. II, 1916, fol.72 recto.

Page 212
The cassone panel with the view of Rome is published in Oswald Sirén's *Descriptive Catalogue of the Pictures in the Jarves Collection, Yale University*, pp.88–89, and also by E. H. Gombrich in *Journal of the Warburg and Courtauld Institutes*, see Note on page 185.

Page 215
The cassone panel with the marriage of Aeneas and Lavinia is published by Paul Schubring in *Cassoni* . . . , as above, Leipzig, 1915, p.256, No.147 and Pl.XXIX.

Dionysius of Halicarnassus tells the later history of Aeneas in *Roman Antiquities*, I, 59–60; Ovid, that of his later life and deification in *Metamorphoses*, XIV.

LIST OF PLATES

INTRODUCTION

BEFORE THE ILIAD

THE ILIAD

THE FALL OF TROY

77. *Achilles catches Penthesilea as she falls from her horse.* From a red-figured Apulian krater, fourth century B.C. Collection of Landgrave Philip of Hesse, Schloss Adolphseck. Photo: Staatliche Kunstsammlungen, Kassel.
78. *Achilles supporting the body of Penthesilea.* Original model, 1837, for a marble relief by Bertel Thorwaldsen. Copenhagen, Thorwaldsen Museum. Photo: Jonals Company, Copenhagen.
79. *Achilles sees Polyxena at Hector's tomb.* Illustration by Jean Mielot from a manuscript of Christine de Pisan's *Épître d'Othéa*, 1461. Brussels, Bibliothèque Royale, MS. fr.9392, fol.98v. Photo: Brussels, Bibliothèque Royale.
80. *The death of Achilles: Ajax rescues his body: Menelaus kills Amasos, an Ethiopian follower of Memnon.* Attick black-figured amphora, sixth century B.C. Philadelphia, University Museum, MS 3442. Photo: University Museum.
81. *A medieval picture of Achilles' death: he is killed by Paris in Apollo's temple.* Detail from a drawing related to a series of fifteenth-century tapestry designs. Paris, Louvre. Photo: Giraudon.
82. *Troilus and other Trojans deliver Briseïde (Cressida) to the Greeks.* From a manuscript of Benoit's *Roman*, Italian, second half of the fourteenth-century. Venice, Biblioteca Marciana, MS.fr.17, fol.105.
83. *Odysseus gives Achilles' son his father's arms.* Attic red-figured kylix by Douris, about 490 B.C. Vienna, Kunsthistorisches Museum, N.3695. Photo: Kunsthistorisches Museum.
84. *Ajax and Agamemnon arm the son of Achilles.* Detail of a late-fifteenth-century Franco-Flemish tapestry. London, Victoria and Albert Museum. Photo: Victoria and Albert Museum.
85. *The theft of the Palladium: Diomedes has taken the image from Athena's altar.* Red-figured Apulian stemless cup by the Diomed painter, early fourth century B.C. Oxford, Ashmolean Museum. Photo: Ashmolean Museum.
86. *Burlesque on the theft of the Palladium.* Red-figured Apulian oinochoe, fourth century B.C. London, British Museum, F.366. Photo: British Museum.
87. *Medieval version of the theft of the Palladium: Ulysses and Diomedes discuss peace with Priam: Antenor arranges for the theft: an eagle snatches the Trojan sacrifice.* Right side of a late-fifteenth-century Franco-Flemish tapestry. Madrid, Collection of the Duke of Alba. Photo: Courtesy of the Duke of Alba, photographer, A. Castellanos, Madrid.
88. *Athena building the Trojan horse.* Attic red-figured kylix, about 470–460 B.C. Florence, Museo Archeologico. Photo: Soprintendenza alle Antichità di Etruria, Florence.
89. *The building of the Trojan horse.* Painting by Giovanni Battista Tiepolo, about 1760. Hartford, Wadsworth Atheneum. Photo: Courtesy Wadsworth Atheneum, photographer, E. Irving Blomstrann.
90. *Laocoön sacrificing: the serpents encircle him and his sons.* Illustration from the *Aeneid*, II, 191–198. Vatican Vergil, fifth century A.D. Rome, Vatican, cod.vat.lat.3225, fol.18v. Photo: Archivio Fotografico Vaticano.
91. *Laocoön.* Marble group, about 50 B.C. Probably a Roman copy of an earlier work. Rome, Vatican. Photo: Archivio Fotografico Vaticano.
92. *Laocoön.* Painting, about 1601–1606, by El Greco. Washington, National Gallery of Art, Samuel H. Kress Collection. Photo: National Gallery of Art.
93. *The wooden horse brought into Troy.* Roman wall painting from Pompeii, second half of the first century A.D. Naples, National Museum, 9040. Photo: Soprintendenza alle Antichità delle Provincie di Napoli.
94. *The Trojan horse, a 'horse of brass', within the walls of Troy.* Left side of a late-fifteenth-century Franco-Flemish tapestry. Zamora, Cathedral Museum. Photo: Federico Heptener, Zamora.
95. *The Trojan horse disgorges its burden.* Illustration from a late-fifteenth-century manuscript of Raoul Lefèvre's *Recueil*. Paris, Bibliothèque Nationale, MS.fr.22552, fol.276v. Photo: Bibliothèque Nationale.
96. *The toilet of Helen.* Painting, 1914, by Bryson Burroughs. Baltimore, Collection of Mrs. Bryson Burroughs.
97. *The meeting of Menelaus and Helen.* From an Attic black-figured neck-amphora, about 550 B.C. New York, Metropolitan Museum of Art, 56.171.18. Photo: Metropolitan Museum.
98. *The meeting of Menelaus and Helen at the fall of Troy.* Attic red-figured skyphos, about 480 B.C. Boston, Museum of Fine Arts, 13.186. Photo: Boston Museum.
99. *The return and reconciliation of Menelaus and Helen.* Illustration from *Le Livre des Estoires dou Commencement dou Monde*, Neapolitan, 1350–1360. London, British Museum, Royal MS.20, D.I., fol.181r. Photo: British Museum.
100. *Neoptolemus killing Priam and Astyanax.* From an Attic red-figured calyx-krater, about 465 B.C. Boston, Museum of Fine Arts, 59.178. Photo: Dietrich Widmer, Basel.
101. *Pyrrhus (Neoptolemus) killing Priam.* Fifteenth-century illustration by Apollonio di Giovanni in a manuscript of the *Aeneid*. Florence, Biblioteca Riccardiana, MS.492, fol.86v. Photo: G. P. Pineider.

THE ORESTEIA

THE ODYSSEY

THE AENEID

INDEX OF MYTHOLOGICAL PERSONAGES AND PLACES

Names of most personages are entered under their most common forms, often latinized Greek, other forms being given in parentheses, as Ajax (Aias), Aphrodite (Cypris, Venus). Latin forms are used in romances, as Jupiter for Zeus, Minerva for Athena.

GENERAL INDEX

Works of art, literature, and music mentioned in Introduction and text, as well as non-mythological personages and places are included here. Dates will be found in the Chronological Appendices, Works of Literature and Music, pp. 217–231; Works of Art, pp. 232–253.

Characters and works listed only in the Appendices are not indexed in detail. Notes are indexed only when they contain important material not otherwise given.